Concerning Death

A Practical Guide for the Living

Concerning Death

A Practical Guide for the Living

Edited by Earl A. Grollman

Beacon Press Boston

To Netta

Copyright © 1974 by Earl A. Grollman
Beacon Press books are published under the auspices
of the Unitarian Universalist Association

Simultaneous casebound and paperback editions
All rights reserved
Printed in the United States of America

9   8   7

Library of Congress Cataloging in Publication Data

Grollman, Earl A.
  Concerning death.
  Includes bibliographies.
  1. Death—Addresses, essays, lectures. 2. Funeral
rites and ceremonies—United States—Addresses, essays,
lectures. I. Title. [DNLM: 1. Death. BF789.D4
G875c 1974]
GT3203.G76   393   73–17117
ISBN 0–8070–2764–2
ISBN 0–8070–2765–0 (pbk.)

Contents

separation? What are the significant guidelines for
helping the child during crises?

When are flat markers and mausoleums appropriate?
What symbols and inscriptions should be used?

Introduction

The evening my husband died had not followed a normal pattern. That Monday, instead of attending my usual meeting, I happened to be at home. I was ironing when the phone rang at 8:35 p.m. A student was calling, saying, "Could you come up and get Mr. Phipps? He isn't feeling well." As I got into the car, I thought, "Boy, when he admits he's not feeling well, there's something wrong." I saw a fire department rescue unit heading for the college but paid it no heed, since it was not going in my direction. But when I pulled up in front of the library, the unit was there; it had come in through another entrance. My thighs felt weak, and sharp pains ran through them, for all I could think of was: "Heart attack!"

One of the librarians had that "Oh, no, it's *your* husband" expression on her face. One of my fellow students (I attended the college's library school) volunteered to go out and sit with my children. I had left them sleeping since I lived only a half mile from the college and had expected to be back right away. I raced up four flights of stairs. In the classroom I saw, and still remember vividly, the faces of my husband's students, his colleagues, and the nurse who blurted out to the rescue unit man, "No pulse! No pulse for ten minutes!" When I saw my husband lying on the floor, I knew. I sat down, waited five minutes, then called my minister. I was a widow, and I knew it.

The questions rolled over me. How do you tell a five-and-a-half - year-old and his almost - three-year-old brother that their father is dead? How should they participate in the coming week's activities? What happens to you and your sense of family identity — and to you and your sense of individual identity? What about lawyers, the will, money, insurance, Social Security? There would be an incredible number of times for me to sign my name to legal documents. I sensed the world shifting about me and became determined to control the forces acting on me.

So Joyce A. Phipps writes in an article, "What Really Happens When Your Husband Dies?"[1]

Do many people deny the reality of death?

To everything there is a season and a time to every purpose under the heaven: A time to be born, and a time to die.

Ecclesiastes 3:1

There is no doubt as to the inevitability of death — that our season will come. Death is the only event concerning the whole psychobiological organism which, once birth has taken place, is predictable beyond dispute. No one can be unaware that life has but a limited span.

And yet, the subject of death is the most significant taboo of our society. There is a vast conspiracy involved in hushing up the new four-letter word of pornography, D-E-A-D. Death has become the forbidden topic, replacing sex as an object of repression.

The French philosopher La Rochefoucald captured this denial insulation when he affirmed: "Neither the sun nor death can be looked at with a steady eye." Death is disguised through euphemistic language. People simply do not die, they "pass on" and "pass away." They "perish." They "expire." They become "defunct" or "deceased."

Death is not only camouflaged; it is avoided. For many, the theme is an obscenity not to be discussed or even mentioned. There is a superstitious belief that if it is not talked about, it will simply disappear. Death itself will "pass away." It is what some social scientists call "The dying of death."

Why is death denied?

For many of our own parents and grandparents, death was considered a customary aspect of life. Because of the high mortality rate, death was a frequent visitor. In contrast, the average child born in America today can expect to live to about seventy, fully twenty-three years longer than he could have at the turn of the century. In the past, multitudes of adults and children would die in the home of bacterial pneumonia, diphtheria, and poliomyelitis. With antibiotics, vaccines, and improved sanitation the once lethal effects of these maladies have now been virtually eliminated. Because our ancestors were in constant contact with death, they were compelled to view terminality as a real and natural phenomenon.

An American experiences death in his immediate family but once in every twenty years. Usually, the event takes place not in the home but away in the hospital. Since there is infrequent exposure, death is not viewed as a pervasive factor of life but as a rare, impersonal, virtually abnormal event. While many people in the past believed in a kind of resurrection and salvation, the present generation's dissolving beliefs and traditions have eroded the consolation of a spiritual and physical immortality.

In addition to the advances of medical science and changing religious philosophies, there are accompanying demographic alterations. Some of you may still recall that grandparents, parents, and children lived in the same household or certainly not more than a few houses or streets away. But at present, with the accent on mobility, members of most families are separated by states and even continents. They are shielded from the ravages of sickness and impending death.

The aged, those most susceptible to death, are kept out of sight. Growing old has become institutionalized in contemporary society. Some are relegated to a retirement village or community of old folk or sometimes, pathetically, to a nursing home. There they await the final solution in the same manner as the leper did in antiquity. As the elderly voluntarily or involuntarily remove themselves from the intimate family circle, the younger members have less and less opportunity to experience death in an immediate, visceral, physical sense, and they are even unable to witness the natural process of growing old.

Twentieth-century man is trying to remove death from life's reality with hopes that he may unravel this final elusive enigma. After all, he has substantial mastery over his physical environment. Space exploration and technological discovery are becoming prosaic and commonplace. He tends to view terminality in a detached, superscientistic fashion. In laboratories around the world, technologists have begun to unlock the secrets of the aging process — and each new discovery improves the prospect that ways may be found to hold back the inexorable gray curtain of senility and prolong the years of youthful vitality. If the major killer of adults — cancer and diseases of the heart, kidney, and blood vessels — were eliminated completely, researchers estimate that perhaps another ten years would be added to adult life expectancy. Some gerontologists have asserted that one may live almost indefinitely. So man talks not about the death of real people but the death of disease through organ transplantation and hemodialysis. He seeks to deny or mitigate death with the primitive belief that death may no longer be inevitable.

How do "modern" people react to death?

Dying and denying are the basic counterparts in our contemporary society. We are not prepared for death. When a loved one does die, the lingering pain, the sudden fury, the sense of outrage, the excruciating feelings of guilt — all of these powerful emotions take us unaware. The shock of mortality never ceases to amaze and overwhelm the living. Each time we are confronted with the crisis of death we ask: "Why?" "Why me?" "What did I do wrong?" "Why am I being punished?" "What can I do to help myself through this terrible ordeal?"

There are as diverse coping mechanisms as there are conceptualizations. Some people will refuse to think about the death at all; others will think of nothing else. Some will vehemently protest; others will quietly resign themselves to the reality. Some will curse God; others will console themselves in a future world-to-come. Some will be disorganized; others will effectively reshape their lives. Some will cry hysterically; others will remain outwardly impassive and emotionless; while still others may even laugh. Some will deify the deceased; others will be angry at the dead person for leaving them alone and abandoned. Some will blame themselves for the death; others will project the guilt upon the physician, the clergyman, or another member of the family. Reactions to death are varied and contradictory; they are neither prescribed nor are they predictable.

Then how can we possibly help people in a culture where death is avoided and evaded?

In helping others to solve the inexplicability of nonexistence, we strengthen ourselves in the realization that dying and death are phases of life and living. Each one of us is a helper — the parent, the physician, the counselor, the clergyman, the attorney, the funeral director, the insurance agent, the teacher, the neighbor, the friend — you!

People generally accept assistance from those whom they can trust. The person needing help may reject offers from those who seek to control, punish, correct, or gain power. Help is most useful when given in an atmosphere of *reciprocal* confidence, warmth, and acceptance. When one feels that his worth as an individual is valued, he is better able to place himself in psychological awareness to receive the necessary aid.

Of course, you do not know precisely what to say. You are most valued when you are both engaged in the *cooperative* quest for understanding. The roles of the two people are interchangeable. Each participant has the intent to learn. The most meaningful relationship is one of common inquiry and quest, of a participatory learning experience.

In order to achieve shared problem-solving there must be a *mutual* openness with both spontaneity and the definiteness of candor. Essential progress is often hindered by fear, punitiveness, and defensiveness. To perform effective grief work, one must know how the other truly feels. Tell it like it is — bitterness, disbelief, loneliness, heartache, guilt. Don't repress true feelings. Deceptions and distortions are harmful to the therapeutic process.

For help is not always helpful — but it can be. The helper and the recipient can both grow and learn when one helps plan *with* another and not *for* another, and when assistance is given in a relationship of reciprocal, cooperative, and mutual trust, joint inquiry, openness, and interdependence.

Is death now becoming a subject of scientific study?

Only within the last decade has the area of death and dying become a respectable concern for the health professional and the social scientist. Heretofore, the topic was limited to theological speculation, philosophical interpretation, and literary expression. Instead of pretending that mortality is not a basic condition of life, the theme of death is now part of the curricula of more than seventy colleges and many high schools and elementary grades. The disguising of death is just too difficult to sustain in a world of war, violence, and potential nuclear devastation.

Yet, despite the proliferation of *new* books, lectures, symposia, television programs, and newspaper interviews, for most of us death is still a forbidden subject. We talk openly about the biological processes surrounding the beginning of existence but still avoid the evidences of the end of the life cycle.

A personal note. I am a clergyman in a congregation that is predominantly professional. Yet all the academic degrees and personal accreditations do not guarantee that one will be able to view death in a receptive, knowledgeable, and balanced manner. There is an abysmal ignorance about practical and inevitable problems: "My mother just died. What do I do?" "How to arrange a funeral?" "To cremate or not?" "How do I select a cemetery, a tombstone, an epitaph?" "What about organ transplantation?"

And the purpose of the book?

No longer can the subject of death be avoided. The world of biology is the world of the living and the dying. There can be no death without life, and, conversely, no life without death. Just as birth is the dawn of humankind's earthly existence, death is the night that must follow. But unfortunately, we are not prepared for this one certainty of existence.

Joyce Phipps writes:

> The evening my husband died did not follow a normal pattern. . . . I was a widow. . . . How do you tell a five-and-

a-half - year-old and his almost - three-year-old brother that their father is dead? How should they participate in the coming week's activities? What happens to you and your sense of family identity and your sense of individual identity? What about the lawyers, the will, money, insurance, Social Security?[2]

One need not wait for tragedy before confronting these fundamental and inevitable questions. This book should encourage the reader to share thoughts, perceptions, and knowledge with the living and to plan as rationally and meaningfully for that unavoidable moment of separation. And when the crisis does come, this volume can be used as a guide for the emotion-laden, death-related situations. The adequacy of your counsel may be the monumental factor in your future well-being as well as for loved ones who remain. This book is then dedicated to the inevitability of death and the preparation for life.

Earl A. Grollman

SUGGESTED READINGS

Berg, David W., and George G. Daugherty, *The Individual, Society, and Death: An Anthology of Readings*, 1972.

Charon, Jacques, *Death and Western Thought* (New York: Macmillan, 1964).

Dumont, Richard G., and Dennis C. Foss, *The American View of Death* (Cambridge, Mass.: Schenkman, 1972).

Feifel, Herman (Ed.), *The Meaning of Death* (New York: McGraw-Hill, 1959).

Fulton, Robert, *Death and Identity* (New York: Wiley, 1965).

Gorer, Geoffrey, *Death, Grief, and Mourning* (Garden City, N.Y.: Doubleday, 1965).

Jackson, Edgar N., *For the Living* (New York: Channel Press, 1965).

Kastenbaum, Robert, and Ruth Aisenberg, *The Psychology of Death* (New York: Springer, 1972).

Kubler-Ross, Elisabeth, *On Death and Dying* (New York: Macmillan, 1969).

Ruitenbeek, Hendrik M., *Death: Interpretations* (New York: Dell, 1969).

Toynbee, Arnold, *Man's Concern with Death* (New York: McGraw-Hill, 1968).

Weisman, Avery D., *On Dying and Denying* (New York: Behavioral Publications, 1972).

Periodicals

Archives of the Foundation of Thanatology. Foundation of Thanatology, 630 West 168th Street, New York, New York 10032.

Omega: The international journal for the psychological study of dying, bereavement, suicide, and other lethal behaviors. Greenwood Press, Inc., 51 Riverside Avenue, Westport, Connecticut 06880.

NOTES

1. Joyce A. Phipps, "What Really Happens When Your Husband Dies?" *The Christian Century*, 230 - 232. Copyright 1973 Christian Century Foundation. Reprinted by permission from the February 21, 1973, issue of *The Christian Century*.
2. *Ibid.*

1

Grief

Should grief be concealed?

How is grief expressed?

When is grief abnormal?

What about grief and guilt?

How to effectively cope with one's grief.

EDGAR N. JACKSON

Although our society seeks to shield us from the stark reality of death, we can never be protected from the overwhelming suffering that follows the loss of a loved one. We need to brush aside the clichés and empty slogans with which most of us tend to overlay our deeply felt anguish. Only through a lucid understanding of sorrow can the grief-stricken be restored to a useful life.

In Dr. Edgar N. Jackson's writings, one finds the most integrated study of the psychological, theological, and philosophical dimensions of bereavement. He is the author of eighteen books, including *Understanding Grief, Facing Ourselves, When Someone Dies, Telling a Child about Death,* and *The Christian Funeral.*

Grief

What is grief?

Grief is the intense emotion that floods life when a person's inner security system is shattered by an acute loss, usually associated with the death of someone important in his/her life.

In more personal terms, grief is a young widow who must find a way to bring up her three children, alone. Grief is the angry reaction of a man so filled with shocked uncertainty and confusion that he strikes out at the nearest person. Grief is the little old lady who goes to the funeral of a stranger and does some unfinished business of her own feeling by crying her eyes out there; she is weeping for herself, for the event she is sure will come, and for which she has so little help in preparing herself.

Grief is a mother walking daily to a nearby cemetery to stand quietly alone for a few moments before she goes on about the tasks of the day; she knows that part of her is in the cemetery, just as part of her is in her daily work. Grief is the deep sympathy one person has for another when he wants to do all he can to help resolve a tragic experience. Grief is the silent, knifelike terror and sadness that comes a hundred times a day, when you start to speak to someone who is no longer there.

Grief is the emptiness that comes when you eat alone after eating with another for years. Grief is the desperate longing for another whose loss you cannot learn to endure. Grief is teaching yourself how to go to bed without saying good night to the one who has died. Grief is the helpless wishing that things were different when you know they are not and never will be again. Grief is a whole cluster of adjustments, apprehensions, and uncertainties that strike life in its forward progress and make it difficult to reorganize and redirect the energies of life.

Grief is always more than sorrow. Bereavement is the event in personal history that triggers the emotion of grief. Mourning is the process by which the powerful emotion is slowly and painfully brought under control. But when doctors speak of grief they are focusing on the raw feelings that are at the center of a whole process that engages the person in adjusting to changed circumstances. They are speaking of the deep fears of the mourner, of his prospects of loneliness, and of the obstacles he must face as he finds a new way of living.

Why do we grieve for a loved one who died?

Usually we do not grieve for the person who has died but rather for ourselves and our own sense of loss. The person who has died is no longer able to use his nervous system to feel physical pain. The person who is still alive and capable of feeling has the emotional response. It is usually a conflicted feeling because he suffers the loss and at the same time has the basic human response of being glad that he is still alive and able to experience sensations even though they may be painful. So grief is usually characterized by ambivalence — of two conflicting types of sensation going on at the same time. As St. Augustine pointed out, grief is a strange mixture of joy and sorrow — joy to be yet alive and sorrow to have life diminished by the loss of one we love.

We grieve because we experience deprivation. Our life has been diminished. We have lost something we cherished and we do not want to admit the loss. Life is made up of deprivation experiences, for every time we make a choice we give up one alternative in order to accept the other. But death is so final and so overwhelming a deprivation that our past experience does not seem to adequately prepare us for its personal devastation. We feel that part of our own being is lost with our deprivation. Because a part of our inner being was invested in another, we have this feeling of being personally reduced.

That is why it is so important to do the work of mourning wisely and well, for it is through this process that we retrieve that part of ourself so that we can continue life as a whole person rather than as one who has been permanently diminished because of his/her loss. Mourning is the process that guarantees that we happen to our grief rather than having our grief happen to us. Mourning is the process of self-mastery that makes sure we remain whole, even though deprived, rather than being destroyed by what has happened to us. Our grief is rooted in emotions that reach out in all directions beyond our physical being. Only as we literally pull up by the roots the feelings that no longer have a soil to sustain them are we able to let them take root again elsewhere and be nurtured with life-giving experience.

What are the manifestations of grief?

Grief can vary considerably depending on the personality and experience of the individual. It is usually characterized by an immediate and overwhelming sense of generalized discomfort. This discomfort may show up in one or more of the organic systems of the individual.

His muscular system may feel weak as if his strength were drained. He may be unable to make his muscles work as he desires, and conflict within the muscle system may show up in tension and tremors. Usually this condition resolves itself in a few hours.

The glandular system may be activated, with different sets of glands working in different ways. The tear glands may overflow at the same time that the salivary glands seem to dry up and the mouth becomes parched. Other glands may overwork for a while with disturbances in digestion, sexual activity, and normal control of disease systems. In acute grief persons tend to be more vulnerable to infections and viral illnesses.

The cardiovascular system may react with high blood pressure, rapid heart action, and changes in body temperature, with alternating cold chills or hot flashes. The respiration may be affected, with changes in the rate of breathing and periods of gasping or deep sighing. The gastrointestinal system may experience malfunction, with difficulty in swallowing, loss of appetite, indigestion, diarrhea, and/or constipation. The skin may react with heightened sensitivity, various forms of irritation, either immediately or over a longer period of time, with increased perspiration or dry coldness. In some cases there may be more acute manifestations such as shingles or boils.

The variations depend upon the person's unique manner of response to emotional stress and may involve opposite extremes. Fortunately not every person will have all the manifestations mentioned above, but any of these can be well within the norm of grief responses.

In addition to physical manifestations there are feeling responses characterized by sorrow, fears, and anxiety and uncertainty about the future. There may also be changes in personality that show up in social behavior and patterns of living. A neat person may become slovenly. A gregarious person may become withdrawn. A person of faith may become a doubter. These changes in personality may indicate special needs and call for professional psychotherapeutic care.

Is grief normal?

Grief is the other side of the coin of love. If you are capable of love you are capable of grief. Only the person who is incapable of loving another is entirely free of the possibility of grief. We would not want to think of life without love. But when you love you become vulnerable, because the one you love may suffer and die and part of you suffers and dies along with him. When anyone dies we all die a little, for we are all diminished and reminded of our own mortal status. But this is not a hopeless state; the death we experience in our grief can be overcome at least in part by healthful mourning whereby our inner being is restored to normal. So grief is normal for normal people.

Is there a distinction between normal and abnormal grief?

Yes, for with normal grief you are able to work your way back to productive and near normal living, while with abnormal grief you develop a chronic state of psychological or physical symptoms that persist for an unreasonable period of time.

Soon after a death, it is difficult to separate the normal from the abnormal. Under the stress of powerful emotions, people say and do things that are quite out of character. We must ask ourselves, then, whether an act that may seem abnormal is part of a whole pattern of unusual actions and reactions or merely an isolated occurrence. And we want to see whether this new way of acting and reacting is becoming more firmly fixed or less so.

The abnormal usually shows up in extremes. Sometimes what we observe is a seeming inability to react emotionally at all. The person who is cold, efficient, impersonal, and dry-eyed under powerful emotional stress may be underreacting. The person who goes all to pieces may be overreacting. We cannot on the face of it say that the seemingly calm person is handling his situation well; neither can we say, in the face of an explosion of grief, that sorrow is shattering to the other.

If the mourner has emotional weak spots in his nature, they may show in aggravated form under the pressure of grief. Danger signals one must watch for are unreasonable withdrawal from normal functions, excessive anger at others, or intense suspicion of others. Anger and/or suspicion may be directed against the physician, the minister, the funeral director, or even toward members of the immediate family. Moods of inappropriate elation or deep depression may also indicate that things are not right.

One of the best ways to gauge abnormal emotional reactions is to observe a person's behavior a month or so after the death. Most people will be quite back to normal by that time. If physical and emotional symptoms persist, and if the person is unable to function effectively after a few weeks, it is a fairly specific indication that he should have some special help in meeting his problems of adjustment.

The exception here might be widows or widowers, where the basic problems of adjustment involve so much of life, its status, and its role relationships, that a longer period of readjustment may well be within the norm.

What about grief and guilt?

Almost always some guilt is present with grief although the guilt may take many forms, some discernible and others obscure. Sometimes it is acted out toward others in unreasonable accusations. Hostility may be an effort to protect oneself against his own guilt feelings. Guilt often shows up as anger against others — a substitute for anger against oneself.

Often guilt shows up in depression where anger is directed inward. Unless resolved, it tends to increase with time. For the more depressed a person feels, the more angry he may become toward himself for his uncomfortable feelings. So it seems to work that the more depressed a person is, the more angry he becomes, and the more angry he is with himself, the more deeply he digs the pit of his depression.

The closer the human relationship, the more chance for guilt to be a part of the response. With members of the immediate family this is often the case. Children feel guilt at the death of parents because of their natural resistance to parental authority. Parents feel guilt at the death of their children because they think of the number of ways they might have done things differently with different outcomes. A son dies in war and his parents feel they should have supported his inclination toward pacifism. A daughter dies in a car crash and they wish they hadn't given her the car for graduation.

Real guilt can usually lead to restitution, but when death comes it is impossible for direct restitution, so reasonable alternatives may become useful. A memorial gift takes the form of a self-punishing fine or penalty and reduces guilt as it gives a form of immortality to the memory of the dead person.

Neurotic guilt, where guilt feelings seem out of proportion to the cause, may usually be relieved through counseling. Talking out the feelings can help to bring them into perspective so they can be understood and controlled.

Existential guilt is a diffused sense of human inadequacy related to our feelings of mortality and our inability to match deeds with dreams and hopes. Here it seems the only resolution of the feeling comes with facing the fact of our limitations and trying to do as best we can with the time and energy we have. Existential guilt gives us an invitation to be kind to ourselves with the implication that life and loss are enough of a burden to bear without adding to it an unreasonable load of unnecessary guilt and self-punishment. Existential guilt often shows up as self-pity and no emotion has yet been discovered that produces so little value in life.

What are the ways of coping with grief?

It is clear, then, that the grief-stricken are highly vulnerable to illness. Other studies show grief as a source of mental breakdown and social maladjustment. Since grief can produce such human suffering it is important for us to discover wise and effective ways of coping with it.

The wise management of grief calls for at least three important steps. First comes the painful task of facing the full reality of what has happened. Bluntly and with determination we must resist detours around the truth. We must realize that there is no easy way to face the death of one who was deeply loved. We need courage to endure the pain, aware that ours is essentially a healthy pain, one that has within it its own healing qualities.

The second step centers around breaking some of the bonds that tie us to the person who has died. This is sometimes referred to as "withdrawing the emotional capital from the past" so that our feelings can be reinvested in the present and the future. Life has been interrelated in many ways with the person who has died. A parent invests his hope in the life of a child. If the child dies he must withdraw the hope, for it is no longer valid. Only as he withdraws it can he look toward the future with complete honesty. When an aged parent dies, adult children must recognize that they cannot have dependent feelings anymore. They must withdraw their dependence and declare their independence; otherwise their lives will be perpetually bound to a false security.

Third, it is vital to develop ways that will make it possible for the surviving person to find new interests, satisfactions, and creative activities for the remainder of his life. New relationships must be formed, new acquaintances made, new challenges developed. The energy of life must be planted where it can be fruitful. The past is past. While its memories may be treasured, one cannot live on memories alone and still be healthy.

How are these goals to be attained? (Grief is relieved by time, by understanding, and by the ongoing creative impulses of life itself.)

When sorrow comes the days drag. The long hours of these slow-moving days are weighted with pain and defeat. But all people in all places have recognized that time has about it a healing quality. As time moves on, things that were out of perspective begin to move back into their proper place. So one must be patient and give psychic wounds enough time to heal.

When we understand what is happening it is easier to bear. It is meaningless suffering that is unendurable. When we can grasp the fact that death is part of the cycle of life, then death in general is not so distressing; rather it is the individual death we contemplate that presents a problem to us. But if the personal loss is related to a larger process, we are then able to see it in the larger perspective that understanding adds to the slow wisdom of time.

Life has about it a certain built-in momentum. It shows up in the meeting of problems and the finding of solutions. The effort to do the next thing that must be done helps us to live beyond our grief and ease ourselves into the future with its claims upon us.

And the things we do together to act out our feelings helps us to wisely cope with them. Ceremonies have a way of helping us to act out feelings that are too deep to be put into words. Through rites and rituals we are aided in facing reality, pouring out our deep and valid feelings and gaining the support of a group of people who give us some of their strength as we act out our emotions together.

We can tell when we have arrived at the place where we have managed our feelings well, for then we can look back on the past with its rich treasure of memory and shared experience free from the pain that was so much a part of our early response to loss. We will have arrived at the place where we can hold on to the things that death cannot take from us, for we will have discovered that beyond the biological event of physical death there is much of life that can never be destroyed by external happenings. We will have discovered the inner dimension of that immortality that remains very much alive within us.

How do we prepare to meet grief situations?

Preparation for coping with personal crises can come in at least three ways.

(1) First, there is education. We can learn through our own experience of deprivation and loss. We can honestly and courageously study the subject. A high-school course in death perspectives can be useful in helping youths face anxiety about death. Study courses in college, and university and adult groups in the community are valid ways of gaining insight into our emotions and what happens within us in times of crisis.

(2) Second, there is our philosophy of life. Often we run away from developing our philosophy of life because the subject is threatening to us. Psychiatrist Avery Weisman points out that unless a person's way of looking at life is broad enough to confront his own death or the death of those close to him, he has an inadequate perspective on life. In some monastic orders the members were expected to spend some time each day contemplating their own death as an essential to discovering how best to live. Each person is constantly busy creating his own way of life. It should be important for each of us to be sure we are not arriving at an inadequate view of death, for it can create an escapist view of life itself.

(3) Third, we can help to build sound community practice at the time of death. Perhaps the most accessible resource in most communities is the funeral, the social and religious rite associated with death. Here three important

things can take place at one and the same time: Members of the community can be helped to do important anticipatory grief work: those most in need of group support can find it; and anyone with unfinished work of mourning is provided an opportunity to accomplish it. For this reason it seems the private type of service is unsound, for it denies the family some of the resources it needs most at the same time that the community is denied some of its best learning experience. If the leaders responsible for developing sound community practice wisely discern the needs of people who confront death, they may see the value of expanding and enriching the resources for acting out deep feelings rather than restricting them.

2

Care of the Dying Person

What is it like to be dying?

How to talk to the dying person.

What are the hidden reactions of dying people?

Can one achieve a dignified death?

How best to help the dying person.

N. H. CASSEM

Mortality, by Webster's definition, is "the nature of man, as having eventually to die." Death is the ultimate existential fact. But what happens to the patient, the family, and the physician when each is consciously aware of the loss taking place.

The Youville Hospital in Cambridge, Massachusetts, specializes in long-term rehabilitative and chronically ill patients and has pioneered in the development of a program for counseling dying patients. The program is directed by the Reverend Dr. N. H. Cassem, the staff psychiatrist, who has been doing research in the field of terminal patient care for the last nine years. Dr. Cassem is also a psychiatrist at the Massachusetts General Hospital.

Care of the Dying Person

What is it like to be dying or to know that you have a fatal illness and your days are numbered?

For whom?

Nobody in particular — I meant it in a general way. I meant more in general. I want to know more about this because I think it is so important to be able to be helpful to people who are dying.

You asked the most important question in caring for a dying person and also suggested one of the major obstacles to accomplishing it. One who can learn what it is like for another dying patient stands a good chance of being one of the most helpful persons during the illness. On the other hand, one of the major reasons so few people can do this is their preconceptions of what it is like get in the way. They spend much of their time trying to fit the dying person's reactions to their preconceived patterns and never listen to what he or she really says. If confronted by a dying person yourself, do you think you yourself could find out from him what it is like?

I don't know. Are you suggesting that I should learn?

Definitely.

But talking about death or what it is like to be dying seems to me to be just about the last thing that would be helpful for a fatally ill person. In fact, isn't that a cruel and sadistic sort of discus-

sion to have with a person who has a terminal diagnosis?

That's the commonest objection aimed at investigators who have worked with dying people. One of the pioneers in this work, Herman Feifel, met the same objections when he began his work. He found the opposite was true. By far the majority of patients were relieved and grateful that they at last had an opportunity to speak with somebody about it.

You say that everyone wants to talk about death and dying. Isn't that in itself a general principle? And if so, aren't you contradicting your former statement that general principles are dangerous?

Good for you! It would be foolish to say for any individual without getting to know him what he wanted to discuss. It still remains important, however, to find out what it is like for everyone. That may mean for some that they want to be totally frank, for others that they want to avoid the subject, and for others that they deny entirely that they are ill. One of the greatest benefits of the studies of Feifel and other early investigators, not often enough emphasized, is that it *is* possible to talk to critically ill persons about their illness and reactions to it.

I'd like to learn about some of that work. Are you suggesting that it's better not to read that work, better not to read about their findings so that I can meet each dying person fresh?

No, we must do both. After you saw a hundred patients you would have your own generalizations (we probably make them after seeing *one* patient!). I agree it's important that we learn everything we can about different ways of adapting to critical illness and impending death, while at the same time doing everything we can to keep an open, fresh mind when approaching a new individual.

What reading would you suggest on the subject?

All the books listed at the end of this chapter are very helpful. Elisabeth Kubler-Ross's *On Death and Dying* is extremely valuable in this regard. She presents a wealth of clinical material in verbatim patient interviews that are both informative and fascinating. She also formulates a series of five states of emotional reactions which dying patients go through.

What are the stages?

The first she calls *Shock and Denial.* During this time the patient's message is, "No, not me." He may feel completely numb or in a state of shock or may not recognize any internal reactions. It may last from a few seconds or for the rest of his life, or it may intermittently return during the course of his illness.

Is it easy to recognize? "Denial" is a very general word — just what is it that the person denies and what form does the denial take?

There are many forms of denial. The patient may deny that he is ill at all, that the diagnosis is correct, that the diagnosis is fatal, that the diagnosis bothers him in any way, that the diagnosis will change his life-style in any way, and other aspects of the illness or its implications. Minimizing the illness or its threatening implications is also considered a form of denial. So you see it's a very general word.

Moreover, the person with a fatal illness may show his denial in ways other than words. He may make unrealistic plans, look forward to events far beyond his life expectancy, continue smoking if he has lung cancer, disobey doctors' orders, refuse to accept limitations, or make overoptimistic statements about his therapy, such as his medication will cure him or his surgery already has.

Do some patients actually say that they do not have cancer?

At least 20 percent say so. I should also point out that 20 percent of patients who have had a heart attack respond exactly the same way and say that they haven't had one.

But isn't that a function of whether they're told or not?

No. If that were taken into consideration the percentage would be far higher. Those figures were obtained from patients who had been told bluntly and openly their diagnosis.

You said that a person's denial can come and go. Does that mean that if he admits he has cancer on one day he may return to his denial at a later time?

It certainly does mean that. In fact, it can be very striking. I vividly remember one patient who told me on Monday that he didn't know what his illness was, that he really didn't care to have much information; on Tuesday that his body was riddled with cancer and he was a goner; on

Wednesday that he didn't know what his illness was and there was no connection between his left arm amputation and the bone pain of his back and lower extremities (which were involved with the same malignancy); and on Thursday that while nobody likes to die, he himself knew full well that he was facing it. Denial fluctuates and it would be a mistake not to remember and respect that fact.

What did you do about it when that patient's denial changed from day to day?

Why would I want to do anything about it?

Isn't denial a bad thing? I would assume that retaining it would just make it more difficult for a person to function.

Which person?

OK, it's bad to generalize, I realize. But you are implying that denial can be a good thing under some circumstances. What are those circumstances and how am I supposed to tell whether it's good or not?

We couldn't get along without denial. Denial is essentially that mechanism by which a person is enabled to put out of mind the morbid, upsetting, frightening, depressing, and pessimistic aspects of his life while he focuses on more constructive issues like the business of living. The reason it fluctuates is probably dictated by the degree of stress he is under at any given time. The amount of denial a person uses is precisely that which is required to get along comfortably. The person who thinks only that pain, breathlessness, another heart attack, or death itself is around the next corner makes a neurotic out of himself.

But how do you tell when it is constructive and when it isn't?

Although at times it is extremely difficult to tell, the best criterion is whether the person is able to do what he himself wants to do with a maximum amount of enjoyment. If his denial is so distorted that a communication barrier has come up between him and the family and he is becoming more and more isolated from them, it is time to break through the denial so that some sharing can take place. If his relationships are good, and he isn't doing anything self-destructive, what is so bad about denial? There is a danger among people who take care of the dying of wanting the person to conform to their standards and expectations, thereby overlooking what is important for the person himself.

But if there are stages, isn't it necessary to stop denying before one gets into the next stage?

No, only for some. The stages, in fact, coexist within the person. For example, persistent denial can be the best stimulus to the expression of anger, such as when the person insists on acting with normal vigor and experiences extreme frustration at the weakness or fatigue that results.

The second stage is called Anger. What happens during that time?

The patient no longer says, "No, not me." He now says, "Why me?" Angry, bitter, and resentful at what has happened to him, he becomes irritable, difficult to manage, and generally out of sorts.

Does he actually say that he's mad about being sick?

Almost never, at least in the beginning. The patient may complain about his treatment, that he's not getting well fast enough, that the hospital food is terrible, or, saying nothing, he appears surly and hostile.

Is the person angry at anyone in particular?

As noted, certain staff members or the physicians may be singled out, but when the person discusses his feelings of frustration and resentment over becoming ill, he often doesn't know whom to blame. Many patients blame God.

Would you expect a devoutly religious person to be angry at God?

Yes. Not every person expresses anger toward God, but many religious people acknowledge that they have angry feelings or resentment toward God. Most often they will say something like, "I never did anything wrong, certainly nothing to deserve this. Why did it have to happen? It's just not fair." Other persons say that they do not blame God but they cannot help feeling resentful or asking the question "Why?"

What can a person do to stop this reaction?

That's exactly what you want *not* to do. Anger is a spontaneous human feeling and most patients are much better off if it is allowed to come out so that they can understand their own feelings better. One of our main tasks should be not to stop a person when he is expressing anger.

How should one help another person get his anger out?

Some need no help and all that's necessary is to listen. From others it helps to get the details of their story: When it started, who was involved, why they say what they say, and so on. Feelings of anger can be like an abscess which needs to be drained.

If the anger is directed at nurses or physicians or at the hospital food or rules, isn't it dangerous to assume that the only anger involved stems from their being terminally ill? Isn't it often true that the food is bad or the treatment is poor? How can you tell when the anger is displaced?

This is why it's so important to get as many details as possible from the person. Sometimes it seems impossible to tell what the truth is. It may take three or four days of hearing the same complaints before one begins to get the suspicion that there is more anger involved than is justified by the complaints.

Are there patients who remain hostile, angry, and uncooperative for a long time?

Prolonged anger and hostile behavior are not rare among chronically ill people. This may in part be due to the unwillingness of those who take care of them to let some of the anger erupt and thereby be dispelled or dissipated. Still, there are some illnesses in which prolonged anger is more common. Young men suddenly paralyzed in an accident may remain bitter and hostile for months.

What's a good way to approach a bitter, angry person?

Slowly, patiently, and with respect. The first step is probably to hear them out several times, yet to keep coming back. Trying too early to get the people to see the brighter side of things will only make them angrier. It can be very helpful to get them talking about subjects other than their illness, such as their past or current events. With some it will seem that nothing works. Patients with prolonged reactions of this kind tax the ingenuity of the most creative persons. In the end it's not the person with many methods or "tricks" who is helpful, but the one who cares enough to keep trying to remain open, to refuse to patronize, to continue to understand the other person better.

What is the third stage, "Bargaining"?

Instead of saying "Why me?" the patient may say, "Yes, it is me, *but* . . . . " The dying person gives provisional acknowledgment to his condition. He now says that he may have a remission, that he hopes he'll live until a special event (wedding, birth, graduation, etc.). One man wanted to see his daughter happily married, a woman hoped to survive until her great-grandchild was born.

And after "Bargaining" comes "Depression"?

The fourth reaction or stage comes at those times when the patient says, "Yes, it is me," and the full impact of his condition hits him. Aware that he must lose all those whom he loves, thinking of the many things he will not live to see or do, and anticipating his steady deterioration, he may become withdrawn, brooding, sad, unconsolable. Despair would seem to be a genuine danger. Surely this phase must be bad for the patient: How can it be prevented, minimized, or reversed? Some depression is inevitable. In fact it would be quite unusual not to find it in normal people. Many people feel better when they are able to express sorrow or weep. So when someone is crying or talking about sorrow, the first thing we should do is hear them out.

What can anyone possibly gain from telling about their misery or crying about it?

People tell their sorrows to someone else for a very important reason. In times of suffering it's very helpful to have the presence of another person who understands something of what the sufferer goes through. If we are able to listen we may be able to become that understanding person whom he needs and seeks. Suffering alone is suffering compounded. All too few people exist who have the capacity to hear out a sad story with compassion. Many a person has said to his spouse, friend, chaplain, nurse, or physician: "I don't think I could have made it through that day without you." So there is a genuine risk in not allowing a patient to express his depressed feelings, namely, that he will be left with the feeling that nobody understands or knows what it's like. It's too easy to then say, "Nobody cares." That feeling or conviction is more likely to produce despair than personal reactions to losses.

Does anyone ever really accept death?

To many a sick room death is a welcome visitor, especially where pain or prolonged suffering cause persons to view death as a welcome release. Others seem quietly ready but, of course, there are always persons who seem to be caught unawares.

Should care of the adult dying patient consist of

helping him to get through the stages one after the other?

No, that's probably one of the least helpful ways of viewing the five stages. It would be better to think of shock, denial, anger, bargaining, and depression as five normal reactions to any momentous loss. They may occur simultaneously, disappear and reappear, and occur in any order.

Isn't there a best way to die? It would seem that a person ideally should accept death after working himself through the other stages, and be in a state of quiet and calm. Wouldn't it therefore be better to encourage the dying to work on the stages, even in sequence, so they can reach acceptance more readily?

There is no such thing as a best way to die. After all, the other person's death is his own, not ours or anyone else's. There is a danger that our expectations of others are selfish rather than altruistic. Some want others to grow old quietly, not because there is anything especially good about that, but only so the old won't be a nuisance and they won't have to think about the old. So too there is a danger we may want others to die quietly, instead of angrily, because it makes us more comfortable. Dying must have as many styles as living, because dying is the living that is done at the end. The more it is consistent with earlier lifestyle, the better.

If a person doesn't know what to expect, how does he know what to do?

If anything it's better not to come to the patient's bedside biased as to what he "should" be doing. The first obligation we have is to find out what's going on with the dying person. It helps to know that we may meet depression, anger, denial, or bargaining. But it's crucial to keep an open mind so that the patient can be himself rather than have to force himself into our categories or expectations. So the first thing to do is to find out what it's like for the other person.

Does that mean that there are no goals for the dying person that we can aim at or try to reach?

There could be no better goal than to keep the person himself. If he has lost the sense of himself as a whole person then it's important to make him himself again. The only way that that can be done is to find out what kind of person he is and what the present situation means to him.

DEALING WITH THE DYING PERSON

What personal qualities do dying persons find most helpful?

Three qualities head the list. Someone who takes an interest and has compassion; someone who listens; and someone who makes an effort to get to know what they're like — this is the sort of person who will be most helpful when life "begins to fail." Those qualities could be summed up quite simply by saying that it's a person who cares.

Are you implying that there is a shortage of these sorts of persons?

Many people have the potential, but unfortunately there are few who develop their skills. The commonest failings of those who take care of terminally ill persons are, first, the inability to listen or to deal with what the person says, and second, failure to learn what the person is really like.

But listening seems so easy. What are the difficulties?

During a conversation a person with a fatal illness usually says one or more things that make his listener nervous. References to fear, resentment, suffering, despair, or death make another person so uncomfortable that he simply pays no attention to them, or literally tells the ill person something like, "Don't talk like that." We always say, "How are you?" to our friends, but always with a tacit understanding that under no circumstances will they say anything except "fine." In fact, we usually get to know persons who answer that question honestly and stop asking it. One woman feels unconsolable because she must die before her younger children are settled in life. Another cannot get relief from pain. Still another is filled with bitterness.

Do dying persons really want to talk about these things?

Most who bring up those kinds of issues do want to talk about them — otherwise they wouldn't have mentioned them. Unfortunately they are very likely to find there is no one willing to listen.

Can anyone serve as a listener? Aren't there some persons whom you would prefer to tell it to and not to others?

Yes, that is very true. One must assume when a subject of this nature is introduced into the conversation, the person wants to talk about it. Usually, however, certain people become special, and more intimate feelings are shared with them. It can be disappointing for friends, chaplains, nurses, doctors, or others who take care of dying persons when they are not the ones the patient chooses to confide certain intimate details of the way he is feeling or thinking. We have to respect this. The main struggle is finding someone who can listen to that kind of thing. But usually people don't come right out and say what's on their minds.

Are dying persons any different?

Dying persons don't tell what's on their minds either. If they did, they would never have any visitors. What they do is to touch on the topic directly or indirectly, such as, "I've been in the hospital two weeks now this time and I don't seem to be getting anywhere," and I reply, "It must be very frustrating," or, "Have you been getting worried?" I may learn what's on his mind. If I say nothing I won't learn what's on his mind whether he wants to tell me or not.

What usually happens after a question like that is asked?

For some it is a chance to explode, discuss their fears, or simply to leave it and not say anything. It often happens that the other person will not follow up on a question. Sometimes statements are made to test the visitors, professionals, or friends. Through the response a person can tell whether what he says will be taken seriously or not. Many suggestive things are said by patients.

What about the risk of fatally ill persons breaking down when questions like this are asked? Isn't it dangerous to pursue some of these concerns with them?

Don't forget it is the fatally ill person who introduced the topic. If by "breaking down" you mean becoming psychotic then the risk is almost negligible. But if by "breaking down" you mean merely getting upset, then, of course, the patient will get upset. But what we don't want to recognize is that the patient is already upset.

But if the patient is already upset, talking about it will make him even more upset. And isn't this harmful for him?

It may not be true that talking will make him more upset. He does not appear upset when he talks because he has had to suppress his feelings and has had no one who has been willing to share with him. When he now has a chance to express how bad he feels or the way he feels in the presence of someone with some compassion and understanding, it is helpful. These feelings do more damage pent up than they do when expressed.

Are there any fears that are common to dying persons?

Several years ago a survey was conducted among terminally ill cancer patients, in which they were asked what their fears about dying were. They had several on the list, such as fear of being disfigured, loss of independence, insanity, and others. The highest ranked fears were: being left alone to die, pain, and suffocation. It is immediately apparent how important listening is for these persons. If you can't find anybody who is willing to listen to what you say, you are essentially abandoned already.

When they really do come to die how correct have they been in their fears?

Because our society has such an aversion for old people and the dying, they usually *are* abandoned. So their primary fear is very well justified. Fortunately, with proper care, pain does not make the top of the list because 90 percent of the patients can be made comfortable. The three greatest physical problems are: nausea and vomiting, difficult breathing or suffocating, difficulty in swallowing and getting food down.

What are the reasons dying persons are isolated or even abandoned?

We always exclude strangers or aliens, as we call them. Basically, they are a large minority group who are discriminated against. Dying persons are foreigners to the living precisely because there are so few people among the living who work hard at finding out what dying is like. When the astronauts come back from outer space we interview them and find out what the experience was like, and we're very much interested. But when Herman Feifel and other early investigators interviewed dying patients and learned what they were going through, their findings were not only unwelcome but usually rejected.

Still most families seem to hold the position that the family member who is dying not only does not want to tell what he is going through but that he must be sheltered from it. Shouldn't they be the best judges of what a person needs?

Families usually suffer from a certain misguided compassion. In their own efforts to pretend or wish that nothing frightening or discouraging will happen to the person they love, they retain the illusion that he, himself, doesn't know about it or doesn't want to talk about it.

Do patients know what they have even if they haven't been told?

Certainly by the time the disease is advanced it's best to assume that everybody knows what he has and that it's extremely serious. One should also assume that almost every one of these persons has thought about dying. Although this is contrary to popular belief, all investigators who have worked with dying persons have found these to be the facts. Because patients *do* realize these things, they naturally have many of the feelings associated with this knowledge we discussed above.

Do you recommend, then, that a visitor or professional should direct the conversation toward the patient's fears of death or other things that might be on his mind?

Of course not. Basically one goes to talk with a dying person because he is interested in him. In the course of listening carefully, if the visitor or professional hears things that suggest fear, discouragement, suffering, or similar concerns, then he should at that point be willing to discuss them more thoroughly. When you find yourself wanting to control the direction of the conversation even before you have seen the person, then you know something is wrong.

Listening is usually considered a passive operation. You make it sound very aggressive. Isn't that the same thing as directing the conversation yourself?

A good listener is about as passive as a good surgeon. If you tell a friend you bought a new car and all he says is "oh," or "that's nice," you realize right away that he is not interested. But if he asks you what kind, what horsepower, what the repair record on that model is, and vhy you preferred it over other models, you not only know that he is interested but you find yourself in the midst of a real conversation. The same is true with the dying person who may want to talk about being discouraged or making out a will. So when a patient says something like, "I've got three years before retirement, but I guess that doesn't make too much difference now," it simply isn't enough to say nothing. "What do you mean?" would be much better.

Still, it is important that the dying person direct the conversation and be able to stop it. The man talking about his car might not want to talk about how much he paid for it or how he was financing it, and anyone who asked a question like that and noticed some hesitancy in the answer should know enough to stop asking it. So too with the dying person. It's important that he be given an opportunity to express something that he may want to express.

What if I am talking to a friend and he asks me what he has?

If you were his doctor I hope you would have already told him. But if you were not, then it's important to find out why he asks the question, why he directs it to you. You may find that out by asking him a question, such as "What do you think you have?" Or "What have you been told?" After that, if one is really interested, one should find out what he knows, what he has been told and by whom, when they told him these things, how it was communicated to him, and whether he thinks the communication has been defective in some way or whether he doesn't believe it. It is *not* safe to assume you know what the patient wants before you have made any effort to find out from him in detail.

What if he asks whether he is dying?

This is a rare question, particularly from patients who have a fair length of time to live. Actually it is more common in patients who face death abruptly, at least in my own experience. Because it is an unusual question, even more care should be taken to find out just why it is asked. The best reply would be another question. "Do you think you're dying?" If he says yes then we must find out the circumstances — namely why, when did he learn, who told him, how does he know, what exactly was said.

What proportion of conversation time with dying persons is taken up with getting at their depressed, angry, or frightened feelings?

No one can promise that no morbid or heavy conversations will occur, but fortunately most of the conversation time with dying persons is not spent on those concerns. In fact, most of the people who work with dying persons find that these kinds of discussions are in a distinct minority.

What should be talked about, then?

Too often we forget that the dying patient is a living person. He has both a past and a present history, his own talents and idiosyncrasies, and unique interests and viewpoints. Dealing with him should be viewed as getting to know him better.

How does one know what to talk about?

Usually the patient gives some clues. Hospitalized persons often have pictures of their families at the bedside. This aspect of the person's life is one of the most important to learn about: his family and how he regards them. Another obvious area to explore is the sort of work the person has done. Hobbies, interests, special talents, all help us know better what the person is like. The more we know the more we will appreciate him as a person.

Are there any areas or topics that should be avoided with dying persons?

No area should be avoided that the person wants to talk about. Of course, learning what the person wants to talk about is difficult but that's the obligation and responsibility of those who really care about him.

So far you have talked about understanding as though it were only communicated in words or conversation. Isn't it true that there are many nonverbal ways of communicating concern and understanding as well?

Sometimes the nonverbal forms of communication convey far more meaningfully our concern than do our verbal communications. Squeezing a hand, a hug, moist eyes during a sudden silence, little acts of thoughtfulness, consistent, unresenting fidelity often tell a fatally ill person far more than words could ever express. There are many shared silences far more profound than words.

Is touch more important with a dying person, such as holding a hand?

Touching surely is one of the most important forms of communication with dying persons and is usually not done enough. The dying are in some sense the "untouchables" of our age. Remembering always to shake a hand, holding a hand, touching an arm, a hand on the shoulder, all these have great potential for comforting a person who is dying.

Isn't it also true that there are some people who don't like to be touched?

Many people have an aversion to being touched. What we forget, however, is that touch is a two-way sense. Not only does touch convey what we mean, but it also tells us a good deal about the person we touch. Touching another person is the quickest way to find out who doesn't like to be touched. Failing, then, to respect that would be a glaring mistake. Touch also reveals taut muscles or sweaty palms. So even touch is another way to learn more about the person we are trying to help.

Because all of this seems so delicate, isn't it inevitable that mistakes will be made?

For anyone devoted to taking care of the dying, mistakes are guaranteed as part of the contract. The important thing is to keep trying our best to avoid them. As long as we do that, they have certain genuine advantages. They remind the other person — and this is a reassuring thing — that we're human too. Our mistakes give the dying person a chance to reassure us. The parents of a ten-year-old boy with terminal malignancy once told me they spent most of their time consoling the people who came to visit them. Paradoxically, of course, the visitors came in an effort to do some consoling but had to be consoled by the parents themselves. What really matters is that we're trying to do the right thing by the suffering people we're with. When we make mistakes and have enough sensitivity to feel bad about it, it gives them a chance to take care of us, which they do very effectively. It also keeps us aware that the relationship is at least equal, and that the roles of helper and helped can frequently be reversed.

To rephrase and repeat, what do you talk about with a person who is fatally ill?

There are three basic ways of thinking about this. In the first place, I talk about those things that make the other person more real to me — his family, his work, his hobbies, his current interests. his loves and hates, particularly as they affect nim now, but with care to include both past and present. That helps me to get to know him and appreciate him better as a person. In the second place, I give some extra thought to what he is like and how that should direct my conversation. For example, if he is frightened or hostile, I know it's important (always assuming that he's willing to share it) to find out what he's scared of or what he's furious about. In those situations getting more information is very necessary. If he is morose and dejected, I know it's more important to adjust myself for a longer siege of repeated visits. Last, as far as he and I are concerned, he needs to be able to count on me as a consistent visitor. I know that in order to return consistently over a long period of time, that I must make the encounters as pleasant for myself as possible. Therefore, I explore and exploit those aspects of a person's history or work or personality that make her or him most interesting and enjoyable to me. The nurse's aide who worked in one of the earliest homes for brain damaged children, the swordfisherman, the professor who had exacting demands of the students in their Shakespeare seminar, all enriched my knowledge and appreciation of those areas. If we can grow to appreciate these things about people, our increased respect for what they are is quite evident to them, too. So one very important aspect of talking to a fatally ill person is thinking about what is required to keep me coming back.

What about the problem of imposing on the other person? Are your visits ever an imposition?

There is no doubt that some visits may be an imposition, including my own, or that a visit may be too long. Perhaps it's helpful to think of oneself as another form of medication, asking what is the dose required to help and beyond what dose do we become toxic? From what the dying say, it seems clear that the majority of people don't have to worry about being "toxic" because they find it simply impossible to visit in the first place. That's why dying people are so afraid of being abandoned.

If a person has told you about all the things that anger, frighten, and depress him, is it more likely that your presence would remind him of those things rather than more hopeful or positive things?

Having someone nearby who understands what you're going through is sometimes more helpful than any other single thing. If there are people around with whom we can share only the best things and not the worst, they really aren't true friends. I remember a man in his mid-fifties who most (including himself) thought would not survive extensive cardiac surgery. Most still thought he would die after he survived surgery. Although profoundly depressed and at times disoriented, he had an excellent sense of humor, which no one seemed either to appreciate or to be able to elicit. His wife once said to me, "You're the only one who can get him to laugh." That surprised me somewhat, but not so much when I learned I was the only one who could get him to cry. It was a good lesson that sharing has to go in both directions, both gloomy and bright.

Throughout all this talk about the "dying" or "terminal" person. How do you define the terminally ill person?

I'm never sure. Life, of course, is a terminal state. Once somebody incurs an illness that he is very likely to die from, he could be called terminally ill. But how "likely" is that to be? The rhythm or march of the illness is very important. If it is likely to recur suddenly without warning, as with heart disease or the remission periods of leukemia, the person may be anxious because he lives under the sword of Damocles. If the disease trajectory is long and slow, as with multiple sclerosis, the person may be dealing more with depression. Whatever it is, he may be mad, sad, or scared, and our task is the same: to find out what it's like for him and how we can help keep him a person.

You said earlier that what the dying person needs is someone who has compassion, who listens, and who will get to know him. Doesn't everyone need that, whether they are dying or not? If so, how are the dying person's needs any different?

They aren't. The well housewife next door with four children has just as much right to hope for your interest and compassion when she is healthy as when she learns that she has an inoperable ovarian malignancy. There is a monumental difference between the two instances but the difference lies not in her but in our own hearts. Assuming that I appreciate and respect her when she is healthy, I would never dream of denying her concern, listening, and personal interest. But when I learn that she has an inoperable cancer I am very likely to feel so devastated, so helpless, and so outraged that I would rather avoid than confront her. The difference is in us.

Those feelings don't sound very professional. What about the danger that being too involved with the person would hurt one's ability to take care of them? If professionals have those feel-

*ings, is it necessary to suppress them or is it
possible to become so accustomed to dying that
one doesn't have them anymore?*

Every honest person, including the professional, has
some or all of those feelings upon confronting a dying person.
Of course, they will be more intense if that other person is
closer to our own age. But the major difficulty in helping
fatally ill persons go on living comes from the feelings of
their helpers. Until we can deal with the feelings we will be
poor helpers. We should respect the diversity of ways in
which people go through these feelings, just as we have to
respect the many different ways or lifestyles that people have.
Some cannot discuss feelings of overwhelming compassion or
sympathy but very skillfully communicate it in nonverbal
ways.

Do feelings get in the way of our efficiency?

Without any doubt. The consequences of this are
much worse for a surgeon than they are for a chaplain. Too
few people appreciate that one of the surgeon's primary
responsibilities to his patient is to make sure that his hands
are steady in the operating room. In this age where it seems
fashionable to castigate physicians, especially surgeons, people forget this. Still, we must remember that from the
patient's viewpoint the person who takes good care of him is
the person who retains the ability to care about him. That is,
the ability to feel sympathy for another person, which literally means that suffering uncomfortable feelings with each new
person is essential to caring about them. Difficult as it is, we
have to be willing to remain vulnerable.

*Isn't there a danger in being vulnerable? Doesn't
it harm the patients to see that professionals or
family members are upset?*

It would upset a person if the professionals taking care of him were unable to do their job. Being able to trust someone else's competence is extremely important. But critically ill people also want to know that those taking care of them are human as well. The absence of any manifest feeling is usually taken as coldness or lack of concern. A woman could well wonder, for example, why her husband joked or talked about the weather all the time he was aware of the fact that she was dying. As long as one does his job well, it's not only not bad but probably important that the patient knows that he or she has feelings.

Are there any other things that can be done for fatally ill persons besides becoming comfortable enough to keep on visiting?

Assuming that the patient's physicians are well versed in the use of narcotics to control pain and alcohol to promote a sense of well-being, one important thing that can be done for the dying person is to make sure that he has access to children. Probably no influence is as successful in cheering up the day of an elderly or dying person as the presence of a child. Hospitals which impose restrictions against children visiting dying persons are inhumane.

Will visiting dying persons do any harm to the child?

The only evidence for trauma in children comes from families in which there is already some conflict. For that reason parents should be encouraged to take their children to visit seriously ill persons whom they themselves might feel comfortable with and with whom the child and his immediate family have no conflict. At St. Christopher's Hospice in London, the staff has a day-care center where children of the staff remain during the day. Patients who are ambulatory are free to visit the playground or playrooms for these children. Far from doing the children harm, this is mutually beneficial. Even though our generation has been deprived of coming to know in a natural manner that death is part of life, there is no need to rob children of that fact so necessary for emotional maturation. The fact is that children have a beneficial effect on the majority of persons afflicted with a fatal or potentially fatal illness. Misguided attempts to deprive them of contact with children constitute cruelty. Most of those who say that children in general cannot tolerate this or don't want to know about it are actually talking about the other child within themselves who wants to deny the reality of death, illness, and suffering.

So far this discussion has focused on being able to talk with dying persons about their fears and reactions to their illness, even about dying itself. What can one do when the patient's physician says that he is not to be told about his diagnosis or prognosis?

That situation is no exception to all the foregoing. The difference lies in one's using that as an excuse to avoid talking to patients when those instructions have been left. With this sort of patient our obligation is no different, namely to get to know him, how he feels, and what we can do to help keep him himself. When that kind of order is issued, it means that someone, usually including the patient, has difficulty with openness. That has to be respected, above all in the patient. If he is deteriorating rapidly, of course, you can again take for granted that he knows his diagnosis and has thought about dying.

How can one deal with a family who insist that

*no one discuss the illness of the sick member
with him?*

Families are crucial in the care of the dying. When
they are present and constructively concerned, the overall
comfort of the patient will be increased manyfold. When they
remain on the fringe or have somehow lost interest in the dying person, then they can be as much a hindrance as a help.
We must not forget that families need help too. Critically ill
persons get all the attention of the hospital staff, while family
members, who may be equally devastated by the illness, are
left to fend for themselves. We must get to know the family,
if at all possible, nearly as well as we know the patient.
Instead of always discussing the patient's health or present
state, we should remember to ask the family how they
themselves are doing and give them a chance to share their
own burdens with someone. "We follow your husband very
closely every day but who worries about *you*? How are you
holding up under all this?" is a question that should be asked
more often of family members. I personally don't believe
that the conspiracy of silence ever helped anybody. But the
interpersonal walls that are built by such conspiracies are not
broken down overnight. As in dealing with the patient, it is
important to draw out the family to give their account of why
they think the patient doesn't know, just exactly what he
knows, how he cannot know, why they think he cannot take
it, if he can't take it what exactly will happen, etc. The family
knows the patient better than anyone else, even though they
may be misusing their knowledge in this situation. It would
be a mistake not to share in that knowledge. It would also be
a mistake to forget that families who say patients shouldn't
have access to the truth are violating the rights of that family
member.

If the patient's rights are being violated, isn't it

necessary and advisable that he be given the truth without further delay?

Only rarely is that true. People who say it's that simple are the ethical bulls in reality's china shop. What is forgotten is that the family who can't be open about tragedy and death is a family that never was fully open about life. The clinical attempts to heal those defects require much more effort and concern.

What should one do with a dying person who says that although he knows, his family should not be informed?

Although he is probably within his rights, he may not be exercising them wisely. Again, as is always the case, it is important to elicit from him in detail everything that went into his request. He may have excellent reasons or he may have reasons that are infantile.

Is it easier for older people to meet death? Is death ever easy for anyone?

Age increases one's capacity to meet death with equanimity as a general rule. Furthermore, it would be an oversight not to mention that for many persons death is a welcome visitor to their sickroom. Especially if physical suffering or personal abandonment are involved, this is likely to be true. Many persons pray that death come. Nor need they be morbid and depressed about it. In fact, some are impatient. A ninety-five-year-old great-great grandmother talked often of how proud she was of all her children and descendants. She had had a lingering breast malignancy since she was ninety-one. "It's time to be in the grave," she used to tell me, "now I just want to be with God." She had an air of calm, sunny composure about her that was striking.

Is it easier for members of an organized religion to meet death without fear?

In general no, only if they are older. Popular myths to the contrary, being a churchgoer doesn't assure one of any increased tranquillity in the face of suffering or death. Of course, most people are probably churchgoers out of habit and for them religion itself is little more than a habit or an attitude. Probably a necessary condition for meeting death with equanimity is the prior realization that loss is real, separation is genuine and painful, and that death brings this life to an end. Some people use religion to delude themselves that suffering and tragedy don't hurt, or that they will never have to face any. There is evidence that those people who confront their religious convictions with these truths actually do manifest less fear of death than those who use religion like a bandage or a set of blinders.

Do you think it's helpful for a religious person to share with a dying person his own insights and religious convictions?

Not unless the dying person wants to hear them. If we really are honest about helping another person religiously, the best thing that we do for him first is get him to share with us his own religious history. Is he a churchgoer now? What was his family tradition? What effect did his present illness have on his religious behavior and beliefs? Where does he think the Lord stands in all this? Is the Lord unfair? Is the illness seen as punishment for something he did? Is he furious with God because he never did anything to deserve this? If he believes in God, what sort of a person or concept does he regard God as being? Of course, if one is a chaplain or a minister, these questions seem natural But even if one is not, these questions, because they are so highly personal, are likely to be very important to the dying person. They are seldom asked, however. Death is a taboo topic but it is not as much avoided as religion.

But the most common reason that those questions remain unasked is not because they are embarrassing (which they are), but because we have such a hard time tolerating anyone with a different theology from our own. So if we learn that the dying person happens to be a Jehovah's Witness, or is devoted to St. Anthony, or is a Trinitarian, or an atheist, it may be that we don't want to hear any more about it — not because it's not important but because we just don't want to hear about it. Only after all that information is elicited and understood would I be willing to say that the patient stands to gain anything from a discourse on someone's personal theology. Unless he asks, of course, which is different. Even if he asks, we should remember that one of the primary reasons for asking about another's religious belief (e.g., in the afterlife), is to see whether or not we might be willing to listen to them about their own belief.

Should one deal differently, then, if the dying person is an atheist or an agnostic?

No. All the same questions apply. All the atheists and agnostics alive in Western civilization now have a history of contact with religion. In fact, it was usually that contact that made them an atheist. It is always of interest to know what that force was and how it came about — provided, of course, they are willing to tell you.

What is the best way to help cheer a fatally ill person?

First of all by giving up your notion that that's what he needs. The first thing that a critically ill person needs is someone to take him seriously, care about him, listen to him, and get to know him as a person so that he is appreciated as such. You do that, and then you'll know what cheers him up.

On the contrary, how can anyone be cheerful around a fatally ill person, especially if it's a young adult in a particularly tragic situation? Isn't that a denial in itself or a form of hypocrisy?

The fatally ill person would be the first to remind you that he is not being waked just yet. It is no easier to tolerate a sourpuss when you are dying than it is when you are in good health; in fact, it's much more difficult. In general, if a fatally ill person is a stranger to you and you are meeting him for the first time it is better to err on the side of being serious so that he will know that he is being taken seriously; but once you get to know him, you will realize that moments of laughter are even more important, more therapeutic, and can be more hearty then they were during periods of better health.

Is it possible to find a lighter side in every case when someone is fatally ill? Are there some people who are miserable and always remain miserable, or should we expect that there will be periods of some hearty laughter for everybody?

A fair ideal would be that everyone could be made more comfortable then they are; but reality forces us to admit that not everyone is a hero and for some the terminal illness seems to be miserable from start to finish despite a good deal of skillful and well-intentioned intervention. One wouldn't be honest if the hope were presented, the expectation presented, that work with every dying person produces tangible satisfaction to the afflicted person. There are people, after all, who have never made good adjustments to most of life's pressures. Those who have been unable to capitalize on other opportunities to grow may also be unable to capitalize on the last opportunity to grow which dying presents.

If a fatal illness is an opportunity to grow, then tragedies must be accompanied by something that is positive. What can that be?

Of and in itself, tragedy never brought anything good to anybody. If it did, everybody would be rich. Much more is needed. What tragedy activates in the persons who suffer is a set of strengths or virtues that have been present all along (even though they may not necessarily have been manifest). Dying has a way of bringing into high relief the important things about living. One poet, after he learned he had a fatal illness, claimed that he saw everything around him as though for the first time. Life seemed more than ever a gift and he appreciated everything more — smells, motion, paintings, sunsets, symphonies. Another couple, one of whom was dying, said that the love and caring support of their friends took on new dimensions and never seemed as real as it did during the days following knowledge of the diagnosis. For those who have the capacity to react, dying reminds them of how precious their relationships are *now*. They realize how foolish it is to postpone reconciliations and to put off mending the rent portions in the tapestry of affections between themselves and those they love. For once, people become more important than stuffy protocols. These kinds of people are inspiring and probably teach us more about the way we should live our own lives than any other single group of people.

Care of the dying sounds both difficult and rewarding. What factors enable those who do it to continue?

First of all there are inspiring people who teach indelible examples about life itself by the way they live. Secondly, it does become clear that people are helped by the efforts. As one husband told the nurse after his wife died, "You know, she really loved you. It made all the difference in the world to have you there." Another family made a special trip back to the hospital to thank the chaplain who had assembled them around the bed of their father at the time of his death. "Without you we could never have done that," one daughter told him, "and it was such a beautiful experience. We'll never forget you." Doing the work one learns to suffer more and suffer longer, not because these are in themselves helpful, but because they are the way we get the deeper appreciation of fatally ill persons and a fuller share in the happier moments. Finally, we get a lot of help and instruction in many things from the dying themselves. Seeing other persons grow is of course satisfying, but it would be foolish to overlook the opportunities that working with them provide for growth in us as well. Dying persons and their families need others willing to explore, understand, and mutually share the growth process they are struggling with. If we can bring ourselves to do this, difficult though it surely is, then we will be of more help to those who need us in these trying times of their lives. Moreover, those who do it on a regular basis will discover that they will learn more than they will teach, receive more than they give, and have more opportunities to grow up themselves than they would have had, perhaps, had they avoided this kind of service.

SUGGESTED READINGS

Feifel, Herman, "Death." In *Taboo Topics*, edited by N. L. Fardero (New York: Atherton Press, 1963), pp. 8 - 21.

Feifel, Herman (Ed.), *The Meaning of Death* (New York: McGraw-Hill, 1959).

Kubler-Ross, Elisabeth, *On Death and Dying* (New York: Macmillan, 1969).

Weisman, Avery D., *On Dying and Denying* (New York: Behavioral Publications, 1972).

Saunders, Cicely, "The Moment of Truth: Care of the Dying Person." In *Death and Dying: Current Issues in the Treatment of the Dying Person*, edited by Leonard Pearson (Cleveland: the Press of Case Western Reserve University, 1969), pp. 49 - 78. The other contributions in this volume are also highly recommended.

Godin, Andre, *Death and Presence: The Psychology of Death and the Afterlife* (Brussels: Lumen Vitae Press, 1972).

Kutscher, Austin H. (Ed.), *Death and Bereavement* (Springfield, Ill.: C. C. Thomas, 1969).

3

The Doctor, Fatal Illness, and the Family

Is fear of death unnatural?

What are the patient's attitudes during long-term illness?

Why isn't the physician more helpful?

What should be the role of the family?

Should the person be told of his fatal illness?

MELVIN J. KRANT

To talk to, work with, and understand the dying person evokes intense personal feelings. What is medicine's responsibility to the individual with a fatal illness? How about the patient attitudes during long-term sickness? What is the role of the family? And to understand dying in others demands that we deal with dying within ourselves.

Dr. Melvin J. Krant is the director of the Tufts University - Medical Cancer Unit, Lemuel Shattuck Hospital, in

Boston. He is president of the Equinox Institute, Brookline, devoted to creating an educational opportunity for understanding the social and the personal meaning of death, dying, and bereavement.

The Doctor, Fatal Illness, and the Family

How have attitudes toward death and dying changed?

Among the many changes in the way people live their lives, the twentieth century has seen two developments which make the physician, or the health-care system, pivotal to the problems besetting a dying person and his family. First, in this very materialistic century, the natural place of death and of the time called dying has by and large been denuded of traditional religious, social, and family forces which previously integrated these phenomena into the person's and family's concept of life. In the past, a firmer religious tradition, a larger family context, and a natural relationship to the land allowed people to participate and understand the dimensions of death as belonging to both God and man simultaneously. In this more traditional structure (if one can look back on previous generations and call them traditional) there was less confusion and less uncertainty as to how to behave and what to do surrounding the issues of dying and death itself. Thus, the sadness and the bewilderment of losing one's own life, or watching the life of a loved one being lost, was less compounded by loneliness and disorganization. The enormous advances of modern medicine have created two illusions operating to the disadvantage of dying people and their families.

The first illusion is that there will always be a treatment, or a medicine, that can prevent death, and therefore one can always play a game around dying as if the physician and the hospital have the power to postpone death indefinitely. The second illusion is that somehow the responsibility for one's personal health resides in the activities and behavior of the individual himself, so that if he does get ill, especially with a fatal illness, in some way he bears responsibility for such illness, as if it was not in nature's domain for natural illness to occur at all.

The first of these illusions seems related to the fact that a large number of therapeutic activities are available for patients with fatal illness that can postpone the moment of dying. With modern surgery, rehabilitation care, intensive diagnostic facilities, and the like, some illnesses, previously fatal, now seem to be curable — even certain kinds of cancer. In addition, some illnesses which are fatal can be prolonged so that an individual recovers for a while as if he were permanently getting better. These victories tend to be short-lived, and people continue to die, only most of us now have the feeling that doctors can still do things to prolong life if only we put ourselves in their hands.

The second illusion is fostered by announcements and pronouncements in the media and in lectures that so much of our health depends on ourselves. Thus, the food we eat, the amount of exercise we get, the rapidity with which we go for a physical examination, all seem to imply that the outcome of our lives, and certainly of our health, depends on our own initiative. In this regard, becoming sick with a fatal illness is clearly failing to take care of ourselves well enough. While there may be an element of truth to that, nevertheless if someone does come down with a fatal illness such as recurrent heart attacks, or cancer, there is often a feeling of having let somebody down, or of having failed in one's own care, which results in bad feelings on the part of patients about themselves, and often a feeling of accusation on the part of family members.

How should we behave in the face of fatal illness?

Since we have come to rely so heavily on the doctor and the health-care system for being professionally responsible for those acts surrounding the process of illness and dying, and because of the changes in our way of life from previous centuries, which has made death and the dying experience foreign to many of us until it happens to strike a loved one quite close to us, we really do not know how to behave — either from the viewpoint of the patient or from the viewpoint of a family — in order to create the most support for an individual facing a serious illness. I would therefore like to look at certain aspects of the problem of fatal illness and dying, and pose a series of questions in search for that elusive word *dignity.*

Since people do die of fatal illnesses, and since we must all die in one fashion or another, we can either die and help others die in a manner we call dignified, or in any other style or manner that can be described as fearful, resigned, abandoned, lonely, or in other appropriate terms. At no point am I claiming that death, coming at the end of a long-term fatal illness, should be seen either as a happy event or a careless event. For those of us who lose a member of our family, death will always be awesome, sad, and frequently filled with great difficulty. For an individual dying his own life, and giving up the many beautiful things life has to offer, we cannot kid ourselves that anything we do will make that death happy or joyful. But dignity is a word that goes beyond simple happiness. It is a word that involves self-control, style, caring, manners, free choice.

Suppose we analyze some of these concepts further, and expand upon the question of dignity. How can an individual have a death with dignity? I have asked this question of many individuals of various ages and my answer is a composite of their particular responses to such a question. The individuals asked have been students in universities and in professional schools, people dying of cancer, family members of such patients, and people in their seventies and eighties, both well and sick.

Most people feel that dignity requires the individual to have a high level of self-esteem. The individual feels at peace with himself, at harmony with himself, and in control of his destiny. For people to feel dignity they must feel a sense of worth both in who they are and in what they are doing. Frequently that sense of worth is a reflection of the way important individuals closely related to a person indicate that he is worthwhile to them. Thus, an elderly woman, who may have found worth in her years of living by being a mother and caregiver to her children, and who now finds in her old age that she has nothing to contribute to the welfare of her children or her grandchildren, can hardly feel self-esteem or self-worth, despite the fact that a daughter or a son may tell her how much he or she still loves her. If in the process of becoming fatally sick the dying woman sees herself as empty of giving or a doing role that previously gave her a sense of worth, then dignity is hard to command.

Inherent in the concept of worth is the sense of being in control of one's life. By control, I mean fundamentally being able to be part of the decisions made concerning one's life, and feeling one is truly a participant in those decisions. Thus, if we find ourselves in a hospital with tests being done to us that we neither understand nor desire, or find ourselves being sent to nursing homes or extended care facilities without our having a say as to where we are going — such events are hardly synonymous with feeling in control of one's destiny, with being involved in decisions necessary to control one's life.

Can a person approach his death with a sense of dignity? Obviously to die with dignity implies that one has been living one's life with dignity up to the moment that death occurs. It is then permissible to ask if one can feel a sense of worth, and be in control of his life, if he does not have two essential phenomena available to him: a feeling of being supported and loved by important people in his life, and a knowledge of the conditions which beset him so that he can make decisions about his living and dying in a meaningful fashion.

What is the nature of the doctor-patient relationship in fatal illness?

Because we have come to rely so heavily on the physician in these matters as a source of information and advice, it is important that we understand the interplay between individual patients, their physicians, and their families if we are to truly dissect out those events relating to the word dignity. Our first serious question is: "Should an individual who develops signs and symptoms of a fatal illness be fully informed about the nature of the illness and its potential outcome by his physician?" This question is usually best answered by looking at the reverse, namely: What happens to a relationship between patient and physician if the patient feels that either he is not being told the truth, or that he is being compromised in some fashion by his physician? Clearly that relationship must suffer enormously, and the patient must feel bewildered and very much alone if he cannot rely fully upon his physician to share all pertinent information about his condition.

We could immediately object that there are individuals who would prefer, under any circumstances, not to know that they have a life-threatening or fatal illness, and would certainly not want their physicians to be sharing such information with them. I agree that there always are a certain number of such individuals. But I think in general the failure to be honest in the relationship between physician and patient is more a matter of the physician's wishing to protect the patient from information he feels the patient could not tolerate, or the physician's avoiding having to deliver bad news to his patient. In either way, over any period of time a patient can only feel alone and confused if he finds or believes that he cannot have an honest relationship with his physician. The less an individual knows about his condition, the less he is in a position to make those choices necessary for the control of his life. If he hands over all decision-making to others, he may be able to get along, but it is hard to believe that such an individual can feel a sense of dignity. In general, I've come to believe that most patients are quite strong, do wish to be informed of the nature and status of their illnesses, and have significant resources for dealing effectively with decisions such as medical care, hospitalization, and the like, if they have information on which to make an adequate decision.

What about patient attitudes during long-term illness?

Simply telling somebody a diagnosis or sharing the implications of a diagnosis in some kind of truth-telling session is not the same as maintaining an honest relationship. By its very nature, truth-telling can be barbaric, painful, and nonsupportive, and can destroy an individual quite easily. Those physicians and others in the health-care sphere who are responsible for giving information to a patient must also bear the responsibility of an ongoing affective relationship with that patient, if the patient is to feel the support necessary to help him make up his mind about important matters. A great problem with modern medicine today, especially as practiced in large hospitals and clinics, is the impersonality of the relationship between doctors and patients, so that there is indeed often a dearth of ongoing support, of warm exchange between an impersonal physician and a patient. Too much specialization and professionalization promotes distance and loneliness when someone is seriously sick.

The course of a fatal illness today, such as cancer, chronic heart disease, or chronic renal disease, tends to extend over a long period of time. There are many treatments and resources available to keep patients alive and in reasonably good health for considerable periods of time. There are also many experimental procedures available today, and many patients find themselves in experimental treatments with drugs or surgery that often extend good living time. Thus a man or a woman who develops a fatal illness may find there is an extended period of time between the moment a diagnosis is made and eventual death. It would be virtually impossible for most people to live in that time if they focused only on the fact that their lives were to end at some indefinite, but possibly near time. Thus, for the very requirements of living, often a patient with a fatal illness and his family will approach their problems as if indeed the illness did not exist. We might call this denial, and in some ways I suppose it is fair to use the word. However, it seems to me that this attitude is more of a necessary adjustment to the fact that life must go on, and that it is extraordinarily difficult to think, on a day-by-day basis, that one's life is finished, when there is indeed living left to be done.

I believe it is critically important that people with fatal illnesses, when they are in the early phase of their disorders, and it appears that a considerable amount of good living time is left, be offered hope and reassurance that the future is indefinite, that life should be led as if they cannot know when the end will come. To focus too early on death would probably be a disservice to most patients and their families in this particular phase of illness.

What stresses do the fatally ill face?

When the disease and its manifestations have progressed, the patient's future is now considerably shortened, and a dying time seems to be at hand, then another type of support is necessary for a dignified resolution of the problem of dying. I cannot say specifically what period of time this is: for some patients it may be days, for others, weeks. Nor can one be sure there won't be better days and worse days even within that block of time, that we can now designate as the dying time. But it certainly is within that framework of time, when the sick individual is stressed by his apparent failing, that concepts such as dignity begin to take on a new shape and a new dimension. Being sick — especially being sick enough to be weak, devoid of appetite, and slipping away from life — causes considerable psychological stress for the patient and his family. Whatever few options are available to an individual are oftentimes cherished, although the individual may recede from people, interests, or events that previously occupied much of his attention. How much the individual may wish to look at these days as days of dying, or how much he may wish to avoid looking at reality and instead focus on minor complaints and minor disorders as if these were all of life, will be different with different individuals. However, I think most people are aware of the fact that they are dying, when such time does come, and that most have the strength to search for a meaningful perspective during that time.

It should not be assumed from the statement that people are strong and have resources to cope with the knowledge of a fatal illness, that such patients are necessarily happy and outgoing individuals. Being informed of fatal illness, or becoming aware that one has limited time left in life, can be a depressing event, leading to much anxiety and other personality disturbances. It is to protect against such depression and sadness that information is often withheld from patients. But sadness and depression are part of life, especially in response to events of great tragic importance, and people should be allowed to have their sadness, their sense of depression, when facing events so crucial as a fatal illness. By themselves, depression and sadness do not prevent an individual from using what time he has left creatively, meaningfully, and with dignity.

What is the role of the family?

But can a dying person, or an individual with a fatal illness, feel a sense of worthiness if he does not have the support of his family? Here again, recognizing that few of us live in isolation, but define the best there is in our lives in relationship to other important loved ones, the absence of their full support at such critical times as when a fatal illness strikes, or when one must deal with his own dying, can only diminish one's sense of self-worth, and diminish the possibility of approaching death with personal dignity. Now family members often wish to protect themselves from facing the issues of losing an important family member, and oftentimes behave as if protecting the dying person from information about himself will help that person be happy. Nothing could be further from the truth.

Oftentimes we find patients attempt desperately to protect their families from knowing what the patient knows, at a time when the family is anxious to protect the patient from what the family knows. Both parties consume enormous amounts of energy in game-playing, and both feel a sense of depression, isolation, and loneliness, in not being able to share openly their awareness that one of them is seriously ill and dying. Frequently a seriously sick individual will try to explore with his family what it means to be dying, and what wishes he or she has in relation to a future in which the person will no longer be present. The family that does not allow the individual this opportunity of sharing innermost thoughts frequently increases the terrible sense of loneliness and distance already felt by the very nature of illness. This is not to say that families and patients spend all their days doing nothing but talking about dying and its meaning. But certainly, the patient who is able to use his family creatively and supportively, and can share with them those inner concerns he has about dying and what will happen after he is gone, and the family which is able to express their good-byes, their sense of loss, their feeling of loneliness and fright at the prospect of the person's death, present a manner of strength to both parties which frequently allows dignity to exist.

How can the physician play a meaningful role?

The physician, or other people in the health-care area, is very apt to create either harmony or disharmony in these relationships by the manner of communicating such information. When a family is told of a fatal illness but the patient is not, then a sense of secrecy and disharmony is immediately created which will be difficult, in the long run, for all to bear. If the physician instructs the family not to tell the patient, or indeed if the physician allows the family to dictate the terms of what is told to the patient, then that same situation of disharmony and distrust is allowed to exist. It may seen natural at first for a family to wish to protect the patient from the devastating information that he has a fatal illness, and in fact such protection may seem to work well in the beginning when the patient first comes home from the hospital.

But over a long period of time, such "protecting" works to the disadvantage of both parties. Certainly there are situations in which a family member might feel that protecting the individual from the knowledge of his illness right to the time of his death succeeded, and that "poor Joe" died without ever knowing what he had. But as a general rule this kind of protective information can only work when a patient is less than mature. I have seen too many situations in which the keeping of secrets has resulted in exaggerated depressions and difficult behavior problems for the patient, for the doctor, and for the family.

How can the patient and his family share supportive feelings?

Families frequently need supportive help themselves, either from the doctor or other health personnel, to allow this open communication to exist. Again, the family must not expect the individual patient will wish to spend every day discussing nothing but his oncoming death. Frequently what happens is that once the air has been cleared, and the patient and the family fully understand what is happening, then the time remaining can be spent in memory, in seeking for common joys in life, and in sharing time creatively. I frequently see exactly the opposite when patients and their families are not in tune with each other. Then it is hard to visit, there are wishes not to be present, and people have little to say to the patient except empty talk while the patient stares at the wall or out the window with a feeling of being totally out of touch with those who were formerly his very dear loved ones. Open communication does not mean that the dying of a family member is a happy event. However, we are not talking of happiness but of dignity. If an individual can feel the support of his family in an effective style during the time of his last weeks and days, then he is more assured of feeling a sense of worth and dignity in his life, than otherwise.

I have also many times been aware that families will put patients into hospitals and/or nursing homes because they are unable to deal with demands and behaviors arising from the patient's feeling of being deceived or being out of touch with reality. I am very impressed that oftentimes a dying person can remain at home to the very end of his life, with relatively little pain and minimal complaints, when he is aware that all that can be done for him medically has been done, and that open communication and full support between him, his loved ones, and his physician exists.

I am not suggesting that all people should die at home, for frequently the last stages of a fatal illness can be exhausting, because of complications, for the patient and especially for the family looking after him. The hospital is frequently the best place for an individual to die when many complications occur. But when there is a loving and supporting family, an individual can stay at home and be in control of those few things he can control during a terminal illness. Being at home may mean control over when to eat, what to eat, who should be visiting, the length of visits, having a dog on the bed, being able to touch the heads of children — small but important things. Many of these are out of his control in the hospital. If they are a source of pleasure that is important to a person, they become critically important during the terminal period of life.

What about the natural fear of death?

However, even in the face of a loving and supporting family, there is oftentimes great anxiety in the patient, and in family members, which prevents warm and sympathetic support of each other. In such situations it is well for the physician and other members of the health-care staff to be aware of such anxiety, and attempt to work out the reasons for them with patient and family. It is not enough to say that anxieties are related to someone's fear of dying. Certainly, most people have a fear of dying even if it represents nothing more than an adventure into the unknown. But an attitude toward that fear can accentuate it to cause disturbances beyond the measure of the dying itself. Such emotional reactions are best looked at as problems of interpersonal communication, indicating areas of unresolved tension between patients and their families. Help in this regard from the physician, or other members of the health-care staff, can frequently smooth tensions, allowing for a peaceful resolution of the dying time. The use of certain tranquilizing drugs may sometimes be effective, but one must be certain the drug is not used to obliterate the personality and stop effective communication.

Outside help is sometimes necessary — how to proceed?

The essential issue we are talking about is allowing a person to stay in control as much as he can, and to feel that loving support which gives him a sense of his own worth, so he can approach death in a courageous and dignified fashion. Since interfamily relationships are often difficult and testy, and since both the act of dying and the act of losing can accentuate preexisting problems as well as cause enormous concerns during the dying time, help is often required for family members, as well as for patients, to bring them together into a more peaceful and unified relationship with each other. For after all, the manner of a person's dying is his last act both for himself and for those he loves, and it can be a heritage he leaves for the memory of those who come after him. Therefore, to be dignified throughout the last days of one's life is more than simply a question of style. It is a question of helping us all feel that the summing up at the end gives a particular kind of importance and majesty to the life that was led.

Frequently it is family members who need the most help in being able to communicate effectively and supportively with somebody they love who is now dying. And frequently it is family members who cause many problems for themselves, for their loved ones, and for the medical staff because of unworked-through tensions in regard to their demands on the dying person. But beyond this, most of us have been so uneducated, unprepared, and unrehearsed as to how to deal with the dying of a loved family member, we simply are stressed by an embarrassment of how and what to do.

We all feel embarrassed when we are inadequate to a task, even though we might not be aware of how inadequate we really are. We feel tense, uncomfortable, avoid people, and then cannot understand why the situation seems so bad. Physicians and other health staff are also beginning to recognize that dying is not just a biologic event but an important psychological and social circumstance requiring the attention of all those most intimate to the process, not just the patient. Helping relationships are beginning to be established, and are functioning in many large institutions where terminal illnesses are common. However, there is a need for much greater expansion of such services, especially where families are small, where the dying person is still intimate with the family process, and where patterns of communication have been poor at best in the time preceding the development of the fatal illness.

4

Children and Death

Can youngsters truly understand death?

How should it be explained?

Is it unwise to take the child to the funeral?

How does the youngster respond to separation?

What are the significant guidelines for helping the child during crises?

EARL A. GROLLMAN

Albert Camus has instructed us: "Men cannot live without meaning." This is true of children, too. Meaning is an answer to "emptiness." Significance cannot be found unless we take death into our living. As we cannot escape this truth in our adult years, so we cannot protect children from it either. Nor should we. Tragedy is not the respector of age. Case studies show that even for very young children, well-developed mental faculties are functioning to help them understand life's final mystery.

Rabbi Earl A. Grollman, D.D., has devoted much of his life to interpreting the emotional reactions of youngsters during the terrible trauma of a death in the family. His *Talking About Death: A Dialogue Between Parent and Child* was awarded the Trends Citation by UNESCO at the International Children's and Youth Book Exhibition in Munich, Germany. He also edited *Explaining Death to Children*, blending in the best insights of psychiatry, sociology, psychology, biology, anthropology, religion, and children's literature.

Children and Death

Why should innocent children be burdened with discussions of tragic death?

A child growing up today is all too aware of the reality of death, perhaps more than parents realize. Even at a very young age children are confronted with that instance when life no longer exists: pet is killed; funeral procession passes by; grandfather dies; leader is assassinated. And, of course, there is television, with the picture of death in vivid color.

The small child tries out the word "death" and rolls it around the tongue. He closes his eyes, lies on the ground, and imagines what death must feel like. He loves to blow out a lighted match and inquires, "Where did the light go? Is it gone forever? If you die, do you ever come back?"

And when death does occur, the bereaved adults are often so upset by their own sense of loss they may say nothing to their offspring. They imagine that either the fact of death is beyond a child's comprehension or that they can protect the youngster from the anguish they themselves feel.

But the child has every right to be included in that situation which seriously affects him both as an individual and as a member of a family. Silence only deprives him of the opportunity to share his grief.

But if the parent is confused, how can he help his offspring?

Of course, the adult does not understand the complete meaning of death. No mortal has ever pierced the veil of its great mystery. Yet the wise parent has the inescapable responsibility to share with his youngster the fragments of adult experience and knowledge. There is no justification in leaving the bewildered child to muddle through as best as he can.

While insight is a gift, parents must first place themselves in a position to receive it. They must prepare themselves for it. They must be quiet and learn to listen to their children. They must sit down and watch them while they work and play. They must observe them in action and hear the tone and timbre of their voices. The youngsters should be encouraged to tell the adults how they feel about death, what they think, what they know, where they need to go. Parents should respond by trying to let the youngsters know that they understand what their children are trying to say. Adults should attempt to answer questions in the spirit in which they are asked.

Do not teach the child as if you have final answers that he must accept. Adults show their maturity when they respond, "Are you surprised that I do not know everything about death? Don't be. Yet we can still talk about it. You can learn something from me. I can learn something from you. We can help each other." As parents confront crucial issues, they will learn along with their children.

Can youngsters understand the meaning of death?

The terms "dead" and "die" are common in young peoples'· vocabulary. But these words may conjure up divergent meanings.

Psychologist Maria Nagy, studying Hungarian

children in the late 1940s, discovered three phases in the child's awareness of mortality. She learned that the child from three to five may deny death as a regular and final process. To him death is like sleep; you are dead, then you are alive again. Or like taking a journey; you are gone, then you come back again. This child may experience many times each day some real aspects of what he considers "death," such as when his father goes to work or his mother to the supermarket.

Between five and nine, children appear to be able to accept the idea that a person has died but may not understand it as something that will happen to everyone and particularly to themselves. Around the age of nine and ten, the child recognizes death as an inevitable experience that will occur even to him.

Of course these are all rough approximations with many variations but may prove of value when children raise questions. Nagy's investigation also demonstrated three recurring questions in the child's mind: "What is death?" "What makes people die?" "What happens to people when they die; where do they go?"

Psychologists point out the interesting fact that some adolescents and adults have childlike views of death. They "know" that death is inevitable and final, but most of their daily attitudes and actions are more consistent with the conviction that personal death is an unfounded rumor.

Should parents share religious convictions with their children?

Religion is concerned with the mystery of death as well as the meaning of life. In giving religious interpretation the most important consideration is honesty. Parents can only teach what they sincerely believe. Religion cannot be taught, it must be caught.

Avoid theological abstractions which would only confuse children. Concepts must be translated into the language and comprehension of the child. It is not necessary or possible that the youngster accept the totality of your religious philosophy. One cannot legislate theology.

Suffering and death should not be linked with sin and divine punishment. Children experience enough guilt without an added measure of God's chastisement.

Are fairy tales a helpful explanation for the enigma of death?

The question arises constantly about what we should tell a child when death occurs. Should we avoid acknowledgment that the person has died? Should we suggest that grandfather became ill and had to go away to a hospital where he could recuperate and become cured, hoping that his memory would gradually fade away and the youngster would come to accept the absence as being the norm?

Evasions indicate the uncertainty the adult has about his child's capacity to deal with existing situations. It encourages him to develop the capacity to "forget about things," and does not prepare him to deal with life's realities. Parents should never cover up with a fiction they will someday repudiate. There is no greater need for a child than trust and truth.

How about, "Mother has gone on a long journey" instead of the harsh words, "Mother has died?"

To say to a child, "Your mother has gone away for a long journey for a very long time," is a statement geared to provide some solace and ease the strain of the mother's disappearance. But the child might interpret this explanation to mean that his mother has abandoned and deserted him without saying good-bye. Far from being comforted and holding the memory of the deceased dear, the child may react with anger and resentment.

The youngster could also develop the delusion that someday Mother will return. Or unconsciously he may assume, "Mommy didn't really care enough about me so she stayed away." Also, if the mother only went away on a journey, why is everyone crying?

There is no need to avoid the word *die*, especially in the age of television when death is referred to so frequently. It is easier for the child to understand a direct statement about death than some evasive term like "going away," which adds fear that one who goes away may never come back.

> *Or, "God took Daddy when he was so young because your father was so good that He wanted your father for Himself."*

Do you really believe that there is a relationship between longevity and goodness? The righteous may surely die young but can also live to a ripe old age.

One little girl said, "Don't Mommy and I need Daddy more than God?" This child developed a deep resentment against a God who capriciously robbed her of her father. One youngster became upset with the thought, "But God loves me too; maybe I'll be the next one He will take away."

> *Why not simply say, "Grandma died because she was so sick"?*

People do become sick and die, but most everyone who becomes ill survives to live a long life. Will the child himself die if he has a cold, the mumps, the measles? How can the youngster make a distinction between a death-producing illness and one not quite so serious? The comparison of sickness to death often brings confusion rather than understanding.

The child who sustains the death of a loved one is often secretly terrified that he may himself die of the same sickness. It is necessary to repeat again and again, "Even though you and the person who died were from the same family, you are different people. And I am happy to truthfully tell you that you are in good health. We expect that you will live a long, long time."

What about the use of the word "heaven" as the new abode of the deceased father?

Heaven is a difficult concept for a child. One youngster asked, "Mother, if Daddy is supposed to be in heaven, then why are they putting him in the ground?"

One should share his religious resources with his offspring but must be prepared for further elaboration for simplistic theological terms.

Is death like sleeping?

It is only natural to draw the parallel. Homer, in the *Iliad*, alludes to sleep (Hypnos) and death (Thanatos) as twin brothers, and many of our religious prayers entwine the ideas of *sleep* and *death*; but you run the risk of causing a pathological dread of bedtime. There are children who toss about in fear of going "forever asleep," never to wake up again! Some youngsters actually struggle with all their might to remain awake, fearful that they might go off to the deceased's type of "sleep."

How should the facts of death be explained to the child?

The answer can be expressed in two words: *naturally* and *lovingly*.

Understandably, it is easier for the parent to respond with fictions and half truths that also make him appear to know all the answers. But the secure adult has no need to profess infinite knowledge. It is far healthier for a child to share the joint quest for additional wisdom than for his immediate curiosity to be appeased by fantasy in the guise of fact.

You might initiate the conversation by talking about the flowers growing in the spring and summer only to be followed by their fading away in the fall and winter seasons. This is the sequence of life; for all living things there is a time to grow, flourish, and then to die.

Explanations should be presented without lurid, gruesome, or terrifying description. Proceed slowly and simply, step by step, with patience and gentleness. Fears will be lessened when the discussion is initially focussed not upon the morbidity of death but upon the beauty of life.

When should the offspring be told of the death of a loved one?

It is important that the youngster be told *immediately*. If possible, he should first receive this information from a parent or from someone close to him. It is wise for the child to hear the sad news in familiar surroundings, preferably in his own home. A delay in informing the child makes it all the more likely that he will be told of the death by the wrong person, in the wrong way, at the wrong place.

Should the youngster go to the funeral?

Death is sad, but sadness is an integral part of the life cycle. The funeral is an important occasion in the life of the family. The youngster should have the same privilege as any other member of his household to express his own love and devotion. To deprive him of a sense of belonging could well impair his future mental health.

Explain in advance of the funeral the details of the service. The child will be more relaxed and less disturbed if he first understands what he will soon witness. All the emotional reactions that a child is likely to experience — sorrow and loneliness, anger and rejection, denial and guilt — can be considerably lessened if the youngster knows what is occurring and that adults are not trying to hide things from him.

No matter how helpful and therapeutic the funeral may be the child should never be forced to attend. If the apprehensive youngster elects to remain at home, do not place any additional "shaming" pressure upon him. Gently suggest that perhaps sometime later, when he so decides, you might visit the cemetery together. If one can anticipate that there might be hysterical outbursts, it might be prudent to keep the sensitive child at home. When the funeral is over, he should then be given the opportunity to remain with the family and share their grief.

Do children experience grief?

Mourning and sadness are appropriate emotions for people of all ages. The more meaningful the relationship, the more intense the feeling of loss. To feel depression and melancholy is not abnormal.

According to Dr. John Bowlby of Tavistock Clinic in London, each child experiences three phases in the natural grieving process. The first is protest, when the child cannot quite believe the person is dead and he attempts, sometimes angrily, to regain him. The next is pain, despair, and disorganization, when the youngster begins to accept the fact that the loved one is really gone. Finally there is hope, when the offspring begins to organize his life without the deceased.

Should the child be discouraged from crying?

Only the insensitive could say of the child who had encountered tragedy and remained dispassionate, "The youngster is taking it so well. He never cries."

The son and daughter whose loved one dies should be allowed to express their grief. It is natural. They loved him. They miss him. To say, "Be brave!" sounds as if one were minimizing their loss.

Don't be afraid of causing tears; they are like a safety valve. So often parents and friends deliberately attempt to veer the conversation away from the deceased. They are apprehensive of the tears that might start to flow. They do not understand that expressing grief through crying is normal and helpful.

Tears are the tender tribute of yearning affection for those who have died but can never be forgotten. The worst thing possible is for the child to repress them. The youngster who stoically keeps his grief bottled up inside may later find a release in an explosion more dangerous to his inner makeup.

Although the parents should not deny the child the opportunity to weep, neither should they urge him to display unfelt feelings. He is likely to feel confused and hypocritical when told he ought to express a sentiment that he does not honestly feel. There are many outlets, and the child should express those emotions that most naturally meet his needs.

What are other responses to death?

For the youngster, death may bring a variety of reactions:

Denial: "I don't believe it. It didn't happen. It is just a dream. Daddy will come back. He will! He will!"

The child may frequently look as if he were un-affected because he is trying to defend himself against the death by pretending it has not really happened. Seeing this the adult may feel the youngster's apparent unconcern is heartless. Or the parent may be relieved and feel, "Isn't it lucky! I am sure he misses his father, but he does not seem to be really bothered by it." Usually the lack of response signifies that the child has found the loss too great to accept, and goes on pretending secretly that the deceased is still alive.

Bodily Distress: "I have a tightness in my throat!" "I can't breathe." "I have no appetite at all." "I have no strength." "I am exhausted." "I can't do my homework." "I can't sleep." "I had a nightmare." The anxiety has expressed itself in physical and emotional symptoms.

Hostile Reactions to the Deceased: "How could Dad-dy do this to me?" "Didn't he care enough about me to stay alive?" "Why did he leave me?" The child feels deserted, abandoned, and angry.

Hostile Reactions to Others: "It's the doctor's fault. He gave him the wrong medicine." Or, "Mother didn't take proper care of him, that's why he died." The resentment is projected outward in order to relieve guilt by making someone else responsible for the death.

Replacement: "Uncle Ben, do you love me, really love me?" The child makes a fast play for the affection of others as a substitute for the parent who has died, which is quite normal.

Assumption of Mannerisms of Deceased: "Do I look like Daddy?" The son attempts to take on the characteristic traits of the father by walking and talking like him. He may even try to become the head of the family, and the mate of the mother.

Idealization: "How dare you say anything against

Daddy! He was perfect." In the attempt to fight off his own unhappy thoughts, the child becomes obsessed with the father's good qualities. The falsification is out of keeping with the father's real life and character.

Anxiety: "I feel like Daddy when he died. I have a pain in my chest." The youngster becomes preoccupied with the physical symptoms that terminated the life of the father. He transfers the symptoms to himself, in a process of identification.

Panic: "Who will take care of me now?" "Suppose something happens to Mommy?" "Daddy used to bring home money for food and toys. Who will get these things for us?" This state of confusion and shock needs the parent's supportive love: "My health is fine. I will take care of you. There is enough money for food and toys."

Guilt: Children are very likely to feel guilt since, in their experience, bad things happen to them because they were naughty. The desertion of the parent must be a retribution for their wrongdoing. Therefore, they search their minds for the "bad deed" that caused it. Many young children harbor all kinds of fantasies that they are responsible for the death in the family. They believe in a primitive magic; that is, if one wishes someone harm, the belief alone will bring results.

A boy says to his sister: "I wish you were dead." Then when the sister dies a year later, the lad is terror stricken by his own powers. Or a youngster may fear that he made his mother work too hard. He can still recall her saying, "You're such a messy kid. Picking up after you will be the death of me yet." This is why it is so necessary to help the child express his own fantasies and fears.

These are some of the reactions of children as well as adults. Some may never appear. Some come at the time of crises. Others may be delayed, since so often the child represses his emotions and attempts to appear calm in the face of tragedy.

In summary, what general guidelines would you suggest to help the child who has suffered the death of a loved one?

Just as you cannot protect yourself from the sorrow surrounding death, so you cannot defend your offspring. The mental health of us all is not the denial of tragedy but the frank acknowledgment of painful separation.

The child should be able to discuss death with his family before crisis strikes. Talk in a quiet, honest, straightforward way so as to encourage further dialogue. The learning process should be in gradual stages according to the youngster's intellectual and emotional capabilities. Begin at the offspring's level and remember that attitude is more important than words.

Never tell the child what he will later need to unlearn. Avoid fairy tales, half truths, and circumlocutions. Imaginative fancy only gets in the youngster's way when he is having enough trouble separating the real from the make-believe.

The very involvement of the offspring in the sorrow of the family can be a source of maturation. Not only does the child receive love but he is given the opportunity to love in return. He gains strength by giving strength. Reassurance comes from the presence of loving people.

Allow the child to give vent to his emotions of grief. Anger, tears, guilt, despair, and protest are natural reactions to family disorganization.

Encourage the youngster to discuss his innermost fantasies and fears and feelings. The child needs to talk, not to be talked to. He should be given every opportunity to reminisce about the person who died, and if he so desires, may express anger as well as affection.

Do not close the door to doubt, questioning, and difference of opinion. Respect the offspring's own personality, for in the long run it is he who must find his own answers to the problems of life and death.

It must be remembered that young people vary in their reactions. There is no single procedure and formula that will fit all youngsters either at the time of death or during the period that follows. There are so many variables: How close was the child to the deceased? How, when, and where were the circumstances of death? What is his concept of death? How do significant adults react? What is the offspring's physical and emotional health? What have been his prior experiences with loss? There are differences in grief reactions because of unique conditions, feelings, and attitudes. Like adults, children, too, must be understood and valued. ,

Talking about death is often a complex and disturbing task. There are times when even the best-informed and well-intentioned parents are simply inadequate. Seeking help from a therapist (psychologist or child-guidance clinic) is not an admission of weakness, but a demonstration of strength and love.

In the end, of course, what you are will determine what you teach your offspring. If parents are disturbed by the thought of death, their children will feel anxieties and tensions too. Regardless of language employed, emotional tones are transmitted. The real challenge is not just how to explain death to your children but how to understand and make peace with it yourself.

SUGGESTED READINGS

Anthony, Sylvia, *The Child's Discovery of Death* (London: Kegan Paul, 1946).

Arnstein, Helene S., *What to Tell Your Child About Birth, Illness, Death, Divorce, and Other Family Crises* (New York: Bobbs-Merril, 1960).

Bro, Marguerite H., *When Children Ask* (New York: Harper & Row, 1956).

Feifel, Herman (Ed.), *The Meaning of Death* (New York: McGraw-Hill, 1959).

Fulton, Robert, *Death and Identity* (New York: Wiley, 1965).

Ginott, Haim G., *Between Parent and Child* (New York: Macmillan, 1965).

Gorer, Geoffrey, *Death, Grief, and Mourning* (Garden City, N.Y.: Doubleday, 1965).

Grollman, Earl A., *Talking About Death* (Boston: Beacon Press, 1970).

Gruenberg, S. M., *The Encyclopedia of Child Care and Guidance* (Garden City, N.Y.: Doubleday, 1954).

Hunter, Edith F., *The Questioning Child and Religion* (Boston: Beacon Press, 1956).

Hurlock, Elizabeth B., *Adolescent Development* (New York: McGraw-Hill, 1955).

Jackson, Edgar N., *Telling a Child About Death* (New York: Channel Press, 1965).

Kastenbaum, Robert, "The Kingdom Where Nobody Dies." *Saturday Review*, January, 1973.

Kutscher, Austin H., *But Not To Lose* (New York: Frederick Fell, 1969).

Lamers, William, Jr., *Death, Grief, Mourning, the Funeral ond the Child* (Chicago: National Association of Funeral Directors. November 1, 1965).

Lasker, Arnold A., "Telling Children the Facts of Death." *Your Child* Winter, 1972.

Lindemann, Erich, "Symtomatology and Managment of Acute Grief." *American Journal of Psychiatry*, 101, 1944.

Nagy, Maria, "The Child's Theories Concerning Death." *Journal of Genetic Psychology*, 73, 1948, 3 27.

Osborne, E., *When You Lose a Loved One* (New York: Appleton-Century-Crofts, 1951).

Parkhurst, Helen, *Exploring the Child's World* (New York: Appleton-Century-Crofts, 1951).

Polner, Murray, and Arthur Barron, *The Questions Children Ask* (New York: Macmillan, 1964).

Ramos, Suzanne, "Learning About Death." *New York Times Magazine*, December 10, 1972.

Wolf, Anna, *The Parents' Manual* (New York: Popular Library, 1951).

5

The Protestant Way in Death and Mourning

Do all Protestants agree to the same rituals and theology of death?

What special customs surround the Protestant ceremony of death?

How is the funeral conducted?

What are the concepts of an afterlife?

How might friends express their condolences?

MERLE R. JORDAN

It is natural to turn to the clergyman during the crisis of death. As an exponent of the mysteries of God, the pastor represents friendship, love, acceptance, forgiveness, and understanding.

Protestant ministers may share differing views, beliefs, and practices. Yet they are united in the goal of giving emotional and religious guidance through "the valley of the shadow of death."

The Reverend Dr. Merle R. Jordan is associate professor of pastoral psychology at Boston University School of Theology. An ordained minister of the United Church of Christ, Dr. Jordan has blended his faith with a dynamic, interpersonal psychology for a more meaningful, spiritual life.

The Protestant Way in Death and Mourning

Is there general agreement among Protestants as to the rituals and theology of death?

There are vast differences within Protestantism in regard to the rituals and theology of death. Even within the same denomination there may be a wide spectrum of beliefs and practices. Pluralism best expresses the Protestant orientation, though it is fair to say that some groups within Protestantism would attest that their theology and rituals are the only authentic Protestant Christian witness. Some Protestant theologies and rituals have helped people to come to grips with the realities and meanings of death as it is experienced in the context of life and life after death; other Protestant traditions are death-denying and may focus so strongly on the "if you are really a Christian, then you will not be sad" approach that the celebration of the gift of eternal life to the deceased is used as a repressive tool to block the authentic grief which needs to be expressed.

Some Protestants view death as the penalty and punishment for man's sin; others see death as a moment of transition when the soul leaves the body for its eternal reward; still others view death as the absolute end. Some of us believe that an adequate theology of death is complex and it has to deal with a larger context in which we seek to understand the dynamic relationship between death and life, the meanings of the finiteness of man and the event of death itself, and the meaning of life after death in relationship to the crucifixion-resurrection experience in particular.

In both Protestant theology and its rituals there are vast differences. There is diversity, for example, in the practice of the open versus the closed casket. Some believe that the funeral service with a closed casket or a memorial service with no casket present are more of a testimony to the joy and victory of the Christian life. Others believe that death is a reality to be faced and not denied, and that the possibility of viewing the deceased may facilitate the grief process for many people and that the task is to face the realities of death in the context of the Christian faith, which can deal genuinely with both sadness and hope.

In spite of the diversity within Protestantism there are some common elements with which many Protestants could agree.

- Death is a mystery, and we cannot fully comprehend the meanings surrounding death.
- Death is a corporate event in the fellowship of believers.
- The impact of death is realized and experienced in the community of faith, and it calls forth the caring resources of the congregation to the bereaved.
- The religious resources and rituals of the faith group are significant to the bereaved in dealing with the death event.

With what special and unique customs does Protestantism surround the ceremony of death?

Unlike some other faith groups, Protestants in general do not have any special and unique customs that are universal, beyond the usual practice of a funeral service and a committal service. However, within the various Protestant denominations there are customs that are practiced by specific religious groups because of their cultural background, or their formal religious rituals prescribed in a denominational book of worship; and because of occasional adaptions to their Protestant practices of customs from other religious traditions in their culture. Thus, for example, some Protestant groups may be at home with the grieving patterns of a wake, which may come from particular cultural and religious backgrounds, while other Protestant groups would be unfamiliar with the wake as a part of the ceremony of death.

Protestants are increasingly emphasizing the significance of "the pastorhood of all believers," in which the care-giving responsibility to the bereaved is shared by the whole congregation and not just undertaken by the professional minister.

How is the Protestant funeral conducted?

For someone who has been an active member of a church as well as for some who have not been so active, the sanctuary of the local church is often the appropriate place for the funeral service. However, for various reasons persons may prefer to have the service held in a funeral home or private home.

The funeral service is a service of worship of the Christian Church. It is conducted by the minister according to the traditions and practices of the denomination and the local church in the context of the particular needs of the mourners and the personal style of the minister. In many Protestant churches it is customary to have a relatively brief service of fifteen to twenty minutes, although the service may be the length of a regular church service.

The elements of the funeral service are largely determined in some major Protestant denominations by the ritual in the book of worship of each denomination. Whether the ritual is formalized in a book of worship or not, it generally consists of the reading of Scriptures and the offering of prayers. Prose and poetry selections may also be included. The funeral sermon or meditation is included in many services. Such preaching is encouraged to be focussed on the mourning process of the bereaved and to speak in relevant terms to the needs of the mourners within the resources of the Christian faith. Either within the sermon or separately, some clergy include a eulogy or a modified eulogy in which the life, personhood, and accomplishments of the deceased are highlighted. Many Protestant clergy do not include any eulogy for a variety of reasons, including the difficulties of either knowing the deceased well or being publicly realistic about the deceased in many instances.

Funeral music, usually played on the organ, is an important part of the service, though there has been much debate about the selection of appropriate music. Sometimes congregational singing of hymns is included and that may help to provide a feeling of solidarity in the sharing of the sorrow and the affirming of the faith.

The committal service is usually a brief service held at the graveside, although because of inclement weather or other reasons the committal service may be held in the church or funeral home as the concluding part of the funeral service.

Particularly in the funeral service at which there is an open casket, it is customary for people who so choose to file by the casket at the conclusion of the service. It is recognized that there are many Protestant variations on the funeral service described above.

Are there contemporary changes in the Protestant funeral service?

The memorial service is the major alternative to the traditional funeral service. In some areas of the Protestant church the memorial service is being used frequently. The memorial service preserves many of the elements of the funeral service. However, it is differentiated by the fact that the casket is not present for the service.

Numerous churches have introduced contemporary worship services for their regular times of church worship, and they have also introduced innovations in wedding services. Some of these changes are just beginning to be reflected in the Protestant funeral, and quite often these changes revolve around the funeral service of a youth or young adult for whom the contemporary innovations seem to be appropriate and which reflect the peer culture in which the person has lived. Thus contemporary music, the use of other musical instruments besides the organ, selected readings from modern poets and writers, and group sharing of memories and feelings about the deceased may be elements of the funeral service.

The contemporary changes can also reflect either a perspective of facing death more realistically and authentically or an attempt to celebrate life to the extent that the realities of death are denied. It is also interesting to note that persons who have been relatively unchurched but for whom there would previously have been a traditional Protestant funeral may now be buried with a humanistic service. The Rev. Paul Irion has compiled *A Manual and Guide for Those Who Conduct a Humanist Funeral Service.*

Is a visitation and/or condolence call appropriate before or after the funeral?

In Protestantism there is no absolute principle in relationship to a condolence call. Such a call should be determined on a prescriptive basis in relationship to the particular situation of bereavement. Some of the criteria in determining the appropriateness of a condolence call before or after the funeral include:

- The local community and church practices should be considered since there may be some expectations and guidelines in the local mores and traditions.
- The feelings and the needs of the potential caller should be considered because this individual may feel within himself or herself that a call at a particular time may be more appropriate to that individual's style of relating to the bereaved. For example, the natural and spontaneous response of many persons is to want to be with a friend who has suffered a loss as soon as possible.
- The kind and quality of relationship between the bereaved and the potential visitor may be a significant factor in the decision. For example, if the visitor is particularly close to the deceased or the bereaved, then waiting until after the funeral to make a call may be experienced by the bereaved as a disappointment, rejection, or hurt.
- The emotional, physical, and spiritual needs of the bereaved are central to the appropriate timing of a call. Some of the circumstances in which a condolence call before the funeral (or even occasionally after the funeral) might not be indicated would be:

   Serious physical problems of the bereaved which might be exacerbated by too many callers or by getting too emotionally upset in dealing with the sharing of grief with the visitors.

   The hysterical nature of the bereaved in which the usual process of carrying on grief work may be counterproductive and the bereaved may be under medication in order to cope more gradually with manageable doses of the sadness.

Certain very trying grief situations, such as a suicide in the family, may mean that the bereaved need the support of friends more at that time or that they want to have some privacy with a select few to work through initially the complex emotions of such a death.

In any event, if there is a question about when or whether to call on the bereaved before or after the funeral, an inquiry to the pastor or to someone in the immediate social network of the nuclear family may give an indication about the appropriate timing of a condolence call. If one is to err, then it is better to make a sin of commission (call and stay briefly) than to make a sin of omission (not to call at all).

Generally, both types of visits are important to the bereaved. Some persons who are particularly influenced by family practices, cultural expectations, and emotional and spiritual needs want to be surrounded by their social network of relatives and friends both before and after the funeral. On the afternoon and evening following a funeral, some people especially want to have family and friends around to share memories, break bread together, and to experience further the supportive fellowship of a caring "clan." Others may want some moments of privacy after the funeral and prefer only the closest of family and friends to be at the home following the funeral service.

It is not uncommon that the major attention to the bereaved is given in the first days following the death of a loved one. However, the loneliness may grow more intense with the passing of time. Thus very often the network of relatives and friends who provide the supportive visits during the weeks and months following the funeral may be the most welcome and may offer a deeply healing ministry to the bereaved.

What expression of sorrow is recommended in

commemorating a deceased Protestant friend?

There are a variety of ways in which one may express his or her sorrow appropriately:

- a sympathy card or letter to the bereaved individual or family;
- condolence visits and/or phone calls to the bereaved;
- a visit to the funeral home during visiting hours, if such are scheduled;
- attendance at the funeral service;
- a memorial gift to a charity or cause in which the deceased and/or the family have shown an interest. Some families are asking that flowers be omitted and a memorial gift be made; however, in many instances where flowers are not requested to be omitted, some relatives and friends express their sympathy naturally through the gift of flowers;
- a willingness to listen, share, and interact with the nuclear family with one's own caring, grief and memories of the deceased. The gift of sharing one's self and being willing to be transparent and vulnerable in the midst of the grief work of the family may be deeply appreciated;
- intercessory prayer for the bereaved who bear the major burden for the loss;
- undertaking of specific action on behalf of the bereaved (such as bringing food or caring for the children at certain times) rather than the general offer of "let me know if there is any way in which I can help."
- The recognition that the bereaved may need your continuing love and support even more in the months of loneliness that follow the funeral, and a realistic concern for the needs of bereaved children who experience various emotions and struggle with questions, fantasies, and mystery.

In carrying out one's expressions of sorrow, the particular needs and wishes of the nuclear family of the deceased should be considered foremost. All too often well-intentioned religious people want to express their caring and love in ways which run counter to the wishes of the family and at times to those of the deceased. The bereaved family are too often criticized for not conforming to the traditional expectations of others in the community in the ways in which they handle their grief and funeral arrangements. Affirming the right of the family to the uniqueness of their style of dealing with grief and with funeral arrangements is of utmost importance. For a friend to demand that he or she carry out his or her own expression of sorrow in a way that will provoke, alienate, and criticize the bereaved family is generally inappropriate as a means of trying to commemorate a friend. We need to learn to live with the plurality of grief and funeral practices among families and religous and cultural groups.

What are the concepts of an afterlife?

Various research studies have pointed out that belief in God is stronger than belief in the hereafter for all Christian faith groups in the United States. Numerous religious people have no belief at all in an afterlife. Others have vague notions about the afterlife. In fact, in an opinion study conducted by the Gallup Organization Inc. in 1968, a representative sample of the American population (1,500 people, 21 and over) revealed the curious fact that more people said that they believed in heaven than in a life after death. The results of that survey are as follows:

	Yes %	No %	No Answer %
Believe in a "life after death"	73	19	8
Believe in "heaven"	85	11	4
Believe in "hell"	65	29	6

In 1964 Glock and Stark surveyed the beliefs of Americans concerning the afterlife according to religious affiliation and also according to five geographical districts of the United States. The proportions in percentages of believers in the hereafter according to religious affiliation are as follows:

"Absolutely Sure There Is a Life Beyond Death" %

Unitarian (9 answers)	0
Congregational (44)	26
United Presbyterian (75)	36
Protestant Episcopal (56)	35
Methodist (217)	42
Presbyterian Church U.S. (40)	43
Disciples of Christ (42)	42
American Lutheran Bodies (145)	52
Total moderate Protestants (628) 41	
Lutheran, Missouri Synod (45)	50
Evangelical and Reformed (28)	50
American Baptist (91)	41
Southern Baptist (187)	65
Other Baptist bodies (90)	59
Sects (128)	67
Total conservative Protestants (569) 59	
Total Protestants (1,197) 50	

The proportions in percentages of believers in the hereafter according to five geographical districts in the United States are as follows:

	East	Midwest	South	Southwest	Mountain & Pacific
"Absolutely Sure There Is a Life Beyond Death"					
Moderate Protestants	31	42	51	52	35
Conservative Protestants	56	64	76	67	45

Studies concerning belief in the hereafter in various countries of the world show that age, sex, occupation, religious affiliation, and nationality may play a part in one's belief in the afterlife. There is also an indication that during the last twenty-five years the belief in a hereafter seems to be decreasing everywhere.*

Protestants vary in belief from those who do not believe in any afterlife to those who may believe in reincarnation. However, the traditional beliefs in the afterlife have focused around the two concepts of resurrection and immortality. While these two concepts have often popularly been used synonymously, many Protestant theologians believe that there is a radical difference between the Christian doctrine of the resurrection and the Greek idea of immortality.

The doctrine of the resurrection includes the following themes: (a) that the powers of evil and death were overcome by God in the crucifixion-resurrection event of Jesus Christ; (b) that the Christian who accepts through faith the grace of God revealed in the crucified and risen Christ receives the gift of eternal life, which is experienced as a new quality of life in the here and now (sometimes spoken of as the new birth, rebirth, or the new being in Christ); (c) that the fulfillment of eternal life is reached only after death occurs, when the Christian enters a new dimension of being. The philosophical concept of immortality focuses on an immortal entity which is inherent in humankind and which continues its existence, uninterrupted after its separation from the body by death. Some Christian scholars assert that the belief in something indestructible in the nature of personhood is not incompatible with the New Testament revelation and the concept of resurrection.

There have also been various understandings of heaven and hell from materialistic conceptions of heaven as a place of golden streets and of hell as a place of raging fires to

* Statistical tables are taken from A. Godin (Ed.), *Death and Presence* (Brussels: Lumen Vitae Press, 1972), chapter one.

more symbolic concepts of heaven as a spiritual realm of being in harmonious relationship with the Eternal and of hell's representing alienation and isolation from the Eternal. Some Protestants may believe in heaven but find they cannot conceive of hell; others believe that one's heaven and hell are experienced only in one's earthly life. While there is no agreement among all Protestants in regard to the concepts of heaven and hell, it may be helpful to identify briefly some differing viewpoints.

For example, hell has been seen by some as the place or realm of everlasting torment for those who have rejected the offer of salvation by God in Jesus Christ. Others cannot believe that a God of love would condemn persons forever and therefore any punishment in the hereafter is remedial and disciplinary so that ultimately all are restored. But others find a major flaw in universal restoration in that it tends to deny the freedom of the person's will to say "no," ultimately even to God. Others cannot believe that, even though sin deserves punishment, hell and the satanic will coexist with God throughout eternity; therefore they affirm that there is no immortality of evil and everlasting torment, that all evil will be annihilated, that there will be a complete and final end to those who have rejected God, and that God and His loving goodness will reign supreme.

Some viewpoints concerning heaven include such ideas as a personal identity that survives the experience of death. While there is mystery about the process and the nature of that inner core of personality which survives death, there is often an affirmation that the essence of personhood lives on in a new realm.

Fellowship with God and communion with the saints is a part of the experience of heaven; there are opportunities for new dimensions of relationship with God and with other persons who are also in heaven. Opportunities for growth are a part of the heavenly experience; there are chances for spiritual development and service. (This concept is in conflict with the idea of heaven as a place of passive rest.)

Again it is important to state that there is a wide spectrum of Protestant concepts of an afterlife, and the above is only a brief synopsis of a few Protestant beliefs in this regard.

How does Protestantism help the mourner to find meaning in life after the funeral service?

Initially it must be acknowledged that too often Protestant churches have not carried on a ministry of caregiving after the funeral is over. However, clergy are increasingly made aware both through their seminary education and continuing education of the importance of the ministry of pastoral care to the bereaved for several months after the initial crisis of the death event. The community of believers is also becoming more conscious of its own continuing ministry to the bereaved through various means of death education carried on within the parish, community, and the communications media.

The sustained ministry of the caring presence of the Christian fellowship with the bereaved is often the key ingredient in helping the grief-stricken person to release as fully as possible the various emotions felt as a result of the death and of subsequent radical changes in his or her life situation. The struggle of coping with life in the face of such a loss; the groping and searching for new purposes, goals, and meanings; and the need for personal acceptance while one is on such a rocky pilgrimage are all a part of the experience that may be shared with persons from the community of faith. Some churches are implementing this "pastorhood of all believers" by scheduling regular visits to the bereaved by both minister and laypersons during the first twelve to eighteen months following the funeral. Some parishes mobilize their caregivers for specific situations so that a couple who have worked through their grief over the death of a child may be particularly effective in ministering to another couple who have recently lost a child. The reentry of the mourner into the ongoing worship and fellowship of the church may also be profoundly sustaining. Death education is beginning in some churches whereby some people may do some anticipatory work on their life situation by facing in imagination potential losses in their family circle.

Thus the network of a caring faith community is primary in helping the mourner find meaning. It may be through the love of God communicated through such people that the realities of the faith make increasing sense and offer sustaining hope to the bereaved. Through the historic resources of the Christian revelation made real through the Christian community, the mourner may gain courage to weave new meanings out of the fabric of life.

Many segments of the Protestant church are moving away from superficial religious clichés, false reassurances, and simplistic, repressive optimism as a means of trying to help the mourner to find meaning in life. A casting aside of the rose-colored-religious-glasses approach to helping the mourner may enable that person to face the actuality of his or her world more readily, to plan the necessary steps ahead more responsibly, and to experience the presence of the living God right in the midst of where one is and where one is in the process of becoming.

Are there special areas of concern for Protestants in their ministry regarding death?

There are many issues that can be touched upon which are significant to some Protestants in dealing with death. Only a few of these concerns can be mentioned here.

- Individuals are encouraged to make a will which should be periodically reexamined and updated if necessary.
- Arrangements should be made for a cemetery lot, if

such burial is desired.

- Serious consideration should be given for granting permission for a post mortem examination, which may help medical knowledge as well as ease the family's mind about the causes of death.
- Vital information that would be helpful to the family in case of your death (such as life insurance policies, etc.) should be kept in some convenient place.
- Consideration should be given to the possible donation of eyes or organs for transplant at the time of one's death. Medical schools are also in need of bodies for educational purposes, and advance permission must be given.
- Written instructions for one's funeral service may be arranged with a member of the family, pastor, and/or a funeral director.
- The ministry to bereaved children must become a more focused part of caregiving within the church so that the needs of the children are not neglected during the crisis of death.
- Since there is often a withdrawing of emotional and spiritual support to a family in which there is a suicide, Protestant churches need to reassess their caregiving to such families and seek to mobilize their concern more effectively to those families.
- Death education programs in the local parish should be encouraged and fostered.
- With the emergence of a variety of lifestyles, the Protestant church must be prepared to minister to persons in grief, whose living arrangements the church may not sanction but whose needs for ministering are still very real and valid. The church should not use the time of death and bereavement as a time for withholding a caregiving ministry in favor of being judgmental upon the surviving member of a

couple who may have been living together without society's official sanction. The church's ministry to the bereaved should be extended to all.

SUGGESTED READINGS

Bachman, C. Charles, *Ministering to the Grief Sufferer* (Englewood Cliffs, N.J.: Prentice-Hall, 1964).

Gatch, Melton, *Death: Meaning and Morality in Christian Thought and Contemporary Culture* (New York: Seabury Press, 1969).

Grollman, Earl A. (Ed.), *Explaining Death to Children* (Boston: Beacon Press, 1967).

Irion, Paul E., *The Funeral and the Mourners* (Nashville: Abingdon Press, 1954).

———, *The Funeral: Vestige or Value* (Nashville: Abingdon Press, 1966).

———, *A Manual and Guide for Those Who Conduct a Humanist Funeral Service* (Baltimore: Waverly Press, 1971).

Jackson, Edgar N., *The Christian Funeral* (New York: Channel Press, 1966).

———, *Understanding Grief* (Nashville: Abingdon Press, 1957).

———, *When Someone Dies* (Philadelphia: Fortress Press, 1971).

Rogers, William F., *Ye Shall Be Comforted* (Philadelphia: Westminster Press, 1950).

Switzer, David K., *The Dynamics of Grief* (Nashville: Abingdon Press, 1970).

Westberg, Granger E., *Good Grief* (Philadelphia: Fortress Press, 1962).

Sample of the Form for Funeral Instructions used by the United Church of Christ, Somerset, Mass.

FUNERAL INSTRUCTIONS FOR . . . .

To asist those responsible for my funeral arrangements I make the following suggestions:

1) I wish to have my service held at:
    ( ) My Church which is: . . . .
    ( ) The Funeral home.

( ) In my own home.
( ) Other directions.

2) I suggest that the following funeral director be called:
. . . .

3) ( ) I have consulted with the above named funeral director and have given him the following directions:
Preference as to casket (. . . . .)
Preference as to vault (. . . . .)
Preference as to urn, if cremation is requested (.)
Other specific directions not covered above: . . . .
Total approximate cost (. . . . . `. . . .)

4) I wish to have:
( ) The usual funeral with graveside committal service.
( ) The funeral service with the committal service as part of it.
( ) A memorial service with private burial before or after it.
( ) My body cremated (with funeral or memorial service as indicated above).

5) I ( ) do ( ) do not wish to have "calling hours" in the funeral home with the open casket.

6) ( ) I would prefer that instead of sending flowers my friends make memorial gifts, if they wish, to: . . .
. . . .

7) I make the following suggestions of material which I would like to have used in my service:
Scripture passages to be read: . . . .
Favorite appropriate poem: . . . .
Prayers: . . . .
Music: . . . .
Other: . . . .

8) ( ) I would like to give my eyes after death to the Eye Bank to help the living see. I have filled out a blank to this purpose and have sent it to:
. . . .

9) ( ) I would like to give my body to . . . .
I have filled out a blank to this purpose and have sent it
to: . . . .

VITAL STATISTICS RECORD

(Last Name)   (First Name)   (Middle Name)
Street   City   State
Date of Birth: Month   Day   Year
Birthplace: City   State
Member of what Church?
(City & State)
Occupation: How Long?
Previous positions held
Name of Father   Birthplace
(City & State)
Maiden Name of Mother   Birthplace
(City & State)
Length of residence in   Years, Resided in
state   years.
Resided in the U.S.A.   years.
If veteran, branch of service, rank, war
Social Security Number
In event of my death please notify:
Relationship: Name: Address: City: State:
. . . .
. . . .
. . . .
. . . .
I wish to be buried in . . . . cemetery
located in
                    (City & State)
The deed to the lot is in the name of   . . . .
and the deed may be found   . . . .

I have made out a will. It may be found . . . .

. . . .

A copy of this record should be given to a member of your family.

A copy also may be left with the church in its files and may be given to the funeral director of your choice, if you wish to do so.

6

The Roman Catholic Way in Death and Mourning

Do all Roman Catholics agree to the same rituals and theology of death?

What special customs surround the Roman Catholic ceremony of death?

How is the funeral conducted?

What are the concepts of an afterlife?

How might friends express their condolences?

RICHARD J. BUTLER

A major function of the Roman Catholic religion is to convey both a theology and a tradition regarding life and death. The meaning is presented within a context of faith in God and the community of faith, the church. There are structured processes for the Catholic who has died — a vigil or wake, funeral Mass, and a ritual at the place of burial. According to the Revised Decree of the

Second Vatican Council: "The celebration of the funeral liturgy with meaning and dignity presupposes an integral understanding of the Christian Mystery and the pastoral office."

Father Richard J. Butler is the executive secretary of the Boston Archdiocesan Liturgical Commission and a columnist for *The Pilot*. He previously served as lecturer in theology at Stonehill College, North Easton, Massachusetts.

The Roman Catholic Way in Death and Mourning

Is there a general agreement among Roman Catholics regarding death?

In the Epistle to the Romans Paul wrote: "If the Spirit of him who raised Jesus from the dead dwells in you, then he who raised Jesus Christ from the dead will also bring to life your mortal bodies because of his Spirit who dwells in you" (8:11). From the Second Vatican Council we read in the 1965 Constitution on the Church in the Modern World, "Pressing upon the Christian, to be sure, are the need and the duty to battle against evil through manifold tribulations and even to suffer death. But, linked with the paschal mystery and patterned on the dying Christ, he will hasten forward to resurrection in the strength which comes from hope . . . . Through Christ and in Christ, the riddles of sorrow and death grow meaningful" (paragraph 22).

These brief statements come to the core of the Christian understanding of death. The paschal mystery is the death and resurrection of Christ. Christian faith holds that in the resurrection death is conquered — not only the death of Christ but ultimately one's own death as well. The sadness and suffering of death are not denied. The victory over death comes not at this hour but in the final hour when Christ will come again.

What are the rituals which the Roman Catholic Church brings to the situations of dying?

The Catholic Church has a ritual of anointing for those who are dying. Until recently this anointing was reserved to the more critical hour of impending death and was spoken of as "extreme unction" or colloquially as the "last rites." In the changes that have been introduced since the Second Vatican Council the anointing is to be done at an early state of any serious sickness.

The Epistle of St. James gives the background for this sacrament of anointing. "Is any one among you sick? Let him bring in the presbyters of the Church, and let them pray over him, anointing him with oil in the name of the Lord. And the prayer of faith will save the sick man, and the Lord will raise him up, and if he be in sin, they shall be forgiven him" (5:14 - 15).

Arrangements for the anointing of the sick are made by contacting the priest in the local parish church. Generally the priest will arrange a time for the anointing allowing the family to be present, when possible, to join in the prayers of the ritual. During the illness the priest should be invited to return regularly and to bring communion to the sick person. At the hour of death itself, communion will be given to the sick person with a special formula; this final communion is called "Viaticum."

Obviously the various circumstances surrounding death do not always allow this scheduling and the ritual allows much variety in the arranging of this pastoral ministry. In sudden deaths the priest should be called. When possible, the anointing and Viaticum would be administered. If the person has died, there would be no anointing but the priest would lead the family in prayers for the person who has died.

How does the ritual of anointing of the sick

differ from the ritual of extreme unction?

Extreme unction is the term applied to the older ritual of anointing, which for the most part was reserved to the critical hours of death. Left to this final hour, the anointing was often done with little ceremony and often with the patient nearly unconscious. The recent ritual of anointing of the sick, promulgated in 1973, is directed to an earlier stage of the process of serious illness. It encourages the patient, when able, to respond. It allows for a communal celebration with the family and friends present.

After the death, how is the Catholic funeral planned?

The funeral is planned by the family, the local parish priest, and the funeral director. In former times this was easily arranged, for generally the local parish priest was present to help the family through the full process of death. Today, as a rule, illness and death are transferred from the local setting to a hospital setting where the hospital chaplain attends the patient and the family. The family should contact their local parish priest and the funeral director after the death and begin planning three phases of the funeral rite: the wake, the funeral Mass, and the burial.

In the questions below, details of these phases are considered, as well as possible exceptions to this normal pattern. The planning process can be somewhat complex and often comes upon families at a time of tensions and anxieties. For this reason it is of great benefit to discuss the various phases, when possible, sufficiently in advance to assure a calm and complete preparation. Planning funeral liturgies during the dying process assures not only a ceremony that includes the wishes of the family but also allows a greater period for counseling from the local parish priest in the whole area of grief and acceptance of death.

What is a wake?

The wake is a vigil or period of waiting for the funeral itself. The custom of wakes varies among ethnic groups and among sectional areas of this country. Both the funeral director and the local parish priest can advise the family in this regard.

Formerly wakes were held in the family home. The body was laid out after embalming and the friends would sit in an all-night vigil. It was an occasion for neighbors and relatives to visit, to sustain the family in the process of grief, to pay respect to the body of the deceased, and to join with one another in an expression of faith. This expression would take different dimensions in different cultural settings. The primary expression was prayer.

In time the wake process was reduced to defined hours, and now, for the most part, it has been transferred to professional funeral homes. Traditions vary from one locale to another on how the wake is conducted. It may be on one or two days. The local parish will usually provide a wake service at a designated hour during the course of the wake. This will include scripture readings and meditative responses. When possible, the priest will invite the family to select the readings and determine other phases of the wake service. Another prayer service, quite frequent at wakes until recently and still observed in some places, is the rosary. This is a devotion centering on meditations of fifteen mysteries of redemption and including a repetitive recitation of the "Hail Mary."

The funeral director will usually arrange the casket in a position for all visitors to pay their respects and also provide an arrangement of chairs for the family to receive the visitors. The family may choose whether the casket is to be closed or opened. The family may determine the extent of flowers to be placed at the casket. The family may choose the arrangement of chairs to provide a more solemn setting or to provide a more informal setting for conversations. In former times the ritual and structure of the wake were quite elaborate and some localities have maintained this. In other situations today the trend is toward simplicity. The new Rite for Christian Burial encourages an avoidance of ostentatious display.

In planning the wake the family should consider the purpose of the wake and the needs of the relatives and friends. The wake is a preparation for the funeral. It should not be so elaborate as to make the funeral itself anticlimactic. The trend to simplicity today has proved quite successful. It should never be carried to a point, however, where rituals that are meaningful, especially to an older generation, are done away with simply for the sake of efficiency.

Both the rituals provided in the church manuals and the many rituals developed in ethnic traditions originated as a service to the family and friends of the bereaved. They serve to define the grief being experienced, the faith that gives meaning to the death, and the supportive dimensions of the community present to the bereaved.

What is the funeral?

The funeral is the service of prayer that is usually incorporated in the celebration of Mass. As a rule it is held a few days after the death to allow for the wake. It begins at the funeral home with a procession to the church. At the church, after all are ushered to their seats, the priest and the assisting ministers meet the body of the dead person at the entrance. There the casket is covered with a white pall, symbolic of the white robe of baptism. The priest himself wears white vestments, emphasizing the joy of faith that overcomes the sadness of death. This is in marked contrast with the black vestments worn until recently when a penitential motif was dominant in much of the funeral liturgy.

After the opening statement, the body is brought to

the head of the aisle. The paschal candle — a sign of Christ present through baptism — is placed at the casket. A liturgy of the Word follows the opening prayer with readings from the Bible. Relatives and friends of the deceased are encouraged to select the readings and to offer the readings. This is one of the points that should be discussed in the initial planning of the funeral. The priest then delivers a homily. While reference may be made to the deceased, this is not in the form of a eulogy. A litany prayer of the faithful concludes the liturgy of the Word.

The liturgy of the Eucharist follows, with gifts of bread and wine brought forth and the Eucharistic Prayer proclaimed. This prayer, which includes several acclamations for the people, incorporates a narration of the Last Supper, a memorial of Christ's death and resurrection, a calling upon the Holy Spirit, and an offering of the sacrifice. The communion follows, with the Lord's Prayer and the reception of the Eucharist. After communion the Rite of Commendation concludes the funeral Mass.

Apart from the selection of texts and the designating of persons for roles of lectoring and bearing the gifts of water and wine, the planning of the funeral Mass should consider the music. Here the director of music in the parish will offer guidelines and note the various acclamations, responses, and chants where music is to be scheduled.

What is the burial rite?

At the cemetery the official rite is quite brief. There is a blessing of the grave, a reading of scripture and of several prayers. Provision is given in the ritual for the development of the rite with the inclusion of litanies, additional readings, etc. When a larger community is present at the burial, singing is sometimes included. As a general rule, the family does not remain at the cemetery for the burial itself; rather they are invited to leave after the ritual. There is a growing practice in some areas for the family to remain while the body is lowered into the grave, thus allowing them to actually experience the burial itself. This is for the family to decide and should be determined in advance.

The custom of having friends return to the home of the family after the burial for a small collation varies from one locale to another.

In what ways do friends express condolence to the family of the deceased?

Presence at the wake, the funeral Mass, and the burial are the standard forms of expressing condolence. In some situations, friends send flowers to the wake. Before sending flowers, however, one should first check the wishes of the family in this regard by contacting them either directly or through the funeral director. Spiritual bouquets — that is, cards announcing the celebration of Mass for the deceased — may be arranged by contacting the local parish; these, or cards announcing donations to a particular charity, may be left at the wake or sent to the family. There is usually a small table near the casket for this purpose.

In attending the wake the hours scheduled should be observed. Visitors generally go directly to the family, offering a brief word of sympathy, and then to the casket to offer a brief prayer. Visitors may stand or kneel for the prayer. When attending the wake service, the visitor should follow the directions given by the leader of the service as to the times for sitting and standing. In most funeral homes there are side rooms for those who wish to extend the visit with additional conversation.

On the day of the funeral usually only immediate friends go to the funeral home and then in procession to the church; others would go directly to the church. Visitors would be seated on arrival. During the entrance rite, all stand. In the liturgy of the Word all sit, except for the gospel reading and the prayer of the faithful, when all stand. As the gifts are brought forward, all may be seated. During the Eucharistic Prayer all would kneel or stand; during the communion and the Rite of Commendation, all would stand.

At the burial the priest or director would lead the people in prayer, explain any responses to be given, and offer any specific directive. After the funeral, when customary, those attending are invited to return to the home of the deceased.

Formal arrangements for visiting the family after the funeral in the days that follow are not usually announced but in most cases such visits prove of great help to the family.

What are some of the exceptions to the normal routine of funerals described above?

On certain holy days, e.g., Christmas and Sundays, funeral Masses are not allowed. In these situations the funeral Mass would be delayed until the following day. On Thursday, Friday, and Saturday of Holy Week no funeral Mass is allowed. On these days a funeral service would be held in the church with a simple liturgy of the Word; burial would follow; in the following week a funeral Mass would be scheduled.

For many years cremation was not allowed for Catholics. The custom of cremation in earlier times included an implicit denial of the resurrection of the dead. This implication is no longer prevalent and accordingly permission can be given for Catholics to be cremated when sufficient reason is present. The wake and the funeral Mass would be as described.

When the body of the deceased is not present, the funeral centers exclusively on the funeral Mass. This situation can arise in the case of drownings and also in the case when provision has been made for the donation of the body for medical science. The donation, however, need not exclude the funeral nor the body being present.

How are military rituals included in the funeral liturgy?

At the wake, military honor guards follow their usual customs. The flag may be placed on the casket. At the church, the flag may continue to drape the casket or the flag may be folded to allow for the white funeral pall. The flag would drape the casket en route to the cemetery and would be formally folded after the burial ritual.

What does the Catholic Church offer the bereaved in the period after the funeral?

Most important for the bereaved is the witness of a community of faith. In the weekly celebration of Mass, the bereaved is given a sign of the death and resurrection of the Lord and the Christian understanding of death today. Through the parish priest, counseling is available to the family of the deceased either on a parochial or on a diocesan level. A month after the death, a Month's Mind Mass is celebrated; each year the family may arrange for an anniversary Mass. In this way, through liturgy and pastoral counseling, the family is brought through the grief process and into an adjusted program of life.

The Catholic believes in a life beyond death. It is there that the kingdom will be finally realized — the kingdom of which Jesus spoke so frequently. The process of entering heaven is not necessarily immediate. There is a purgative process in which the mystery of love is perfected. In this stage, the prayer of the Christian community can aid a fellow Christian who has died. This is a continual concern of the Church. Beyond this the great concern of the Church in the scene of death is the support of faith and the fellowship of love to be witnessed to those who suffer the loss and the sadness of death.

Is there a glossary of often-used words in Roman Catholicism relative to death?

Anointing of the Sick. A ritual in which oil is applied to the body of a sick person as prayers are offered for the forgiveness of sin and the restoration of health. The oil used is blessed by the Bishop during Holy Week. Formerly this ritual was delayed to the critical stages of illness near death and was called extreme unction. Today it is done at an earlier stage.

Funeral Mass. This is the celebration, usually on the day of burial, in which scripture readings are offered on the Christian meaning of death and a eucharistic prayer and communion rite follow. The Mass is begun with a rite of greeting the body of the deceased and it is concluded with a rite of commendation. In the old rite this was sometimes referred to as a "Requiem" Mass — the title coming from the first word of the Latin text of the introit of the Mass.

Month's Mind Mass. This is the title given the celebration of Mass a month after the death and funeral liturgy. Provision is also made in the rituals for a special celebration of Mass on an annual occasion which is called an anniversary Mass.

Pall. This is the covering placed over the casket in the initial rite of greeting at the funeral Mass. The prayer said at the time notes the symbolism of the white garment given a Christian at baptism and orients the theme of the funeral liturgy to the baptismal theme.

Paschal Candle. The high point of the liturgy of the year comes during the Easter vigil when the fire is lit and the candle is blessed and lit from the new fire symbolizing the new life of Christ. This candle stands in a prominent place in the church throughout the year and is lit at funerals and baptisms to relate these liturgies with the Easter vigil liturgy.

Viaticum. The title given to the Holy Communion given to a person near the hour of death. Holy Communion is the consecrated bread, the "Body of the Lord," eaten during the celebration of Mass. Hosts are reserved from the Mass, in the tabernacle, for distribution to the sick. On the occasion of bringing Communion to one who is dying special formulas are provided to aid the sick person at the point of death.

Wake. The title given to the period from the hour of death until the funeral Mass. It is generally defined for a special period of hours during which friends may visit with the family of the deceased and may offer a prayer at the casket.

APPENDIX

THE ROMAN RITUAL

Revised by Decree of the Second Vatican Council and Published by Authority of Pope Paul VI

Rite of Funerals

In the funeral rites the Church celebrates the Paschal mystery of Christ. Those who in baptism have become one with the dead and risen Christ will pass with him from death to life, to be purified in soul and welcomed into the fellowship of the saints in heaven. They look forward in blessed hope to his second coming and the bodily resurrection of the dead. The Church therefore celebrates the eucharistic sacrifice of Christ's passover for the dead, and offers prayers and petitions for them. In the communion of all Christ's members, the prayers which bring spiritual help to some may bring to others a consoling hope.

In celebrating the funeral rites of their brothers and sisters, Christians should certainly affirm their hope in eternal life, but in such a way that they do not seem to neglect or ignore the feeling and practice of their own time and place. Family traditions, local customs, groups established to take care of funerals, anything that is good may be used freely, but anything alien to the Gospel should be changed so that funeral rites for Christians may proclaim the Paschal faith and the spirit of the Gospel.

The bodies of the faithful, which were temples of the Holy Spirit, should be shown honor and respect, but any kind of pomp or display should be avoided. Between the time of death and burial there should be sufficient opportunities for the people to pray for the dead and profess their own faith in eternal life. Depending on local custom, the significant times during this period would seem to be the following: the vigil in the home of the deceased; the time when the body is laid out; the assembly of the relatives and, if possible, the whole community, to receive hope and consolation in the liturgy of the Word, to offer the eucharistic sacrifice, and to bid farewell to the deceased in the final commendation, followed by the carrying of the body to the grave or tomb.

The rite of funerals for adults has been arranged in three plans to take into account conditions in all parts of the world.

(a) The first plan provides for three stations: in the home of the deceased, in the church, and at the cemetery;

(b) the second plan has two stations: in the cemetery chapel and at the grave;

(c) the third plan has one station, at the home of the deceased.

When particular rituals are prepared in harmony with the new Roman Ritual, the conference of bishops may retain the three plans for funeral rites, change the order, or omit one or other of them. It may be that in a country a single plan, for example, the first one with three stations, is the only one in use and therefore should be retained to the exclusion of the others; in another country all three plans may be necessary. The conference of bishops, after considering pastoral needs, will make suitable arrangements.

After the funeral Mass the rite of final commendation and farewell is celebrated. This rite is not to be understood as a purification of the dead — which is effected rather by the eucharistic sacrifice — but as the last farewell with which the Christian community honors one of its members before the body is buried. Although in death there is a certain separation, Christians, who are members of Christ and are one in him, can never be really separated by death. The priest introduces this rite with an invitation to pray; then follow a period of silence, the sprinkling with holy water, the incensation, and the song of farewell. The text and melody of the latter should be such that it may be sung by all present and be experienced as the climax of this entire rite. The sprinkling with holy water, which recalls the person's entrance into eternal life through baptism, and the incensation, which honors the body of the deceased as a temple of the Holy Spirit, may also be considered signs of farewell. The rite of final commendation and farewell is to be held only in the funeral celebration itself, that is, with the body present. In the United States, however, although the rite of final commendation at the catafalque or pall is excluded, it is permitted to celebrate the funeral service, including the commendation, in those cases where it is physically or morally impossible for the body of the deceased person to be present.

In celebrations for the dead, whether the funeral service or any other, emphasis should be given to the biblical readings. These proclaim the Paschal mystery, support the hope of reunion in the kingdom of God, teach respect for the dead, and encourage the witness of Christian living.

The Church employs the prayer of the psalms in the

offices for the dead to express grief and to strengthen genuine hope. Pastors must therefore try by appropriate catechesis to lead their communities to understand and appreciate at least the chief psalms of the funeral liturgy. When pastoral considerations indicate the use of other sacred songs, these should reflect a "warm and living love for sacred scripture" and a liturgical spirit.

In the prayers, too, the Christian community expresses its faith and intercedes for adults who have died so that they may enjoy eternal happiness with God. This is the happiness which deceased children, made sons of adoption through baptism, are believed to enjoy already. Prayers are offered for the parents of these infants, as for the relatives of all the dead, so that in their sorrow they may experience the consolation of faith.

In places where, by particular law, endowment, or custom, the Office of the Dead is usually said not only at the funeral rites but also apart from them, this office may continue to be celebrated with devotion. In view of the demands of modern life and pastoral considerations, a vigil or celebration of God's word may take the place of the office.

Christian funeral rites are permitted for those who choose to have their bodies cremated unless it is shown that they have acted for reasons contrary to Christian principles. These funeral rites should be celebrated according to the plan in use for the region but in a way that does not hide the Church's preference for the custom of burying the dead in a grave or tomb, as the Lord himself willed to be buried. In the case of cremation any danger of scandal or confusion should be removed. The rites ordinarily performed at the cemetery chapel or at the grave or tomb may be used in the crematory building. If there is no other suitable place for the rites, they may be celebrated in the crematory hall itself, provided that the danger of scandal and religious indifferentism is avoided.

In funeral celebrations all who belong to the people

of God should keep in mind their office and ministry: the parents or relatives, those who take care of funerals, the Christian community as a whole, and finally the priest. As teacher of the faith and minister of consolation, the priest presides over the liturgical service and celebrates the eucharist.

Priests and all others should remember that, when they commend the dead to God in the funeral liturgy, it is their duty to strengthen the hope of those present and to foster their faith in the Paschal mystery and the resurrection of the dead. In this way the compassionate kindness of Mother Church and the consolation of the faith may lighten the burden of believers without offending those who mourn.

In preparing and arranging funeral celebrations priests should consider the deceased and the circumstance of his life and death and be concerned also for the sorrow of the relatives and their Christian needs. Priests should be especially aware of persons, Catholic or non-Catholic, who seldom or never participate in the Eucharist or who seem to have lost their faith, but who assist at liturgical celebrations and hear the Gospel on the occasion of funerals. Priests must remember that they are the ministers of Christ's Gospel to all men.

The funeral rites, except the Mass, may be celebrated by a deacon. If pastoral necessity demands, the conference of bishops may, with the permission of the Holy See, permit a lay person to celebrate the service. In the absence of a priest or deacon, it is urged that in the funeral rites according to the first plan the stations in the home of the deceased and at the cemetery be conducted by lay persons; the same holds for vigil services for the dead. In the United States, the local ordinary may depute a lay person, in the absence of a priest or deacon, to lead the station in the church (i.e., the liturgy of the Word and the commendation).

Apart from distinctions based on liturgical function and sacred orders and the honors due to civil authorities according to liturgical law, no special honors are to be paid to any private persons or classes of persons, whether in the ceremonies or by external display.

The priest should consider the various circumstances, and in particular, the wishes of the family and the community. He should make free use of the choices afforded in the rite.

The celebration of the funeral liturgy with meaning and dignity and the priest's ministry to the dead presuppose an integral understanding of the Christian mystery and the pastoral office. Among other things, the priest should:

1. Visit the sick and the dying, as indicated in the relevant section of the Roman Ritual.

2. Teach the significance of Christian death.

3. Show loving concern for the family of the deceased person, support them in the time of sorrow, and as much as possible involve them in planning the funeral celebration and the choice of the options made available in the rite.

4. Integrate the liturgy for the dead with the whole parish liturgical life and the pastoral ministry.

SUGGESTED READINGS

Brett, L., "The Revised Funeral Rites." *The Living Light*, Spring, 1970, volume 7, pages 71-83.

Chilson, R., *An Introduction to the Faith of Catholics* (New York: Paulist Press, 1972).

Corrigan, J., "Future Revisions of the Anointing of the Sick." *Homiletic and Pastoral Review*, April 1968, volume 68, pages 600-602.

Dewart, L., "The Fact of Death." *Commonweal*, November 14, 1969, volume 91, pages 206-208.

Dunn, J. A., "What Happens to You After You Die?" *U.S. Catholic* 37:6-12, November, 1972.

McManus, F. R., "The Reformed Funeral Rite." *American Ecclesiastical Review*, January-February, 1972, volume 166, pages 45-59, 124-139.

Nowell, R., *What a Modern Catholic Believes About Death* (Chicago: Thomas More Press, 1972).

Simpson, M., *Theology of Death and Eternal Life* (Cork: Mercier Press, 1971).

Veatch, R., and E. Wakin, "Death and Dying." *U.S. Catholic*, April, 1972, volume 37, pages 6-13.

Wagner, Johannes (Ed.), *Reforming the Rites of Death* (New York: Paulist-Newman 1968).

FURTHER READINGS

Where is the official text for the funeral liturgy found?

Rite of Funerals (Washington, D.C.: United States Catholic Conference, 1971).

Where can options for the official text be found for those planning the wake and the funeral Mass?

The Lord Is My Shepherd — A Book of Wake Services (Notre Dame, Ind.: Ave Maria Press, 1971).

Champlin, J., and J. Flynn, *Toward a New Life* (Notre Dame, Ind.: Ave Maria Press, 1971).

7

The Jewish Way in Death and Mourning

Do all Jews agree to the same rituals and theology of death?

What special customs surround the Jewish ceremony of death?

How is the funeral conducted?

What are the concepts of an afterlife?

How might friends express their condolences?

EARL A. GROLLMAN

Death is a crisis of life. How a Jew handles death indicates much about the way he views his religious life.

Over the centuries rabbis have evolved distinctive patterns and rites which demonstrate both a respect for the dead and a deep concern for the living. Jewish laws of mourning revolve around a community structure enabling the bereaved to better confront those inevitable moments of darkness and despair.

Rabbi Grollman has been the spiritual leader of the Beth El Temple Center in Belmont, Masssachusetts, since 1951. He has served as president of the Massachusetts Board of Rabbis, the only rabbinical group in the Commonwealth that serves the needs of Orthodox, Conservative, and Reform Jews. A former chairman of the United Rabbinic Chaplaincy Commission, Rabbi Grollman has lectured at seminaries and clergy institutes throughout the country.

The Jewish Way in Death and Mourning

Is there a general agreement of Jews as to the ritual and theology of Judaism?

Judaism is more than a creed; it is a way of life. And death is a reality of life. Since there are diverse ways in which Jews throughout the ages have viewed life, so there are different approaches by which Jews practice the rites of death.

There are those who believe in a fixed authority derived from supernatural revelation. Others recognize the principle of development in religious life and would affirm the right of the individual to follow the dictates of his own conscience.

Over the centuries the rabbis have evolved patterns of practices for the rites of death. Even though Judaism recognizes the value of historical continuity and tradition, there is no single path to the varied rituals and theology of death. For example, traditional Judaism is opposed to cremation as a denial of belief in bodily resurrection. On the other hand, a prominent liberal rabbi in Cleveland writes, "I have no particular faith in physical resurrection. About one in ten funerals in which I officiate involves cremation." Although a few rabbis might still forbid the cornea transplantation, among most of the Orthodox scholars permission would now be granted, on the grounds that organ donation would help restore sight to the living.

Thus, there is no unanimity of acceptance as to the rites of burial and manners of mourning. One can offer only general guidelines. If there are further questions, the rabbi in your community would be only too happy to give you specific information.

With what special and unique customs does Judaism surround the ceremony of death?

For the Jew the ceremonies of death are of enormous significance. The Hebrew religion suggests rites that play a vital role in the healing work of grief. The bereaved must realize that a loved one is gone and that the void must be filled gradually in a constructive way. He should not suppress memories, or the disturbing, even guilt-producing recollections which are an inevitable part of all human relationships. Shock and grief are structured by defined solemn procedures. Joshua Liebman in *Peace of Mind* points to the wisdom of the sages in assigning a definite period of mourning participated in by the entire family.

One becomes a mourner (Hebrew, *Ovel*) upon the death of one of seven relatives: father, mother, husband, wife, son or daughter, brother or sister, including half-brother or half-sister. A child less than thirteen years old is not obliged to observe the rituals of mourning.

From the moment that one learns of the death of a loved one there are specific religious rites which help to order his life. A most striking expression of grief is the rending of the mourner's clothes (*Keriah*). In the Book of Genesis, when Jacob believed that his son, Joseph, was killed, the father "rent his garments" (37:34). Today, many mourners indicate their anguish by cutting a black ribbon, usually at the funeral chapel or at the cemetery prior to interment. The ceremony is performed standing up, to teach the bereaved to "meet all sorrow standing upright." For a parent, the tear is made on the left side over the heart; for others, it is on the right. *Keriah* is visible for the week of *Shiva.*

Shiva (meaning *seven*) refers to the first seven days of intensive mourning beginning immediately after the funeral, with the day of burial counted as the first day. One hour of the seventh day is considered a full day. Mourning customs are not observed on Sabbaths and Festivals.

The bereaved remain at home receiving a continuous stream of condolence calls. Difficult as this may sometimes be, it helps in keeping the bereaved ones' minds active and attentions engaged. Also, it is important because the companionship lends the comfort of the loving concern of family and friends.

Even though a minor is exempt from many of the mourning rites, the youngster should not be arbitrarily dismissed from the family gathering. He should be afforded the chance to face grief and mingle with his loved ones. Some enlightened adults have helped a child feel that he is important by allowing him to share in the family duties such as answering doorbells and telephones, helping with chores, and even in the preparation of the *Seudat Havra-ah,* the meal of consolation. He is given the opportunity to help them and be helped by them.

Immediately upon returning from the cemetery the *Shiva* candle is kindled and remains burning for the entire seven days. Before his death, the great sage Judah Hanasi (135 - 219) instructed that a light should be kept aflame in his home, for "light is the symbol of the divine. The Lord is my light and my salvation."

Following the *Shiva* comes the *Sh-loshim,* the thirty days. The mourners resume normal activity but avoid places of entertainment. At the end of thirty days, ritualistic mourning is over except in the case where the deceased was a parent, when mourning continues for an entire year.

The adult might attend the *Minyan* (daily worship) and the Sabbath services. He reads aloud the *Kaddish* prayer, originally not a liturgy for the dead, but a pledge from the living to dedicate one's life to the God of Life, "Magnified and Sanctified." This is the highest approach to commemorate the memory of a loved one. Each time during the year that the mourner recites the *Kaddish*, he reinforces both the reality of death and the affirmation of life. He openly displays his own needed concern and profound feeling of being a good son, father, brother, or husband. He participates with others who are also suffering the emotional trauma of bereavement. He belongs to the largest company in the world — the company of those who have known anguish and death. This great, universal sense of sorrow helps to unite human hearts and dissolve all other feelings into those of common sympathy and understanding.

The complete mourning period for those whose parents have died concludes twelve months from the day of the death. For other relatives *Sh-loshim* concludes the bereavement.

The anniversary of the death (*Yahrzeit*) is observed annually on the date of death, commencing on the preceding day and concluding on the anniversary day at sunset. *Kaddish* is recited in the synagogue and the *Yahrzeit* candle is kindled.

The service of commemoration of the tombstone or plaque is called the "unveiling." The time of the unveiling may be any time after *Sh-loshim* and usually before the first year of mourning is over. Unveilings, of course, are not held on the Sabbath or Festivals. Any member of the family or a close friend may intone the appropriate prayers, usually a few Psalms, the *El Molay Rachamim* ("God, full of compassion") and the *Kaddish*. Visitation at the grave may be made as often as one wishes following the initial thirty-day period.

The memorial prayer of *Yizkor* ("May God

remember the soul of my revered") is said four times a year during the synagogue worship: *Yom Kippur, Shemini Atzeret, Pesach,* and *Shavuot.* It is not recited during the first year of mourning.

Jewish rituals are community rituals. They are performed by those who share a religious sameness. The traditions create a sense of solidarity, of belongingness, the feeling that one is a member of the group with all the comfort and gratification that such a cohesiveness brings.

Judaism is strict in limiting mourning to the given periods and the customary observances. Excessive grief is taken as want of trust in God. The faith holds it as desirable that with time the havoc wrought by death should help to repair itself. Though no one is ever the same after a bereavement, he is expected, when mourning is over, to take up existence for the sake of life itself. The garment that the pious mourner rends can be sewn and worn again. The scar is there, but life must resume its course. The approach of Judaism is the climb from the valley of despair to the higher road of affirmative living. The observance of the Jewish laws and customs of mourning helps the mourner face reality, gives honor to the deceased, and guides the bereaved in the reaffirmation of life.

How about the Jewish funeral?

Your loved one has just died. There is sudden shock, pain, and disbelief. You can't think! You don't know what to do.

In the wake of your confusion, remember one important fact. *Call your rabbi immediately.* He is the one who can help not only to comfort you in your sorrow but will advise you as to procedure and arrangements. Final plans as to time and place of service should never be completed until your rabbi is consulted.

However, there are those who have little or no relationship with a rabbi or synagogue. In this case the funeral director should be contacted for referral. You will aid the funeral director by making known your needs as to type of funeral service desired. He would then attempt to match the clergyman with your religious requirements.

The rabbi will help to plan the funeral service. He will first question the survivors as to their choice of funeral director. Unfortunately, too often the bereaved have never considered a possible selection. In their sudden grief, they may now make an immediate decision which may not reflect ultimate wisdom. Before tragedy occurs, it is wise to formulate a judgment as to that funeral director who will inspire the family's confidence and trust.

The rabbi will visit your home, assess the immediate needs of the bereaved, and offer faith and understanding in your time of need. Together with the funeral director, arrangements will be made for a Jewish funeral that is tailored to your wishes.

Before the funeral, the question of an autopsy may be raised to establish the cause of death. Generally, Judaism approves the relatives' permission as a means of discovering the origin and hopeful cure of disease and thus saving the lives of others who may suffer the same malady. The autopsy need not delay preparations for the funeral service.

The Jewish funeral is a unique event in the life of your family. There are no two services exactly alike; yet each is an experience of value if it meets the needs of those who mourn. This is why it is necessary to communicate to both the rabbi and the funeral director your values and desires.

The Jewish funeral is a rite of separation. The presence of the casket actualizes the experience. Denial is transformed to the acceptance of reality. The public funeral affords the community an opportunity to offer support and share sorrow. All the emotional reactions that the bereaved are likely to experience — sorrow and loneliness, anger and rejection, guilt, anxiety about the future, and the conviction that nothing is certain or stable anymore — can be lessened by the support of caring friends.

Jewish rites and ceremonies help bear the painful loss. The rabbi will recite those prayers which are expressive of both the spirit of Judaism and the memory of the deceased. The most commonly used Psalm XXIII expresses the faith of the members of the flock in the justice of the Divine Shepherd. From the various Psalms, "O Lord, what is man" is epitomized the thought that although "our days are a passing shadow" there is immortality for those who have "treasured their days with a heart of wisdom." During the recitation of the prayer *El Molay Rachamim,* the name of the deceased is mentioned. The eulogy of the dead (*Hesped*) is usually included in the service to recognize not only that a death has occurred but that a life has been lived.

Rabbis deem it a most worthy deed for the friends not only to attend the funeral service but to follow the procession to the Jewish cemetery. This, the *Halvawyat Hamat,* is the ultimate demonstration of honor and respect. At the graveside, the burial service is concluded. After the recitation of the *Kaddish,* the prayer of condolence is offered: "*Ha-maw-Kom Y'na-chem Es-chem B'soch Sh'aw A-vay-lay Tzee-yon Vee'roo-shaw-law-yim* — May the Eternal comfort you among the other mourners for Zion and Jerusalem." By accepting death as a part of God's order for the world, we make death another part of your life plan. When death comes, there is no need to walk the lonely road alone. Judaism offers meaningful ceremonies to help along the way.

Do you suggest visitation or a condolence call before or after the funeral?

Unlike many other religions, the Jewish burial usually takes place within a day or two after death. Thus the bereaved have immediate and pressing concerns in the arrangement of the funeral.

Unless one is an especially close friend of the mourners, he would not disturb the family during the brief period between death and burial. This would allow the survivors the necessary time to work through the many details of the funeral as well as afford them the opportunity to share their own personal grief. In the *Pirke O'vot* (Ethics of the Fathers), "Do not appease thy fellow in the hour of his anger, and comfort him not in the hour when his dead lies before him."

It is preferable to pay your respects to the deceased by attending the funeral service and then by offering your condolences by visiting the home during the mourning period.

What expression of sorrow would you recommend in commemorating a Jewish deceased friend?

The most important expression of condolence is your own presence at both the funeral and the house of bereavement.

When one comes to the *Shiva*, it is not necessary to say, "*Shalom*, How are you?" Such a question indicates a lack of understanding and could appear offensive to the sorrowing heart. Nor, when an elderly person has died, does the cliché, "Well, he lived to a ripe old age" bring a healing balm when at the moment the terrible pain of separation appears as irreparable. The prophet Ezekiel affirms that the mourner should be able to "sigh in silence." By your attendance, you testify in a nonverbal way that the mourners are not left alone in their grief.

An especially difficult time is when the seven days of

mourning are over, and the house suddenly becomes lonely and desolate. This is another crucial opportunity for you to demonstrate that even though individuals may die, good friends still remain. Even after the *Shiva*, people need other people to help them return to the mainstream of life.

What might you take with you to the house of bereavement? The sages tell us that material gifts are of small solace to those experiencing personal disorientation. On the other hand, bringing food for "the meal of condolence" was always considered acceptable.

How about flowers? In ancient days, Rabbi Jannai commanded his sons that when he died, they would place myrtle twigs upon his deceased body. According to the Talmud, fragrant flowers and spices were utilized at the funeral, ostensibly to offset decaying odors. However, today many Jews regard the use of flowers as pagan and discourage their use. If you have any doubts as to their propriety, consult the newspaper obituary. It would be incorrect to send flowers if there is a notice requesting that they not be sent.

Often, in the death notice, other suitable suggestions are offered: "In lieu of flowers, contributions may be made to the synagogue . . . or a hospital . . . or to medical research for the disease which afflicted the now deceased." This is the family's recommendation for remembrance but does not necessarily exclude other forms of expression. A contribution to any worthwhile charity is a fitting memorial to the memory of the deceased.

It is always appropriate to express condolences with a sympathy card or preferably an individual letter. To share with the bereaved your own personal memories is to give them a meaningful record which they can read and reread in the future. By your demonstration of sorrow, you testify that even though a loved one has died, memories live forever.

What are the concepts of an afterlife?

Jewish people pray to the God of Abraham, the God of Isaac, and the God of Jacob. The God of each is the same God; but each has to find God in his own way. In a concept of death, each person differs in his reactions and belief. Judaism has no dogmatic creed. During the course of the centuries, many ideas have been presented.

The great scholar George F. Moore enumerated the many speculations of death in Jewish literature and stated, "Any attempt to systematize the Jewish notions of the hereafter imposes upon them an order and consistency which does not exist in them."

In the beginning of the first Christian century, the party of the Sadducees actually rejected a belief in an afterlife, while at the same time the Pharisees proclaimed that there was a world to come. The bitterest complaint against the doctrine of the hereafter was that by directing minds heavenward, it diverted people from taking action to correct social evils and encouraged a toleration of unfortunate contemporary conditions.

Many who believed in a life beyond considered it futile to speculate on the nature of the world to come. "Such knowledge," says the Psalmist, "is too high. I cannot attain it." The sages quoted with approval the stern caution of Ben Sirach: "Do not inquire what is beyond thine understanding and do not investigate what is hidden from thee."

The Jewish philosopher Moses Maimonides asserted that when we discuss this subject we are like blind men trying to understand the nature of light. "Know that just as a blind man can form no idea of colors nor a deaf man comprehend sounds, so bodies cannot comprehend the delights of the soul. And even as fish do not know the element fire because they exist ever in its opposite, so are the delights of the world of the spirit unknown to this world of flesh."

Judaism, then, has not wholly harmonized or integrated a precept of death and the hereafter. However, in spite of the varied beliefs throughout its circuitous history, there are observed certain central and unifying patterns. These concepts follow.

The Inevitability of Death

"The Lord God formed man of dust from the ground, and breathed into his nostrils the breath of life, and man became a living being" (Genesis 2:7). So the Psalmist says that when God sends forth His breath, living beings, whether men or animals, are created, and when God takes His breath away, they die (Psalms 104:29 - 30). When man's "breath departs, he returns to his earth" (Psalms 146:4).

Death is regarded by Jews as real — quite dreadfully real. It is the completion of life conceived in its concreteness, the rupture of the pleasures of family and friends, the destruction of the possibility of man's enjoying the praise of God. The "wise women" from Tekoa in 2 Samuel 14:14 remark, "We must all die; we are like water spilt on the ground, which cannot be gathered up again." According to Ecclesiastes 9:5, "The dead know nothing." *Sheol* is "the land of gloom and deep darkness, the land of gloom and chaos" (Job 10:21 - 22) and "the land of primeval ruins" (Ezekiel 26:20); "the land of silence" (Psalms 94:17). "In death there is no remembrance of Thee; in *Sheol* who can give Thee praise?" (Psalms 115:17).

No form of human existence can escape the democracy of death. It is part of the processes of birth, growth, and decay. He knows that "like the grass of the field, he is one whose place will know him no more" (Psalms 103:15). "Man that is born of woman is of few days . . . he comes forth like a flower, and withers; he flees like a shadow, and continues not . . . his days are determined, and the number of his months is with Thee, and Thou hast appointed his bounds that he cannot pass" (Job 14: 1 - 5).

In Judaism, death is both real and inescapable. A

person should know that he must die, for death is an organic, natural, and logical part of life. For what man can live and never see death?

The Deathlessness of Man's Spirit

With the development of the beliefs of other religions in retribution and resurrection, Judaism turned its attention to what happens after death. Whatever one's belief in a world to come, there is the acceptance that man transcends death in naturalistic fashion. Man is immortal; in *body*, through his children; in *thought*, through the survival of his memory; in *influence*, by virtue of the continuance of his personality as a force among those who come after him; and *ideally*, through the identification with the timeless things of the spirit.

A commentator of the Bible explained this immortality of influence in a discussion of "And Jacob lived" (Genesis 47:28). Of how few individuals can we repeat a phrase like, "And Jacob lived"? When many people die, a death notice appears in the press. In reality it is a life notice because, but for it, the world would never have known the person had ever been alive. Only he who has been a force for human goodness, and abides in hearts and in a world made better by his presence, can be said to have *lived*. Only such a one is heir to immortality.

Death is not the end of life — not just in terms of another possible world, but in the real and tangible sense of ongoing ideals and influence that continue shaping the affections one has held and served. Life points always to the future, when one shall become another heritage and influence, whether in ordinary personal memory, or through the thoughts and acts and decisions that give a lasting grace to ongoing human existence. The ancient Egyptians buried their dead with all the things a person needs, such as clothes, weapons, and food, and were more preoccupied with death than with life; the Hebrews, on the other hand, believed that in the hour of man's departure from this world, neither silver nor gold nor precious stones nor pearls accompany him, but only study and good works.

"The rabbis," wrote Louis Ginzberg in *The Legend of the Jews*, "believed in another world and often spoke of rewards awaiting the righteous after their death. Nevertheless, the development of the religious thought of the Jews showed a marked tendency to fix the center of gravity of religion not in the thought of a world beyond but rather to foster and establish it in the actual life of man on earth. In this respect the scribes and the rabbis were the true successors of the prophets."

Recompense

Concerning the final outcome of man's career, many affirmed a belief that death was not nor could be the end of life. Should there not be reward for the righteous as well as punishment for the wicked? It was true that Judaism taught that people should not serve God in the spirit of "bondsmen who tend their master for the sake of wages." Still, it was held that virtue must be repaid and iniquity punished. If God is a God of Justice, and if man does not meet with perfect equity during his lifetime, then he must find it afterward. In the hereafter, the "crooked will be straight, and to each will be given according to his deserts." Thus, this world becomes an antechamber of the world to come where recompense and punishments are to be meted out. "Man is reminded that he must give an account to the Eternal Judge. None will escape His punishment, and no virtue will be unrewarded" (*Mishna, Aboth*, 4:16 - 17). "He who labors before the Sabbath [that is, in this world] will eat on the Sabbath [that is, in the world to come]; but if a man does not labor before the Sabbath, how can he eat on the Sabbath day?" (Talmud, Abodah Zarah, 3B).

There was postulated a continued existence of the soul after death. The Hebrew expressions for soul in the Bible (*Nefesh, Neshamah, Ruach*) indicated a principle of the human body which was the vehicle of all the functions of life. In the last centuries before the Christian Era, the idea developed that there was a distinction between the body and the soul. The soul was the immortal part of man that was independent of the body. "The soul," says the *Midrash*, "may be compared to a princess who is married to a commoner. The most precious gift that the husband brings to his princess fails to thrill her. Likewise, if one were to offer the soul all the pleasures of the world, it would remain indifferent to them because it belongs to a higher order of existence." The soul is the unwilling partner of the body, unwilling to be born and unwilling to die. "Man is born perforce and dies perforce."

Before the body comes into being, the soul already exists. It is pure and untainted. Every morning the devout Jew prays, "O my God, the soul which Thou gave me is pure." The exact place of the soul cannot be determined, and this is another of the mysteries of life.

Resurrection

Still another concept of the hereafter is resurrection (*Tehiyyath Hamethem*). The earlier religion of Israel was more concerned with nationhood and conceived of retribution in national terms. Rewards and punishment were indissolubly related to the corporate people, Israel; not to the single individual. It was later that resurrection was interpreted as the reunion of body and soul together standing in judgment before God. The dead will rise and then be judged as to whether they will share in the blessings of the messianic era.

Soul's Transmigration

For others there is the belief in the transmigration of the soul (*Gilgul Hanefesh*), where human beings after death would enter another body and thus a new life. This doctrine's acceptance was widely held by the mystical *Chassidim*. According to the *Kabbala*, the soul of Aaron was first reincarnated in Eli and then in Ezra.

Reform, Orthodox, Conservative

O. Lazarus, in *Liberal Judaism and Its Standpoint*, summarizes a Reform Jewish attitude toward death:

> We cannot believe in the resurrection of the body that perishes with death. We feel, however, that there is that within us which is immortal, and is not bounded by time and space. It is this, man's soul, as it is called, which continues, so we believe, to live after the death of the body. To it, death is but an incident of life. It brings no violent change. The mere fact of death does not turn a wicked soul into a good one. When we enter the future life, our reason leads us to think that we are, at first, morally and spiritually (dare one add, even intellectually?) the same as we were before we embarked upon the adventure of death. How we progress and develop towards goodness, what suffering of purification we may be called upon to endure or what rewards of pure joy we may experience, we do not know. We cannot regard death as an evil. It is universal — part and parcel, so it would appear, of God's scheme of things. It comes from Him, even as we believe life does. Both must therefore be good. Both are natural and inevitable. Why should we fear?

The Orthodox Jew is committed to a belief in recompense, immortality, and resurrection. The scales of cosmic equity will end up in balance with the body of the dead arising from the grave to be reunited with the soul. In the presence of all the multitudes of all generations, God will pronounce judgment of bliss or damnation.

The Conservative movement has retained some of the prayers in the liturgy where belief is expressed in resurrection and immortality of the soul. For many, the concepts are not regarded literally but rather figuratively and poetically. Some retain the speculative rabbinic and medieval view of the soul as a distinct entity enjoying an independent existence.

Even within each of the three Jewish movements there is the widest possible latitude for differences of opinion. There are many thoughts, yet none is declared authoritative and final. The tradition teaches, but at the same time seems to say there is much we do not know and still more we have to learn. And even then, only God can completely discern the mysteries of life and death.

How does Judaism help the living to find meaning in life?

Moses Maimonides, one of the greatest of the Jewish philosophers, wrote: "People complain that life is too short, that man's life ends before he is done preparing himself for it. The truth is that while our life is short, we live as though we had eternity at our disposal; we waste too much of life. The problem is not that we are allotted a *short* life, but rather that we are *extravagant* in spending it."

Death makes life more precious. We want to attach our fragile and fleeting existence to that which is eternal and enduring. The personal tragedy, the waste, lies in what we can do with life — but do not: the love we do not give; the efforts we do not make; the powers we do not use; the happiness we do not earn; the kindnesses we neglect to bestow; the gratitude we have not expressed; the noble thoughts and deeds that could be ours if only we would realize the sanctity of life.

In Judaism, the living person must utilize his existence to perpetuate the memory of his deceased. Only then can he ennoble ignoble misfortune. In many a sigh is found an insight; in sorrow a jolt out of complacency. The maxim of Jewish philosophy is, "This also for good." Every experience — even death — may be "for good" if the bereaved transforms the value potential into an instrument of spiritual stature, of enlarged sympathy, courageous acceptance, and active determination. Even as the darkness eventually changes into light, so adversity may be converted ultimately into good.

No one can determine how each individual will react to the fact of death. The mystery still walks with our imagination and lurks in our dreams. It is good to remember that courage is not the absence of fear, but the affirmation of life despite fear. For as far as we know, only man faces life with the certain knowledge of having to die. This knowledge, this loss of innocence, can lead him to the edge of the abyss and threaten all his actions with meaninglessness and futility. Or he can seek a bridge that will span the chasm and affirm those things which really give him life — friendship, honor, a desire for justice, love, dignity, family, friends, country, and humankind.

By facing the meaning of our limits as seen in death, one comes to accept the limits and possibilities of life realistically. He sees the parallel between the acceptance of his biological death and the facing of limit and loss in everyday life. Judaism's concern is more with life in the "here" than in the "hereafter," with this world's opportunities rather than with speculation about the world to come.

Judaism helps the adherent to face death and to face

away from it. It aids him to accept the reality of death and protects him from destructive fantasy and illusion in the unconscious denial of fact. Most important of all, the Jewish religion offers an abundance of sharing religious resources in the encounter with helplessness, guilt, loneliness, and fear. Though reason cannot answer the why, and comforting words cannot wipe away tears, Judaism offers consolation in death by reaffirming life.

Is there a glossary of often-used words in Judaism relative to death?

The following explanation of terms may prove helpful:

Alav Hashalom (pronounced Ah-la-hv Ha-shaw-lome) "Peace be upon him." Phrase often used after the name of a departed male is mentioned.

Alehaw Hashalom (All-leh-haw Ha-shaw-lome) "Peace be upon her." Phrase used after a departed female is mentioned.

Avelim (Ah-veh-leem) "Mourners." Laws of mourning apply in case of death of one of seven relatives: father, mother, husband, wife, son or daughter, brother, and sister.

Chevrah Kaddisha (Chev-rah Ka-dee-shaw) "Holy Brotherhood." Society whose members devote themselves to burial and rites connected with it.

El Moleh Rachamin (Ale-moh-lay Ra-cha-meen) "God full of compassion." Memorial prayer recited at funerals. Dates from the seventeenth century. Popular Yiddish name is "Molay."

Gilgul Hanefesh (Gil-gool Hah-neh-fesh) Transmigration of the soul. According to *Zohar*, "Truly, all souls must undergo transmigration" (III, 99b). Kabbalistic School of Rabbi Luria (1534 - 1572) believed that a soul which had sinned returned to its earthly existence in order to make amends.

Hesped (Hes-peed) Eulogy delivered by rabbi for deceased.

Orations date back to biblical times, and contain an account of life accomplishments of the departed one.

Kabbala (Kah-bah-lah) "Tradition." Applied to important complex of Jewish mystical philosophy and practice. Basic work is *Zohar* ("Splendor"), which appeared at end of thirteenth century.

Kaddish "Holy" or "Sanctification." Aramaic prayer for the dead. Essentially a doxology, praising God, and praying for speedy establishment of God's kingdom upon earth. Recited by mourners for period of eleven months from date of burial.

Keriah (Ka-ree-ah) "Rending." Custom of mourner tearing a section of his garment or a black ribbon as symbol of grief. Rite performed before funeral. Rent made over the left side, over the heart. To be performed standing up, for the mourner is to meet sorrow standing upright.

Matzevah (Mah-tzave-vah) Tombstone that is erected toward the end of the first year of interment.

Midrash "Exposition." Books devoted to biblical interpretations. In form of homiletic expositions, legends, and folklore.

Minyan "Number," or "Quorum." Minimum number of ten Jewish males above the age of thirteen required for public services. According to Jewish law, *Minyan* is required for community recital of the *Kaddish*.

Mirrors Practice of covering mirrors is not based on explicit Jewish law. Some authorities regard practices as superstitious and discourage use. Others interpret the rite symbolically. "We ought not to gaze upon our reflection in the mirror in the house of mourning. In so doing, we appear to be reflecting upon ourselves."

Olam Haba (Oh-lam Ha-baw) "World to come." Maimonides explains: "The wise men call it world to come not because it is not in existence at present, but because life in that world will come to man after the life in this world is ended."

Rabbi Leader and teacher in the congregation. Conducts the funeral service, answers many ritual questions regarding the ceremony of death, and aids in important approach of *Menachem Avel* (Mine-a-chem Ah-vel), comforting the bereaved.

Seudat Havra-ah (S-oo-dat Chav-vey-rah) Meal of consolation.

Sh-loshim (Sh-lo-sheem) "Thirty." Mourning begins on first day of the funeral and ends on morning of the thirtieth day.

Shiva (Shee-vah) "Seven." Refers to the first seven days of mourning after burial.

Soul Biblical expressions: *Nefesh* (Neh-fesh), *Neshamah* (N'sha-ma), and *Ruach* (Rue-ach), derived from roots meaning "breath," and "wind." Soul is the source without which there can be no life. Maimonides asserted that only that part of the soul which man develops by his intellectual efforts is immortal.

Tachrichim (Ta-ch-re-cheem) "Shroud." Robe in which some dead are buried. Made of white linen cloth.

Tehiyyath Hamathem (Th-chee-yaht Ha-may-teem) "Resurrection of the dead." Belief that at the end of time the bodies of the dead will rise from the grave.

Unveiling Tombstone consecration in which special prayers are recited, such as *El Moleh Rachamin* and the *Mourner's Kaddish.* Customary to cover the tombstone with a veil and during service for one of the mourners to unveil the stone or plaque.

Yahrzeit (Yohr-tzite) Yiddish term for the anniversary of death. Observed by reciting the *Kaddish* in the synagogue and lighting memorial light in home.

Yahrzeit Light or Candle Well established practice to have candle or special lamp in house of mourning for 24 hours on the anniversary of death.

Yizkor Prayer, "May God remember the soul of my revered. . ." Recited on *Yom Kippur, Shemini Atzeret,* last day of *Passover,* and second day of *Shavuot.*

SUGGESTED READINGS

Barish, Louis, and Rebecca Barish, *Basic Jewish Beliefs* (New York: Jonathan David, 1961).

Bookstaber, David, *The Idea of the Development of the Soul in Medieval Jewish Philosophy* (Philadelphia: Maurice Jacobs, 1950).

Davis, Daniel L., *What to Do When Death Comes* (New York: Federation of Reform Temples).

Gittelsohn, Roland B., *Man's Best Hope* (New York: Random House, 1961).

Gordon, Albert I., *In Times of Sorrow* (New York: United Synagogues of America, 1949).

Greenberg, Sidney, *A Modern Treasury of Jewish Thoughts* (New York: Thomas Yoseloff, 1960).

Grollman, Earl A. (Ed.), *Explaining Death to Children* (Boston: Beacon Press, 1967).

Hertzberg, Arthur (Ed.), *Judaism* (New York: Washington Square Press, 1963).

The Holy Scriptures (Philadelphia: The Jewish Publication Society of America, 1917).

Jacobson, David S., "Death." In *Universal Jewish Encyclopedia,* 3 (New York: Universal Jewish Encyclopedia Company, 1943).

Karp, Harold, *The Spirit Returns to God Who Gave It* (Chicago: Rabinnical Council).

Katz, Robert L., "Counseling the Bereaved." *Central Conference of American Rabbis Yearbook*, LXIII, 465 - 469, 1953.

Lamm, Maurice, *The Jewish Way in Death and Mourning* (New York: Jonathan David, 1969).

Lasker, Arnold A., "When Children Face Bereavement." *Conservative Judaism*, XVIII, 53 - 58, 1964.

Lazarus, O., *Liberal Judaism and Its Standpoint* (London: Macmillan, 1937).

Liebman, Joshua L. *Peace of Mind* (New York: Simon & Schuster, 1946).

Moore, George Foote, *Judaism* (Cambridge: Harvard University Press, 1946).

Noveck, Simon, *Judaism and Psychiatry* (New York: United Synagogues of America, 1956).

Pool, David de Sola, *Why I Am a Jew* (New York: Bloch, 1951).

Rabinowicz, H., *A Guide to Life, Jewish Laws, and Customs of Mourning* (London: Jewish Chronicle Publications, 1964).

Spiro, Jack D., *A Time to Mourn* (New York: Bloch, 1967).

Steinberg, Milton, *Basic Judaism* (New York: Harcourt, 1947).

8

The Law and Death

How does the attorney assist in preplanning?

Is a will necessary?

How are estates taxed?

What are the administrator's responsibilities?

What about the survivor's budget?

MATTHEW H. ROSS

The attorney plays a vital role both in preplanning before death, and after death in helping his client to administer the estate. There are crucial questions all people must ask. Should everyone have a will? How about a trust fund? Should property be held in the name of both spouses? How are estates taxed? What considerations should be given to the decedent's business affairs?

Matthew H. Ross is a partner in the New York law firm of Blumberg, Singer, Ross, Gottesman, and Gordon. A graduate of St. John's University, Mr. Ross received his LL.B. degree from Virginia Law School. He is a member of the Board of Directors of the Foundation of Thanatology.

The Law and Death

What can be done to minimize a widow's or widower's anguish, concern, and difficulties in dealing with the financial and business problems that often follow the death of a spouse?

The agonizing responsibilities with respect to money matters should be considered and discussed during the lifetime of both mates. Preplanning is the most significant factor in diminishing the confusion that follows a loved one's death.

Should planning involve the combined efforts of both husband and wife?

Of course. The preparations should be arranged by both spouses. If the surviving mate understands what has been programmed, agrees with the contents, and is familiar with the people he or she will be working with, there are apt to be fewer unanticipated problems and unexpected decisions.

What are the key areas which should be taken into account in projecting financial and business problems following the death of a mate?

It isn't possible to anticipate all problems that may arise. Indeed, the questions are as varied as the people and respective family situations. However, if the most general issues are anticipated, the survivor's task will be considerably lightened. For example, consideration must certainly be given to such factors as a last will, selection of an appropriate administrator of the estate, funeral and burial arrangements, taxes, the handling of the family residence, the winding up of the business affairs of the decedent, selection of an attorney or advisor for the survivor, the advisability of holding property in joint names, the survivor's anticipated income, expenses, and budget, and the advisability of establishing trusts for beneficiaries.

Should everyone have a will?

With very few exceptions (with which the average person need not concern himself) the answer is yes. If a person dies intestate (without a will), his or her property will pass according to intestacy laws of the state where he or she resides. Such laws may provide, for example, that if a husband dies survived by a widow and two children, his estate should be divided equally among the three of them. This distribution may not only be entirely unsuitable to the family and financial situation of a particular decedent but may also be contrary to his wishes. Through a will, a testator (person who makes a will) can virtually dispose of his property as he wishes (there are statutory rights for the benefit of a surviving spouse which vary from state to state which are limiting and in some states impose limitations on gifts to charities). State laws of distribution may change and thus require periodic rechecking.

In addition, every decedent's estate requires someone to administer it. The administrator (person or persons) may be designated by the decedent in his will or a financial institution authorized to administer estates may handle it. In the absence of a will the administrator is designated by the court, usually from among family members in the succession established by the statute. The selection of the individual to administer the decedent's estate may be one of the more important considerations in connection with estate planning. Last, but equally important, is the fact that a court-appointed administrator of a decedent's estate is usually required to post a bond with the court for the faithful discharge of his duties. The bond can be both costly and unnecessary. By will, the decedent can waive posting a bond. Since the person selected as executor is someone the decedent holds in high regard, usually the bond is waived by the decedent and the cost saved.

Except in the simplest of family and financial situations, a will is essential in order to reasonably and responsibly make provision for the handling and disposition of the estate.

A word of caution in connection with the last will: a will is a highly technical instrument. Its preparation requires training, skill, and experience, and one should not undertake the responsibility by himself but should have professional help.

What are the duties and responsibilities of the person who administers the decedent's estate?

The person named by a decedent in his will to administer his estate is generally known as an executor. This person is charged with the responsibility of collecting the decedent's assets, winding up his affairs, paying his debts and funeral expenses, settling his tax liabilities including estate taxes, disposing of property which should be sold, and ultimately distributing the estate to the persons whom the decedent has directed in his will.

The individual designated by the court to administer the estate of a decedent who dies intestate is usually called an administrator. His duties are substantially those of the executor. The authority of the administrator is fixed by statute. The executor's authority and duties are likewise provided for by statute but may be enlarged or limited by the decedent and tailored to his wishes and requirements. For example, an administrator normally would have no authority to invest in a private business venture. The testator could give him such power if it was decided that this was the expedient thing to do. Needless to say, where there are complicated business and financial affairs the selection of an executor can be singularly important. Likewise, the selection of an executor acceptable to the surviving principal beneficiary could minimize difficulties and avoid unnecessary grief.

What is the purpose of establishing a trust fund?

A trust fund is designed to have assets held in experienced hands until such time as the testator has directed that they be disbursed and, pending this, to pay out, accumulate, or apply the income as directed. Essentially, when a trust is established, property is given to the trustee to hold, administer, and dispose of according to the testator's directions. Trusts are established for a variety of purposes. For example, to leave a bequest for minors or persons with little experience in the management of money, or to provide income for a given person during his or her lifetime, or until the happening of a stated event with the principal going to others thereafter, or to have the income applied for specific purposes, such as education or medical bills, or distribute small amounts over a period of years. The trust may also be used as a device to effectuate tax savings. As an illustration, by leaving property in trust with the income payable to a child and principal on the death of the child to a grandchild, the child will enjoy the entire income of the fund. His or her estate will have no estate tax to pay on the principal, which will pass directly from the testator to the child.

The testator may name anyone of his choosing as trustee, including a financial institution authorized to act as a trustee. Indeed, in the case of very large funds the testator will usually appoint more than one trustee. While the trustee's duties and authorities are generally prescribed by statute, they may be limited or enlarged by the provisions of the will and tailored to suit the circumstances.

As a case in point, investment powers may be restricted to certain types of securities, or the trustee may be authorized to continue certain business ventures which he might not have the authority to do under the statute. With respect to the disposition of the income and principal, the trust can provide for virtually any terms and conditions to meet the testator's wishes.

As stated earlier, the trust can provide that the income be applied for education and maintenance, or to pay medical bills. It may also maintain that the trustee may invade the principal for that purpose. Provisions can be made for the payment of principal at stated ages — for example, at age twenty-one and age twenty-five so as to assure that the beneficiary does not have the entire fund at one time, or from time to time as the trustee deems appropriate. The relationship between the trustee and decedent and the ability, character, and age of the beneficiary are the factors which must be taken into consideration in this regard. Or the trust may provide for fixed payments to a person over a period of years or until a stated event with the principal going to a third person thereafter.

The trust is a useful device to ensure expert management of the funds until such time as the decedent deems appropriate to have them distributed to the beneficiary and, pending that time, to accumulate, apply, or pay out the income, and in some instances to effect tax savings. The establishment of a trust involves many technical considerations and one should not undertake to deal with the problems involved without expert help.

What preplanning should be done regarding funeral arrangements, burial, or cremation?

The decision of burial versus cremation should, if possible, be made during the joint lifetime of the spouses. If not, it must be made almost immediately following death and, needless to say, can be a most distressing decision for the survivor at a most difficult time.

If burial is preferred, the plot should be selected and, if possible, all financial arrangements regarding it should likewise be concluded in the joint lifetime of the spouses. This will not only avoid the survivor's having to make a hasty decision (which is ofttimes unsatisfactory and excessively costly) at a time when he or she is least able to exercise good judgment, but will also provide the opportunity for intelligent selection and the making of reasonable financial arrangements.

It would not be amiss for persons during their lifetime to decide what they regard as a dignified and meaningful funeral and try to determine and agree upon the approximate expenses to be incurred. Funeral costs should be investigated. It is helpful if the survivor understands how funeral charges in the community are computed. This could be investigated during the lifetime of the spouses. The survivor will be saved the task of making a judgment with respect to these matters at the height of his or her bereavement.

The funeral expenses, cost of burial or cremation, and usually the cost for arranging for perpetual care of the plot are considered proper estate expenses and deductible for tax purposes. The funeral director should be asked to render his bill to the estate.

Should property be held in the name of both spouses?

Property held in joint names passes to the survivor on the death of one of the joint owners. Obviously this arrangement is useful only where it is intended that the survivor inherit the entire property held in joint names. Such property passes to the survivor without the necessity of being administered as part of the decedent's estate, and, as a consequence, administration expenses are sometimes saved. However, particularly where the wife is the sole executor and trustee and there are other assets which have to be administered, the saving, if any, will probably not be significant. In a simple estate where there are some bank accounts and possibly some securities, joint ownership may serve as a convenient vehicle for transferring the decedent's entire interest to his wife, without the necessity for a formal estate administration.

While savings accounts, securities, and some real estate holdings lend themselves to joint ownership, it is not generally convenient to hold business interests and important investments in that manner. Where partners are involved, they generally object. Furthermore, very often the property is not available for the payment of the decedent's debts, which could embarrass the estate.

Generally speaking, there is no tax advantage in holding property in joint names. The taxing authorities will assume that this device is merely a matter of convenience and will endeavor to tax the property in the estate of the person who bought and paid for it, lacking clear proof of a gift. Moreover, usually the taxing authorities will endeavor to treat the joint property as taxable in the estate of the first of the joint tenants to die unless there is substantial proof that it was bought and paid for by the survivor. Ofttimes this is difficult to establish where you have spouses who are both income-producing and intermingle their accounts.

Should one make gifts during his lifetime as a means of minimizing taxes?

An individual can make gifts totaling $30,000 in his or her lifetime and a married couple can make gifts totaling $60,000 during their lifetime without being obliged to pay any gift tax, though the gifts must be reported to Internal Revenue Service. In addition, an individual may make gifts of up to $3,000 per year to each of as many persons as he or she may desire, and a married couple may make gifts of up to $6,000 to each of as many persons as they may choose, without being required to pay any tax on the gifts or to report them to Internal Revenue Service.

The rate of tax on gifts is about three-fourths of the rate of tax on estates. Exempt gifts completely escape estate and gift taxes. Property which is the subject of a nonexempt gift is subject to a lower rate of tax than it would be if it were taxed as part of an estate. However, there are practical considerations which should be taken into account. One has to consider how much of his or her estate may reasonably be given away during the donor's lifetime without adversely affecting one's security. Further, the income on property intended as the subject of a gift if held during the balance of the donor's lifetime may, in some instances, more than offset the difference in tax which may have to be paid on death.

How are estates taxed?

The estate of every decedent is subject to a federal estate tax, and a state inheritance tax in most states, except where the estate is exempt because of size. The first $60,000 of an estate is exempt from federal estate taxes. Hence an estate of $60,000 or less would not be subject to federal estate taxes. Most states likewise provide for exemptions. The federal estate tax is graduated, from 3 percent on the first $5,000 of the taxable estate to 77 percent on the taxable estate over $10 million. Most state inheritance taxes are likewise graduated but the rate is lower than the federal rate.

Needless to say, on large estates the tax burden can be very substantial. In every situation, however, consideration should be given as to how the necessary funds will be generated for the payment of estate and inheritance taxes so as to avoid the necessity for sacrifice sales of valuable property in order to raise cash for taxes. Many persons after estimating their estate taxes purchase life insurance with their estate as beneficiary to provide the cash for such purposes. Persons with funds principally invested in closely held corporations should give consideration to the special machinery provided by the tax laws which allow for the withdrawal of cash from such corporations on a tax-free basis for payment of estate taxes. Consideration should also be given as to whether the estate, if it is deemed useful, will be able to avail itself of the provisions in the estate-tax law for the payment of taxes in installments. Both the provisions for payment in installments and for withdrawal of funds from closely held corporations are extremely technical, and expert advice should be sought in this regard. In every case one should endeavor to estimate the estate and inheritance taxes to which his or her estate will be subject and to provide the means for their payment.

What is the marital deduction?

Estate taxes may be minimized dramatically by the married taxpayer who avails himself or herself of the marital deduction. The estate-tax law allows a married person to bequeath to a spouse a portion of his or her estate, known as the marital deduction, tax free. Such portion of the estate, while not taxable in the donor's estate, is taxable as part of the surviving spouse's estate if not disposed of prior to death. While the determination of the amount of a decedent's estate which is available for the marital deduction involves a technical computation, generally speaking it is equal to approximately one-half the decedent's estate.

To qualify as a marital deduction gift and not to be taxable in the donor's estate, the gift to the spouse must be either outright or in trust with the income payable to the spouse coupled with the right on the part of the spouse to dispose of the principal either during lifetime or by will. No other restriction may be imposed. In deciding whether to utilize the marital deduction, consideration must be given in at least the first instance to the size of the respective spouses' estates. If the beneficiary has a larger estate than the testator there may be no advantage because the amount received by the beneficiary would be added to his or her estate and would be taxed at a higher rate than it would have been in the decedent's estate. On the other hand, in such a case one would have to balance this consideration against the advantage of having the use of the tax funds during the balance of the survivor's lifetime against the increased tax burden.

A few examples of how the marital deduction works may be helpful. Assume the husband with an estate of $250,-000 and the wife with only a minimal estate. If the husband bequeathed approximately $125,000 to the wife, his taxable estate would be only $125,000, less the specific exemption of $60,000 (there are, of course, other deductions such as administration expenses which have not been taken into account). Hence, both the husband's estate and the wife's estate (assuming nothing transpired to affect the value of the wife's estate following the husband's death), would each be taxable at the rate applicable to $60,000. In the same example, if the wife's estate was $750,000 instead of minimal, the $125,000 which she would receive as the marital deduction bequest would be taxed at the higher rate applicable to such $125,000 as part of her $875,000 estate. The $125,000 would, in effect, be taxable at the highest rate applicable to the estate. Obviously, it would have been cheaper for the husband not to have availed himself of the marital deduction and to have paid the tax on his $250,000 estate. In this example, assuming both spouses were close in age, the use by the wife for life of the funds which would have had to be paid as taxes on the $125,000 on the husband's death would probably not have compensated for the extra estate tax which would be involved.

Obviously, while taxes are an important consideration, they are not the only items which must be taken into account in determining whether one should avail himself of the marital deduction. In some instances, one might be willing to sacrifice the tax benefits, if any, because of his or her reluctance to put so large a portion of his or her estate in the hands of the spouse with the right to dispose of it without restriction. Needless to say, the decision as to whether to avail oneself of the marital deduction involves careful evaluation of the respective estates, computation of estimated taxes, and consideration of the family situation. It should not be undertaken without expert counsel.

What consideration should be given to the decedent's business affairs?

If the decedent is an employed person one should determine whether as part of his employment he is entitled to pension or life insurance benefits on death and, if so, how payment has been provided for. Very often by directing payment to be made to a specific beneficiary as distinguished from having it paid to the decedent's estate, some tax savings can be effected. Usually the employer will be in a position to advise on the various aspects of the pension and life insurance plans provided by it.

If the decedent is in business for himself, careful consideration should be given during the lifetime of both spouses as to what should be done with the business after death. Should the survivor continue to operate the business? Should the business be liquidated? If so, what would be the most economical way to do it? Should the business be sold? If so, what is the best way to sell it and how should the price be determined and paid? Ofttimes a business is operated as a partnership. Consideration should be given as to whether the survivor should succeed the deceased partner, or whether the deceased partner's interest should be sold to the surviving partner, or to a stranger. If it is decided that the deceased partner's interest should be sold to the surviving partner, it may be useful for him to negotiate terms and conditions on which his interest will be purchased by the surviving partner. During the lifetime of both partners neither knows who will be the first to die and, therefore, usually a fairer deal can be made. Furthermore, terms and conditions will have been discussed between the two persons who know the business and its value best. Obviously, if there is an agreement pursuant to which the surviving partner will purchase the deceased partner's interest, the task of the surviving spouse is minimized since all that has to be done is to implement the agreement. The same observations are applicable in the case of closely held corporations. The stockholders can agree among themselves for the purchase of each other's stock on death.

Needless to say, not all the decisions made during one's lifetime will be able to be carried out after his death. For example, a decedent may think his business can be sold and yet it may have to be liquidated because a buyer cannot be found. However, if careful consideration has been given to all aspects of the problem while the operator of the business is alive, and the survivor has had the benefit of his views, the survivor will be in a better position to deal with the problem then if consideration is given to the question for the first time after the death of the operator of the business.

What about the survivor's budget?

When the income producer in the family dies, usually the survivor's mode of living has to be changed dramatically.

Unfortunately, this often comes as a surprise. During their joint lifetimes, the parties should evaluate what the net estate will be after taxes and administration expenses and what income it can reasonably be expected to produce. They should also consider how the survivor is to arrange his or her affairs so as to live on that income. For example, it might be determined that the family residence cannot be continued to be maintained and that it should be sold. In such case, consideration should be given to what might be realized from the sale of the residence. Consideration could also be given as to the terms and conditions of any lease one should sign on a rental apartment since this might be a continuing obligation of the estate, the burden of which might be too great for the survivor. In short, some evaluation should be made as to how the survivor is to readjust his or her affairs following the death of a spouse based on the anticipated income of the estate. If this is done carefully, the survivor will suffer a minimum of surprises and will make the transition with a minimum of difficulty taking into account the circumstances.

What about an advisor for the survivor?

Generally speaking, the surviving spouse will require the services of an advisor, who may be the executor of the decedent's estate, his attorney, a financial advisor, or even a friend (one person may serve in one or more of these capacities). During their lifetime the parties should consider what advice the survivor will require and the person or people who will be expected to serve in that capacity. The person so designated should be acceptable to both spouses.

It is helpful if such person participated in all the considerations involved in the planning. It is not difficult to understand that the surviving spouse will find it much easier when he or she begins to deal with the decedent's affairs if the person or persons he or she will have to deal with are known to him or her and have participated in the planning than if they were strangers or if known, were not previously consulted.

What about the death of persons other than a spouse?

The questions and answers set forth above address themselves to the problems of a surviving spouse. Most of the problems and considerations suggested in these questions and answers are equally applicable in the case of the death of any person with whom the survivor had a close relationship.

9

Insurance and Death

Why should you own insurance?

How to select a reputable company and competent agent.

Are there alternatives to insurance?

What about Social Security, Civil Service, Veterans' and/or Servicemen's benefits?

Where should policies and valuable papers be kept?

ANDREW J. LYONS

Most Americans have some type of insurance to protect their families in time of death. Few people understand how their insurance works, the various types of policies, the methods of selecting a competent agent, and how to collect life-insurance proceeds. Terms such as *actuary, maturity value, reinstatement,* and *settlement options* are bewildering terms for those knowledgeable in other disciplines of life.

Andrew J. Lyons, C.L.U., is second vice president of the Massachusetts Mutual Life Insurance Company of Springfield. His background includes completion of management, business insurance, and programming courses.

Insurance and Death

What is the purpose of insurance?

It is a plan in which many people join together to share a potential risk they could not bear themselves. In order to share the risk a large number of persons, usually referred to as policyholders or policyowners, agree to pay a predetermined sum of money, usually known as the premium. The insurance company underwriting the plan specifies in a legal document (the policy contract) the risk that is covered and the conditions under which the claim will be paid. This is true whether the insurance is for death, disability, old age, health, fire, automobile damage, etc. Through their pooling of the risk, each policyholder knows, in advance, the gross amount of premium he must pay. If it is a life-insurance policy, the annual premium is established for the term of the contract, and as a matter of convenience, the policyowner may pay his premium annually, semiannually, quarterly, or monthly.

What are the major kinds of insurance?

The most well known types of insurance coverages are:

- Life insurance
- Health insurance, including hospitalization, major medical, and insurance which provides income in event of total or partial disability

- Fire and casualty insurance
- Homeowners policy
- Liability

Since the types of insurance policies cover a wide range of risks and benefits, this chapter will focus its attention primarily on life-insurance coverage, with a brief reference to related governmental benefits.

Why are there two kinds of life-insurance companies?

To answer this question first requires a description of the two kinds of life-insurance companies, mutual and stock. A stock company is one that is owned and controlled by a relatively small group of stockowners. A mutual company is one which is owned by the policyholders and is managed by a board of directors chosen by the policyholders.

Generally stock companies issue only nonparticipating contracts — those policies which do not pay dividends to the policyholder — although some companies do issue participating policies as well. Thus only the stockholders share in the profits of the company.

A mutual company usually issues policies on a participating basis. In other words, any profit is returned to all policyholders in the form of dividends. Generally speaking, the gross premium of a life-insurance policy with a mutual company will be higher than that of a stock company. Since the mutual company usually pays dividends, in most cases the net premium of a mutual company, over a period of time, is generally lower than that of a stock company.

What kind of life insurance should you own?

Most life-insurance companies offer a wide variety of coverages and plans with premiums varying depending upon the benefits provided and the length of time coverage is offered. One type of policy might be better for you than another, and this can best be determined with the aid of a competent life-insurance representative. If you depend upon a "do it yourself" technique, your widow may find, at the time when the coverage is needed most, that it is not available.

How can you select a good company and a competent life-insurance agent?

All states license life-insurance companies and have strict laws regulating what they may or may not do. In selecting a life-insurance company first determine if it is licensed to sell insurance in your state. If there is any doubt in your mind this information can be obtained from the insurance commissioner at your state capital.

In addition, your agent should be willing to give you detailed information about the company he represents, furnish you with a copy of the latest annual report, and/or be able to refer you to other persons in the community who are satisfied policyholders of his company.

Since most agents are compensated on a commission basis, it costs you no more to have the best. If you do not already have a competent life-insurance agent, try to find one who is well trained and who knows his business, for his guidance and counsel are invaluable. In most states today the agent must pass a written examination to qualify for his license but this will hardly give you much of a measure of his competency. Find out if the agent is a member of the local National Association of Life Underwriters, or if he has received his Chartered Life Underwriter Designation. This designation, C.L.U., is awarded to those agents who have completed an intensive, lengthy, college-level course of study in insurance and other financial subjects. In addition, a competent agent is willing to refer you to satisfied clients who have used or are using his services.

What types of questions should be asked, and of whom?

The major key to easing the widow's financial worry is to make sure that thought and planning have been given *during the lifetime of both the husband and wife* and the impact of death upon either spouse is understood and planned for. Since no one person has all the answers, here are some questions that should be explored with your life-insurance representative, attorney, and/or financial advisors.

Is property presently held in the name of both husband and wife? What problems could that create at the death of either person? If the surviving spouse wishes to sell the property, can lengthy delays be avoided? This could occur if there is difficulty in establishing the rightful owner or if the property is to be sold by the executor of the estate. This could include residence, automobiles, stock or bonds, business interests, other real estate, etc.

Do both the husband and wife have wills? State laws provide for the disposition of the deceased's estate in the absence of a will; however, the legal disposition is rarely satisfactory to all the survivors and frequently is not the way that the deceased expected or intended to leave his property.

Have you unknowingly disinherited your children or some member of your family? Have you named a guardian for minor children or do you prefer that this be done by the probate court? Since they generally follow the wishes of the deceased, during your lifetime you have the opportunity to discuss your desires for the upbringing of your children with a chosen guardian. But in the absence of a will, if both parents are deceased, the courts will name a guardian of your children and you then have had no chance to indicate your wishes as to how they will be cared for.

Does the size of your estate suggest consideration of a trust? If the surviving widow has had little experience with financial affairs, the creation of a trust and the naming of a bank or trust company to handle the financial affairs may be desirable.

Obviously, the questions raised here are complex and there are no simple, general answers that will apply to all circumstances or individuals. The best solution frequently has a significant impact on the kind of insurance you should buy. It is vital then that the husband and wife allocate time while both are alive, and in good health, to discuss their financial plans with their life-insurance agent and other financial counselors. Proper planning can eliminate or minimize many potential financial problems.

How much insurance is enough?

Again, there is no stock answer. Have you determined the amount of cash and income your spouse would need following your death? What bills might suddenly become due, such as current charge accounts, debts, outstanding loans, funeral expenses, etc.? If you have estimated the funds needed to pay these bills, do you have adequate life insurance and other liquid assets that will guarantee funds will become available when needed? Is there a need to continue monthly income to the widow? Since family financial situations rarely remain static there is a need for periodic review of family finances. In most cases once a year is satisfactory. A competent life-insurance representative is trained and experienced in these matters and can assist you in determining how much is enough for you.

Is it necessary to review my insurance regularly?

Definitely yes! While many families will not, or cannot, provide adequate funds for the survivors, one of the most frequent oversights which can cause great problems relates to the named beneficiary of the life insurance and/or other assets that most people own.

Upon marriage, divorce, remarriage; a death, birth, or adoption; or upon occurence of some other major event, many people unfortunately forget to review the beneficiary who is to receive the proceeds of their insurance upon their death. Since your life-insurance policy is a contract, the insurance company is required to pay the proceeds to the beneficiary(ies) currently named in the policy. Nothing can create more misunderstanding at the time when the widow is emotionally disturbed than to be told that the life-insurance proceeds that she planned on to provide her a monthly income will now be paid to another person. This pitfall can be simply avoided by keeping your beneficiary up to date. Again, an annual review of your life-insurance program is one of the easiest ways to guard against this oversight.

What about Social Security, Civil Service, Veterans' and/or Servicemen's benefits?

Lump-sum and income benefits are payable to eligible survivors covered by the Social Security, Civil Service, Veterans' and/or Servicemen acts. The two most common lump-sum benefits are the maximum of $255 paid by the Social Security Administration and $250* paid to most survivors of veterans and/or servicemen, both benefits being provided under the current law.

In addition, monthly income benefits are payable to eligible survivors from one or more of the previously mentioned sources. The exact amount depends upon established

* Plus an amount of $150 for plot allowance where interment is not in a national or governmental cemetery.

eligibility requirements, such as the income earned by the insured person (in most cases, the husband), the length of time covered, the number of dependent children, etc. Civil Service benefits parallel those paid under the Social Security Act so a person cannot collect payments from both sources. These government benefits are usually significantly large and the monthly income provided can go a long way toward easing the eligible widow's financial burden.

Specific information regarding government benefits may be obtained from several sources. Your local Social Security and Veterans Administration offices can be a source of information regarding these benefits. In addition, information regarding Civil Service benefits may be obtained from the Civil Service Commission, Washington, D.C. Be sure to give them complete identifying information, such as the name in full, date of birth, agencies in which employed, and dates of employment.

Ask your life-insurance man the approximate amount of the benefits payable under each of the acts. While they are estimates, the information can serve as a guide in determining the amount of monthly income the widow will have.

Remember that payments are not made automatically under either Social Security or Veterans' acts. They must be applied for, and any unnecessary delays in filing will delay the time when the payments will begin. In most instances, assume that there will be a delay of approximately three months from the date of filing before you receive your first income check from the Social Security or Veterans Administration office.

Can people lose their eligibility for Social Security benefits?

Governmental programs spell out the survivor qualifications necessary to receive benefits as well as the other eligibility requirements. Generally speaking, Social Security survivorship benefits are paid only if the survivor was married to the deceased at the time of death. If the children and/or widow have income in excess of specified limits, they may lose their eligibility to receive benefits. In addition, in order to receive benefits the insured individual must have been covered for a specified period of time.

While there are some variations in eligibility requirements with respect to service, for Civil Service and Veterans' and/or Servicemen's benefits, the same general rules as for Social Security apply.

Are there alternatives to insurance?

Life insurance is not the sole answer to solving all an individual's or family's financial problems. There are other types of assets that may provide as good or better alternative solutions, depending upon the facts of the individual case. No one would disagree that a bank account, bonds, stocks, real estate, all have their proper place in a sound financial program. However, care should be used in selecting the best financial vehicle to achieve your desired objectives and in assuring that it will be available at full value when needed.

How do you collect life-insurance proceeds?

Collecting life-insurance proceeds is a comparatively simple procedure and the following steps may serve as an effective guide:

1. Notify your insurance representative and/or the company in which the deceased was insured. If more than one company is involved select one life-insurance man to handle all the details for you.

2. Gather together all the life-insurance policies and certificates. Be sure not to throw any of them away simply because the premium has not been paid. Oc-

casionally all or part of the benefit has been continued automatically under the policy provisions, so you may receive some funds of which you were not aware.

3. Request that the life-insurance company forward all necessary forms either directly to you or to the life-insurance agent that you have selected.

4. Your life-insurance representative will assist you in completing the required forms and ask that you supply him with the required number of copies of the death certificate.

5. If the date of birth shown on the death certificate and the date of birth shown on the application for life insurance are different, you will be asked to furnish additional evidence of the correct date of birth. If you wish to speed this process, here is a helpful hint. During the lifetime of the insured the policy can be returned to the company with a copy of the birth certificate and endorsed to indicate the proper birth date. This will eliminate the necessity of offering further proof of the correct date of birth.

6. While a few policies are restrictive, in general the proceeds of a life-insurance policy may be paid to you in several ways or in almost any combination you desire. It can be paid in one lump sum, in installments over whatever period of time you specify, as income for the rest of your life, or left with the insurance company at interest.

Generally speaking, the best advice that can be given to a widow is based on the old adage "act in haste, repent in leisure." In the majority of cases, the best course of action for the widow is to leave the proceeds of her husband's life insurance with the company at interest, reserving the right to withdraw all or part of the funds, or to select some other method of payment. During a period of grief there is a natural tendency to act quickly and withdraw the funds. Well-meaning friends can suggest placing the funds in the bank or some other investment that currently provides a higher level of income. Experience has indicated that in many cases these "investments" don't always turn out the way they are expected. You are better off to sacrifice a few dollars of interest income for a few months, until that time you are in a position to realistically evaluate your financial situation; then take whatever action seems advisable, and if it is in your best interest to continue to leave the proceeds with the life-insurance company or have it paid as monthly income, you have retained the contractual right to select these options.

In what ways can your life-insurance representative be of service?

Earlier in this chapter the importance of selecting a qualified and competent life-insurance man to assist you with your financial affairs was pointed out. In the vast majority of cases life-insurance proceeds represent the only cash funds available to many widows, so it is important that you have a frank discussion of your financial affairs with your life-insurance representative. This should be done not only when you are planning your financial program, during your lifetime, but as soon as it is practical after the death of the husband. He can explain the various benefits and how they can be coordinated with your other assets, and he can help you complete the necessary forms which will minimize delays in receiving benefits. In many instances his working relationship with your accountant, attorney, trust officer, and/or executor can be most helpful during your time of grief. Some of the benefits which you should receive as a life-insurance policyholder are the individual services which the agent can offer during this difficult time. Your agent can best assist you if you give him your full confidence and carefully consider the advice he gives you.

Where should life-insurance policies and other valuable papers be kept?

In a safe location known to more than one person. Many times when death occurs it is difficult to locate insurance policies, stock certificates, wills, and other valuable papers. If there are minor children and one of the parents is deceased, some other responsible person should know the location of these items.

A Brief Glossary of Life Insurance Words and Phrases

Accidental Death Benefit. A death benefit paid when death occurs as a direct result of accidental bodily injury independently of all other causes and within a given period after such injury was sustained (usually ninety days).

Agent. Anyone, not a duly licensed broker, who solicits insurance or aids in the placing of risks, delivery of policies, or collection of premiums in behalf of an insurance company. The acts of an agent are binding upon the company only to the extent specified in his contract or otherwise authorized. He cannot bind the company by any statement contrary to the provisions of the application or policy. The agent cannot delegate his rights or powers unless expressly authorized. In most states an insurance solicitor is regarded as the agent of the insurance company and not of the insured.

Automatic Premium Loan Option. An option which provides that the payment due is automatically paid by a loan on the policy, the contract continuing in force for the face amount less the amount of the loan and interest thereon. When the total payments charged as loans equal the cash value, the policy expires.

Beneficiary. The person to whom the proceeds of a life-insurance contract are payable at the death of the insured.

Chartered Life Underwriter (C.L.U.). A designation conferred by the American College of Life Underwriters in recognition of the attainment of certain standards of education and proficiency in the art and science of life underwriting. The right to the designation is open to any salesman of life insurance, fraternal or old-line or weekly premium, who meets the preliminary requirements and can pass the series of examinations.

Conditional Receipt. The receipt for the payment of the first premium which assures the applicant that, if he is insurable on the date of completion of the company's underwriting requirements, for the amount and plan applied for, and the correct premium has been paid, the insurance will be effective even though the policy has not been issued or delivered.

Contingent Beneficiary. In arranging for the settlement of a policy, provision must be made for the contingency that the named beneficiary or one or more of the several named beneficiaries may die between the time the agreement is executed and the last payment of the proceeds. The persons to whom certain benefits accrue in the event the original beneficiaries are dead are called "contingent" beneficiaries.

Contract. The "Law of Contracts" specifies four requirements for the formation of a simple contract: (1) parties of legal capacity; (2) expression of mutual assent of the parties to a promise, or a set of promises; (3) a valid consideration; and (4) the absence of any statute or other rule declaring such agreement void. A life-insurance policy qualifies as a contract under the above definition. Ordinarily, however, better public relations result from the use of the word "policy" than from the use of the word "contract."

Convertible Term. Some term policies provide that they may be converted to relatively permanent forms of insurance without medical examination if the conversions are made within a limited period as specified in the policy. The conversion may be made as of the original date of issue, provided the insured pays the difference in back premiums with interest thereon, or as of the attained age of the insured at the time of conversion.

Dependency Period Income. One of the basic uses for life insurance. Income for the family during the years until the youngest child reaches maturity.

Disability. A provision covered by a rider, or included in the policy itself, for either (1) waiver of premiums or (2) waiver of premiums and the payment of monthly income during the insured's incapacity should he become disabled within its terms.

Disability Income. A disability benefit provided by a rider attached to a regular life insurance policy or by a disability income policy providing for a monthly income and waiver of premiums in the event of total permanent disability after a fixed waiting period.

Dividend. A dividend on participating life-insurance policies is the refund of that part of the premium paid at the beginning of the year which still remains after the company has set aside the necessary reserve and made deductions for claims and expenses. The dividend may also include a share in the company's investment, mortality, and operating profits.

Dividend Additions. Participating policies usually provide that the policy dividends may be used as single premiums at the insured's attained age to purchase paid-up insurance as additions to the amount of insurance specified on the face of the contract.

Educational Insurance. Insurance proceeds arranged to provide a child with a given income during the educational period.

Emergency Fund. One of the basic uses for life insurance. A reserve death benefit fund provided by the insured to protect his family against sudden large, unbudgetable expenses such as accidents, operations, etc. The increasing loan value of a life insurance policy also constitutes, and often is referred to as, an emergency fund for the insured while he is living.

Endowment. A life-insurance policy which provides for the payment of the face amount at the end of a fixed period, or at a specified age of the insured, or at the death of the insured before the end of the stated period.

Face Amount. Since the amount of insurance protection provided under a given policy is stated on the face or first page of the contract, the term "face amount" is sometimes used in lieu of "sum insured." The actual amount payable by the company may be increased by dividends or decreased by loans.

Grace Period. Most life-insurance contracts provide that premiums may be paid at any time within a period varying from twenty-eight to thirty-one days following the premium due date, the policy remaining in full force in the meantime. If death occurs during the grace period, the premium is deducted from the proceeds payable. As a general rule, no interest is charged on overdue premiums if paid during the grace period.

Group Life Insurance. A form of life insurance usually covering not less than twenty-five (sometimes fifty) employees of a common employer. It may be issued to the employer, and with premiums paid either exclusively by the employer or by employer and employees jointly. Where premiums are paid jointly, there is a maximum beyond which the employees may not be charged, and at least 75 percent of all employees must be insured to overcome any danger of adverse selection. Each covered employee is issued an individual certificate briefing his benefits which are shown under the master contract in detail. Usually written on renewable term basis.

Incontestability. Life insurance policies provide that they shall be incontestable after a stated period from date of isssue, usually two years, except for nonpayment of the premium and sometimes for other specified reasons.

Irrevocable Beneficiary. A beneficiary who has a vested or contingent right to the proceeds of a policy since the insured has made the beneficiary designation without retaining the right to revoke or change the designation.

Lapse. This term is sometimes loosely applied to insurance that goes off the books in any manner other than by death, maturity or expiry of policy term, but technically refers only to contracts which become void when default is made in payment of premium before a surrender value has been established.

License. Certification, issued by state department of insurance, that an individual is qualified to solicit insurance applications for the period covered. Usually issued for period of one year, renewable on application without necessity of the individual's periodic repetition of the original qualifying requirements. Each agent should study carefully the licensing laws and regulations of his own state. Permit issued to a life insurance company to operate in a given state.

Life-Insurance Trust. Life insurance companies usually cannot act as trustees or guardians, nor exercise discretion in making payments to beneficiaries. In some cases it is advisable to have the policy proceeds paid to a trust company and distributed under the terms of a trust agreement, thereby permitting greater flexibility in the distribution of the proceeds. Such an arrangement constitutes an "unfunded" life insurance trust. Under a "funded" life-insurance trust, the trustee is given not only control over the policy proceeds but also securities or other property to provide funds out of which to pay the premiums.

Maturity Value. The proceeds payable on an endowment contract at the end of the specified endowment period, for example, or payable on an ordinary life contract at the last age of the mortality table if the insured is still living at that age. The maturity value of such a policy is the same as its face amount; of a retirement income policy it is usually a larger amount; in either it is equal to the reserve value of the policy on its maturity date. The actual amount payable by the company may, of course, be increased by dividend additions or accumulated dividend deposits, or decreased by outstanding loans.

Misrepresentation. Making, issuing, or circulating, or causing to be issued or circulated, any written or oral statement which does not represent the correct policy terms, dividends, or share of surplus thereon, or the use of a name or title for any policy or class of policies which does not reflect the true nature thereof. Generally classified as a misdemeanor, subject to fine, revocation of license, and sometimes imprisonment.

Mutual Company. One which has no capital stock, is owned by the policyholders, is managed by a board of directors chosen by the policyholders, and usually issues participating insurance only.

National Association of Life Underwriters. An organization of life-insurance men and women formed for the sole purpose of benefiting the man in the field. Membership in the Association gives the underwriter a place to meet others in the same work, where ideas and experiences can be exchanged and where there is opportunity to listen to successful leaders in the business.

Nonparticipating Policies. Policies which bear a relatively low guaranteed premium, on which no refunds or dividends are paid.

Ordinary Life, Whole Life, Straight Life. These terms are synonymous and are applied to the type of policy which continues during the whole of the insured's life and provides for the payment of amount insured at his death, or at age 100 on the basis of the CSO Table if he still is living at that age. These are not the only designations given this plan of insurance. Convertible life is an example of individual company usage.

Paid-Up. A policy on which no future payments are to be made, and under which there are outstanding benefits provided by the policy's terms.

Participating Policies. Policies which share in the distribution of "dividends" out of the surplus earnings of the company.

Premium. The term used on old-line insurance for the charge made for a given form of insurance or annuity policy at a given age, or the amount payable to the company for the benefits provided under a certain policy.

Proceeds. The net amount of money payable by the company at the death of an insured or at the maturity of a policy.

Reinstatement. By the terms of most life-insurance policies the policyholder has the right to reinstate a lapsed policy within a stated time after lapse, provided he presents satisfactory evidence of insurability. The right is usually denied if the policy has been surrendered for its cash value.

Renewable Term. Some term contracts provide that they may be renewed on the same plan for one or more years without medical examination but with rates based on the advanced age of the insured.

Retirement Income. One of the basic uses for life insurance. Life income, beginning at a selected retirement age, derived by applying contractual settlement options to policy or annuity cash values. Often the name of a policy providing both insurance and retirement income. The definition may apply to individual or to joint lives.

Revocable Beneficiary. A beneficiary whose rights in a policy are subject to the insured's reserved right to revoke or change the beneficiary designation and the right to surrender or make a loan on the policy without the consent of the beneficiary.

Settlement Options. Nearly all life-insurance policies now issued provide for several optional modes of settlement in lieu of payment in a single cash sum. The usual options are: interest; installments for a stated period; life income with a stated number of years' payments certain; fixed income as long as proceeds will last.

Stock Company. One that is owned and controlled by a group of stockholders whose investment in the company provides the safety margin necessary in the insurance of guaranteed, fixed premium, nonparticipating policies. The stockholders share in the profits and losses of the company. Some stock companies also issue participating policies.

Suicide. Most policies provide that if the insured commits suicide within a specified period, usually two years, after date of issue, the company's liability will be limited to a return of premiums paid.

Term Insurance. Insurance protection during a limited number of years but expiring without value if the insured survives the stated period. The protection period may be one or more years but ordinarily is five to twenty years since such periods usually cover the need for temporary protection.

Twisting. The practice of inducing a policyholder in one company to lapse, forfeit, or surrender his insurance for the purpose of taking out a policy in another company. Generally classified as a misdemeanor, subject to fine, revocation of license, and sometimes imprisonment.

Underwriter. The word commonly given to the home office individual who accepts and classifies the life-insurance risk. It is also used occasionally to describe the agent who solicits insurance.

Waiver of Premium Disability. Nearly all life-insurance companies will add to their policies, upon payment of a small additional premium, a clause which provides that in the event the insured is totally disabled within its terms, his insurance policy will be continued in full force even though the payment of further premiums is waived by the company during the disability period.

Warranties and Representations. Under the laws of most states all statements made by the applicant, whether in the application blank or to the medical examiner, are considered, in the absence of fraud, to be representations and not warranties. A warranty must be literally true, and a breach of warranty is sufficient to render the policy void whether the matter warranted is material or not and whether or not it had contributed to the loss. A representation need be only substantially true. As a general rule, representations are considered fraudulent only when they relate to a matter material to the risk and were made with fraudulent intent.

Widow's Life Income. One of the basic programmed uses for life insurance. Life income for the widow starting at death of the insured or after the children have reached maturity.

SUGGESTED READINGS

"Your Life Insurance and How It Works"
"A Wife Looks At Life Insurance"
"Understanding Your Life Insurance"
    (All available from The Institute of Life Insurance, 277 Park Avenue, New York, New York 10017.)
"Income and Outgo"
"What Does She Do Now?"
"Personal Papers, Records"
    (All available from LIAMA, 170 Sigourney Street, Hartford, Connecticut 06105.)

10

The Coroner and Death

Is there a difference between coroner and medical examiner?

What are the coroner's duties and responsibilities?

What is an inquest?

What procedures does the coroner follow on being notified of death?

CYRIL H. WECHT

The coroner and/or medical examiner have major duties and responsibilities in probing deaths that are sudden, violent, or appear to be surrounded by suspicious circumstances. They also examine deaths of persons who were not under the care of a licensed physician. What procedures do they follow on being notified of death? Can burial or other disposition take place before a permanent certificate of death is issued? The inquest — what is it? What type of training should a coroner or medical examiner have?

Cyril H. Wecht, M.D., LL.B., J.D., the coroner of Allegheny County, Pennsylvania, is a diplomate in forensic pathology, and, as an attorney, is the director of forensic sciences at the Duquesne University School of Law. He serves as editor of *Legal Medicine Annual* and as editorial consultant of *Medical Economics*.

The Coroner and Death

What is a coroner?

A coroner is an elected official in most jurisdictions throughout the United States, although in a few scattered municipalities the coroner is appointed. The office of coroner developed in England approximately 800 to 900 years ago. Coroners were originally referred to as "crowners," the name deriving from the fact that they were officially appointed by the Crown to represent the King's interests in the investigation of violent, unexplained, and suspicious deaths, and more importantly, in the disposition of any personal or real property that became available under the existing laws following a homicide or suicide. The Latin word for crown is *corona,* and hence in later years the name of the office came to be called coroner.

During the development of the British Colonies in America, the Anglo-Saxon common law was adopted by the English colonists and was incorporated into their formal laws. As a matter of fact, the office of coroner came to be a constitutional office in many jurisdictions, a development which has produced considerable difficulty insofar as proponents of a medical examiner system are concerned. In these jurisdictions, the coroner's office cannot be abolished without a constitutional amendment, a legislative feat not too easily accomplished.

In England the coroner's office began to acquire the trappings of a political office because of its obvious influence.

and impact in many critical areas of death investigation. This approach and philosophy of the coroner's office were carried over to the various colonies. After the formation of the United States, each state adopted the office of coroner with little or no change from the manner in which these offices had been run previously. Thus, until changes were made in several jurisdictions many years later, all coroners in the United States were determined by political election, with no specific qualifications having been established as prerequisites for the office.

What is a medical examiner? Are the two offices (coroner and medical examiner) the same?

A medical examiner is an appointed official at a city, county, or state level. He must be a physician and, in almost all jurisdictions today, is a trained pathologist. As a matter of fact, in all large metropolitan areas the medical examiner is also a forensic pathologist — one who has acquired additional formal training in the performance of autopsies and investigations in certain kinds of cases, e.g., sudden, suspicious, violent, unexpected, unexplained, and medically unattended deaths.

The medical examiner is appointed by the chief executive officials of the city, county, or state jurisdiction, or by an independent commission. He is usually obliged to take a competitive examination along with other applicants for the position, and his appointment is based upon specific qualifications in the field of general pathology and forensic pathology. Education, experience, formal recognition by the American Board of Pathology, achievements in his profession, etc., are all factors considered by the appointing authorities.

Thus it is quite clear that there are significant differences between the traditional office of the coroner and the office of medical examiner. The former is a political office which, with few exceptions in the United States, is open to anybody who chooses to run for the office. In many instances coroners have no training in either law or medicine, and have no knowledge, experience, or education whatsoever in the handling of medical-legal death cases.

On the other hand, most medical examiners, certainly those functioning in larger metropolitan communities, are trained forensic pathologists whose educational background enables them to determine the cause and manner of death in a scientific, objective fashion. Medical examiners are most often affiliated with medical schools on a part-time basis and participate in the overall training, research, and educational programs at the medical school in their community.

> *How does one become a coroner or a medical examiner? What type of training is necessary?*

Coroners require no training whatsoever except in Ohio and Louisiana, where the state law requires that they have a medical degree. Of course, this is quite inadequate, for a medical degree by itself means nothing insofar as the role of a medical examiner is concerned. It is absolutely essential that a functioning medical examiner have extensive training and experience in the field of general pathology and forensic pathology.

A forensic pathologist, i.e., medical examiner, is a medical doctor who has spent five years as a resident in general and forensic pathology. Usually, four years are spent in a residency program studying anatomic and clinical pathology. This is followed by a fifth year in forensic pathology at one of the approximately fifteen approved and accredited medical-legal investigative training centers throughout the United States.

Following the training, the pathologist takes national examinations which are given each year by the American Board of Pathology. If he passes these examinations he is then certified by the American Board of Pathology as a diplomate in anatomic and clinical pathology, and then separately, following additional examinations, he may be certified by the American Board of Pathology in forensic pathology.

What are his duties? What are his responsibilities?

The medical examiner or coroner must assume jurisdiction in all cases in which a doctor was not in attendance or is unable to certify the cause of death with reasonable professional certainty. All homicides, accidents. and suicides fall within the jurisdiction of the coroner's or medical examiner's office. All deaths of a sudden or suspicious nature must be examined by the coroner or medical examiner, including deaths that occur in jails and other similar governmental institutions. Industrial deaths; unexpected deaths at hospitals, particularly those in which there is a possibility of medical negligence; poisonings; drug overdose fatalities — these are all examples of the kinds of cases which a medical examiner must deal with daily.

The responsibilities of a medical examiner or trained coroner are to see to it that proper scientific studies are performed. This includes an autopsy, toxicology tests, microscopic slide examinations, bacteriology, chemical analyses, and whatever other studies are deemed to be appropriate and necessary in specific cases. These findings are then prepared in formal official fashion and made available to appropriate interested parties including attorneys, hospitals, physicians, courts, law-enforcement agencies, prosecuting and defense attorneys in criminal cases, families, insurance companies, etc.

What procedures does the coroner follow on being notified of death?

In part, this depends upon the particular laws of the jurisdiction involved. Generally, all violent, suspicious, unexplained, unexpected, and medically unattended deaths are reported to the coroner by the police, hospital authorities, physicians, or on occasion, private citizens. The coroner immediately commences his investigation of such cases to determine whether or not the body should be brought to his facility for the performance of an autopsy and toxicology tests.

Sometimes further investigation reveals that the individual was under the care of a physician, and the coroner or medical examiner may decide to release the body. Most often, however, it is necessary to bring the body into his facility for the necessary scientific studies.

Can burial or other disposition take place before a permanent certificate of death is issued?

Yes, if the coroner or medical examiner is involved. No, if a private physician or hospital is involved.

If a coroner or medical examiner has assumed jurisdiction in a case, and if he is not satisfied initially following his investigation or the gross autopsy examination that he can certify the cause of death, he may issue a temporary death certificate in which the cause of death is listed as "Pending." Then, further scientific tests are done in the ensuing days and weeks, depending upon the nature and complexity of the case, following which definitive diagnoses are determined. Then a corrected final certificate of death is issued by the coroner or medical examiner.

It should be pointed out that on occasion even the most thorough and painstaking scientific investigation may not reveal a definitive cause of death. Most good medical examiners' offices are not hesitant about issuing a death certificate which lists "Undetermined natural causes," or similar terminology, in a few cases each year.

What kinds of investigations does he make? What are the purposes?

The investigations include all kinds of scientific analyses, including pathology, toxicology, chemistry, bacteriology, histology, immunology, serology, odontology, anthropology, and criminalistics. The medical examiner or coroner may call upon consultants in different fields such as radiology, dentistry, anthropology, criminalistics, entomology, biology, engineering, and other scientific fields to assist him in the investigation of specific cases.

The purpose of these investigations is to determine as accurately and scientifically as possible the specific mode of death (natural causes, accident, homicide, or suicide), and the exact cause of death. Many times it is necessary to identify bodies which have been badly mutilated in accidents, conflagrations, or other traumatic incidents. Bodies also become decomposed when they are not promptly discovered, and identification becomes a problem in such instances.

The medical examiner or coroner must document and certify death in all such cases in order to ensure that the civil and criminal justice systems are properly served and that the needs of the community are fully met. The health and welfare of the community's residents are matters of prime concern and importance to any good medical-legal investigative office.

A trained medical examiner also makes significant contributions to many other community programs such as suicide prevention, drug-abuse education, crib-death research, medical-legal education of attorneys and physicians, environmental control, and so forth.

What is an inquest? What is the coroner's responsibility in this matter?

An inquest is a formal investigation conducted by a coroner or medical examiner into deaths in which there is a possibility, a suspicion, an allegation, or actual knowledge of criminality on the part of some individual. Traditionally, six jurors were convened by the coroner to render a verdict in these cases. These jurors were unilaterally selected by the coroner and usually were old friends and cronies. This system still exists in many jurisdictions throughout the United States today!

In some jurisdictions, particularly those where a medical examiner system has been adopted, inquests may not be conducted at all. In other jurisdictions the medical examiner may conduct an inquest, with or without a jury. At the inquest, which is a quasijudicial proceeding presided over by the coroner or medical examiner, or their solicitor, the basic facts are presented by different witnesses. These usually include law enforcement officers, the pathologist who performed the autopsy, and any lay witnesses who have something to contribute.

In those cases in which police have arrested an individual and charged him with a particular crime, usually murder, the defendant may testify at an inquest if he wishes. Usually his attorney does not wish him to testify at an inquest. If the coroner and/or the coroner's jury determines that a prima facie case has been presented — that is to say, if sufficient facts have been introduced to indicate that a criminal act was performed by the particular individual charged, and that a criminal act played a role in bringing about the death of the named decedent, the defendant will be bound over by the coroner for the grand jury. Then, the case is heard by the grand jury, and the defendant is either indicted and held for trial, or as happens occasionally the case may be dismissed by the grand jury.

Some coroners' offices hold a preliminary hearing instead of an inquest. In essence, a preliminary hearing is the same as an inquest except that no jury is involved. The coroner or his solicitor handles the case himself and makes the necessary legal determination based upon the evidence introduced by various witnesses.

How does the role of the coroner differ in various states and localities?

It should be pointed out that coroners' laws do vary somewhat from jurisdiction to jurisdiction, although basically the philosophy, modus operandi, and objectives of the office are the same. To a great extent it is a matter of how the laws are interpreted by the individuals who act as coroners and medical examiners, and what the traditions of the medical-legal investigative office are in that particular community.

Of course, sometimes the authority of the coroner or medical examiner may be challenged, and such cases are then adjudicated by the courts.

SUGGESTED READINGS

Camps, Francis E. (Ed.) *Gradwohl's Legal Medicine* (Bristol, England: John Wright & Sons, 1968).

Camps, Frances E., and J.M. Cameron, *Practical Forensic Medicine* (London: Hutchinson Medical Publications, 1956).

Curran, William J., and E. Donald Shapiro, *Law, Medicine and Forensic Science* (Boston: Little, Brown, 1970).

Curry, Alan S., *Poison Detection in Human Organs* (Springfield, Ill.. Charles C. Thomas, 1963).

Gonzales, Thomas A., *Legal Medicine, Pathology, and Toxicology* (New York: Appleton-Century-Crofts, 1937).

Snyder, Lemoyne, et al, *Homicide Investigation* (Springfield, Ill.: C. C. Thomas, 1944).

Wecht, Cyril H., *Legal Medicine Annual* (New York: Appleton-Century-Crofts, 1969 - 1972).

Wecht, Cyril H., *The Medico-Legal Autopsy Laws of the Fifty States, the District of Columbia, American Samoa, the Canal Zone, Guam, Puerto Rico, and the Virgin Islands* (Washington, D.C.: Armed Forces Institute of Pathology, revised edition 1971).

11

The Funeral and the Funeral Director

Why a funeral?

What is the role of the funeral director?

What is involved in the cost of a funeral?
Is prearrangement helpful?

What is embalming?

Should the body not be present and not be viewed?

What are memorial societies?

HOWARD C. RAETHER and ROBERT C. SLATER

A loved one dies. You are about to make arrangements. You must consider many details: What funeral director to call. Whether the service should be private. Should the body be present and viewed? How much should a funeral cost? How can the funeral director be of assistance during the period of crisis?

Howard C. Raether, Ph.B., J.D., has served since 1948 as the executive director of the National Funeral Directors Association. A member of many governmental agencies, he was awarded the highest honor the U.S. Army makes to a private citizen — the Distinguished Civilian Service Award. Mr. Raether is a member of the National Council on Tissue Transplantation and Utilization as well as the author of *Successful Funeral Service Practice.*

Professor Robert C. Slater is the director of mortuary science at the University of Minnesota. He has written *Funeral Service — A Heritage, a Challenge, a Future* and more than fifty articles in numerous magazines relating to death and the funeral.

The Funeral and the Funeral Director

SOME INTRODUCTORY THOUGHTS

Talking about death is often difficult. A death in the family may create problems for survivors which can sometimes be alleviated by discussions about what the options are when death requires certain decisions to be made.

The inherent uncertainties make it highly desirable that professional counseling be secured from a funeral director. He will gladly assist you at no cost or obligation. If in your discussion there are matters which go beyond his field, he will suggest you contact a person competent in that area. Always bear in mind that the funeral director is there to serve you. Remember, too, that experience dictates that it is difficult to be specific about matters, including costs, without knowing when, where, and under what circumstances death will occur.

With these basic thoughts in mind, the following questions and answers were prepared and will cover most of the concerns a person will have when death comes into his family.

What is a funeral?

West coast psychiatrist William M. Lamers, Jr., says, "The funeral is an organized, purposeful, time limited, flexible, group-centered response to death." To this should be added that the response involves rites and ceremonies during some or all of which the body of the deceased is present.

When did the idea of funerals first evolve in history?

Prehistoric man had sophisticated burial practices. The Smithsonian Museum of Natural History displayed a 30,000-year-old "corpse" of a Paleolithic man found in a state of preservation in a cave in Spain. But even before then, man had associated himself with burial practices. A cave in northern Iraq revealed to archeologists that flowers were a part of a Neanderthal burial about 60,000 years ago. Undoubtedly the practices of ancient civilizations and those of the early Egyptians provided the basics for rites and ceremonies within the Christian tradition, which in turn were derived from Hebrew religious and ethical concepts. Since the beginning of recorded history, man has publicly viewed his dead and buried them with ceremony.

What is the purpose of the funeral?

A funeral is *of* the person who has died as it provides for the disposition of his body with rites and ceremonies attendant thereto. The funeral also meets the needs of the survivors. These needs may be personal while at the same time involve the community and the religious beliefs of the deceased or his family. University of Minnesota sociologist, Robert Fulton, says that the funeral is not only a declaration of a death that has occurred but it is also a testimony to a life that has been lived.

Is there a difference between a "funeral director," "mortician," "undertaker," or "embalmer"?

Generally speaking, no. These are names given to persons licensed by the state in which they practice and who serve the living as they care for the dead. Specifically, there could be a difference. All states and the District of Columbia license embalmers. These persons are educated and trained to prepare human remains for a funeral and burial. Most states license funeral directors, who serve the public in all aspects of funeral service, excluding embalming. Some states have a single license which covers both funeral directing and embalming. About 75 percent of all funeral-service practitioners are licensed to perform all the tasks required of a funeral functionary.

Is there a difference between an "undertaking establishment," a "funeral home," a "funeral chapel," a "mortuary," or a "memorial home"?

No. These are names given to a place or premise devoted to or used in the care and preparation of human dead for the funeral and burial. Facilities will be provided for the convenience of the bereaved for viewing, visitation, and the providing of funeral services with accompanying rites or ceremonies.

What facilities go to make up a funeral home or mortuary?

Most funeral homes or mortuaries consist of an entrance foyer, a preparation room, an arrangement room, a casket selection room, a visitation or "in state" room, which might also be used for the funeral service, a room for the clergy, an office, lounges, and service areas. Most have chapels. Some also have living or sleeping quarters for the owner and/or members of his staff.

How does one become a funeral-service licensee — that is, a funeral director and/or embalmer?

The requirements for licensure generally include: (1) the minimum of a high-school graduation; (2) in four states, one year of college; in twenty-one states, two years of college; (3) in every state at least an academic year in a professional curriculum in a college of funeral service education or mortuary science; (4) passing a state board licensing examination; and (5) in every state a period of internship or apprenticeship, ranging from one to three years, with the norm being one year.

What does a funeral director do to help in the arrangements and conduct of a funeral?

After being selected by a family to serve them, the funeral director removes or arranges for the removal of the deceased to the funeral home. Information for the death certificate and obituary notice is secured as early as is convenient for the family. The funeral director is responsible for the proper completion and filing of the death certificate, at which time the burial or transit permit is secured.

The funeral director makes an appointment to discuss the various phases of the service. These phases include: the place of service — church or funeral home; the time of service; the clergyman or other person who will officiate at the funeral — always contacting him before the time and place are finally determined; selecting cemetery space — which may mean the purchase of a cemetery lot or arranging for the opening of a grave in the family plot; or if final disposition is to be cremation, securing permits and making arrangements with the crematory; music for the service, including organist, singer, and selection of music to be used; contacting fraternal officials (if any); notifying casket bearers; selecting the clothing necessary; and choosing the casket and outside receptacle. These preliminary arrangements are usually subject to subsequent checking and organization of details. Additional arrangements are considered in the event the deceased is to be transferred to some other city for services and/or interment.

On the day of the services, which may be one, two, three, or more days from the time of death, the funeral director attends the floral arrangements, arranges for the physical facilities, provides cars for the family and casket bearers, receives and ushers friends to their seats, coordinates the service with the clergyman, organizes the funeral cortege, and has a car available to send flowers to the cemetery. The many separate details in the funeral service require the careful attention of the funeral director and his assistants.

Usually there will be a few further items that will be dictated by the particular service, appearing only as that service is planned and arranged. The family's wishes and desires will modify some of the details, for each entire funeral must be in keeping with the preferences of each family and the sensitivities and desires of the family members.

After the service, the funeral director assists the family in filing necessary claims for Social Security, veterans and union benefits, and insurance. Often the funeral director serves a family for several months following a funeral until all matters and details are satisfactorily completed for the family.

What is embalming?

Embalming is the replacing of the fluids in a dead body with chemicals for disinfection and temporary preservation.

How is embalming accomplished?

The licensed embalmer will carefully wash and cleanse the body with particular attention to the hands, face, and hair. The preserving chemicals will be injected into the body, under carefully controlled pressure, through an artery. The body fluids will be removed through a vein. Ordinarily, the embalming process of both injection and drainage will be accomplished through one incision in the vascular system.

Is embalming ever required by law?

Embalming is sometimes required by law to permit a body to be transported. Sometimes it is mandatory if final disposition of the body is not within a prescribed period of time. Also, it may be essential to protect the public's health when death was due to certain infectious diseases.

What is the primary purpose of embalming?

The temporary preservation is to permit the body to be present for the period of the funeral, including the visitation or wake, and for the funeral service.

Is it important to have the body present?

Man makes meaningful associations with persons and significant objects. When someone dies, a life on earth has ended. What remains is not that living person; it is the body of a man, woman, or child who once was loved and who loved in return. When we remember a person we have known, we always think of them in terms of their physical being — their body.

That is why it is difficult for many survivors to disassociate themselves immediately from the lifeless body. The finite mind requires evidence that an earthly existence has ended. With the body present, the opportunity is thus provided for recall and reminiscence, both of which help in accepting the reality and finality of the death that has occurred.

Should a body be viewed?

If it can be made viewable, yes! This is perhaps of greater importance today than ever before. Many people die away from home, often in distant medical institutions. There are some deaths which follow a devastating, lingering illness. There are also persons whose lives end under tragic circumstances. Several helpful purposes are served by the custom of viewing:

Realization. Viewing the dead body makes those who survive more aware of the reality of sudden, accidental, or lingering death. Seeing is believing. Often much time, effort, and money are expended to recover a missing body for the purpose of confirming the fact that the death has occurred.

Recall. Before a long, lingering death, the face of someone loved may be lined with the evidence of pain or malignancy. With accidents and violence, the entire body may be disfigured. Proper preparation and, when necessary, restoration help to modify and remove the marks of violence or the ravages of disease. Preparation, restoration, and the use of cosmetics are not meant to make the dead look alive. They provide an acceptable image for recalling the deceased. Viewing is therapeutic for people, regardless of age. It is especially helpful for a child who has experienced the death of one loved. Instead of fantasizing in his vivid imagination, with the body present he is able to comprehend the real meaning of death.

When once the funeral service begins, should the casket remain open?

Some people want it that way; but it is recommended that just before the service begins, especially if it is religiously oriented, the casket be closed.

What is involved in the cost of a funeral?

Four separate and distinct categories of charges make up the cost of a funeral. They are:
- Those which specifically involve the funeral director, including his professional services and those of his staff, the use of the facilities and equipment he has available, and the casket and the vault as selected by the family.
- Those dealing with the disposition of the body. If earth interred, there is the cost of the grave (if no cemetery lot is previously owned) and the charge for opening and closing same. If cremated, there is the charge for the cremation, plus the cost of an urn, if one is desired, in which to place the cremated remains.
- Those for memorialization, such as a monument or marker for the grave or a niche in a columbarium for the urn of cremated remains.

• Those miscellaneous expenses paid by the family directly or through the funeral director. These include such items as: honoraria, flowers, newspaper death notices, additional limousines, burial clothing, and out-of-town transportation of the body.

What should a funeral cost?

This is hard to say. The value of a funeral as it meets the needs of those who mourn should never be determined in terms of dollars expended. The funeral is usually selected by the family of the deceased. Their needs, desires, and demands must be considered. Their decision is often rooted in religious and ethnic customs, family preferences and traditions, and, of course, the customs and usages of their particular community. Then, too, the economy of an area has its effects on funeral prices just as it does on the cost of other services and commodities. In addition, there are the expenses of the funeral home essential to provide a variety of choices. All who are selecting a funeral should be able to choose the kind of funeral they want. In doing so, all except the less fortunate must share in the cost of making the choices available.

Where does the money come from to pay for funerals?

Money for funeral and burial purposes usually comes from one or more sources. Some of the proceeds of life insurance (once called death insurance); allowances of governmental agencies (Social Security, Veterans Administration, workmen's compensation, welfare, and others); union and fraternal organization benefits; and savings and estate funds are the primary sources. Sometimes there is also specially designated insurance such as funeral insurance, which provides funds for the beneficiary to use for funeralization and final disposition and burial insurance which provides services and merchandise.

Suppose a person dies leaving no one to pay for the funeral and no money from any source, governmental or charitable. What then?

There are few instances like this. Most times these persons leave no relatives or friends or none with sufficient interest to claim the body for funeralization and/or final disposition. Such bodies are released to the state anatomical board for use in medical research.

Is the casket an American "invention"?

No. As was said earlier, for thousands of years man has viewed his dead and buried them with ceremony. This is done whether the body is embalmed or not, whether or not there is a funeral functionary, and whether the rite is primitively simple or highly organized. Most times there is some sort of container for the body for the funeral ceremony and in which to transport the remains to the place of final disposition. The receptacles range from a wooden box to a highly ornate coffin or casket. The first coffin makers in America were craftsmen, most likely cabinet makers who migrated from Europe, where coffin making is still a skilled craft.

Is there a difference between a coffin and casket?

Yes. A coffin is a burial receptacle which tapers out from the head to the area for the shoulders, where it is the widest, and then tapers in to the foot. A casket is rectangular.

Is there any other function or purpose for the casket?

Yes. Besides being the receptacle used during the period of the funeral and for transporting the remains, it most times is the receptacle which encases the body in or above the ground. The casket is also the last material gift the survivors can give the body which once was a person. It adds to the esthetics of the funeral setting and to the repose of the body.

How does one determine the selection of a casket?

This is a matter of personal or family preference, sometimes involving something the deceased did or liked. Then, too, the sex of the deceased, height, weight and other physical features should be taken into consideration. Most funeral homes offer a range of twelve to thirty-six caskets from which a family can make its choice. Material, design, color, and construction are some of the variables available to a family.

What is a burial vault?

A burial vault is an outer enclosure into which the casketed remains are placed. The purpose is to provide protection against the elements and to bear the earth load. It is made of concrete, steel, fiberglass, and copper. For those who do not use a protective vault, many cemeteries require the use of some type of outside enclosure to reduce the possibility of a grave cave-in. These can come in the form of a sectional concrete or a wooden outside enclosure.

Is a vault required by law?

No. But courts have upheld the right of a cemetery to regulate relative to some form of outside enclosure.

What are the common means of final disposition?

Interment. This is the most common procedure. The deceased is buried (interred) in the earth in dedicated ground called a cemetery or memorial park.

Cremation. In this procedure the dead body is reduced to ashes by means of intense heat (approximately 2,-200 degrees Fahrenheit). The residue or ashes that remain after the casketed body has been cremated may be buried, scattered, or placed in an urn (inurned) and deposited in a columbarium. A columbarium is a special room with niches (small storage places) in a crematorium where the inurned ashes may be placed.

Entombment. The casketed body is entombed in a specially constructed above-ground mausoleum. There may be individual mausolea, family mausolea (for two to twelve entombments), or large public mausolea for large numbers of entombments.

Should those who go to the funeral service also go to the committal?

Yes. It is the final farewell to the deceased. The earthly relationship between the person who has died and those who loved him ends at the grave, the mausoleum, or the crematory. It is a temporary hurt. The healing process is helped by the presence of those who care as the finality of the death is realized by those who mourn.

Going to the committal generally involves a

funeral procession. Can this be dangerous?

It need not be. It can be orderly and safe. The traffic hazards involved in a funeral procession are probably not nearly as great as those around places where athletic events are staged, shopping centers, drive-in theaters, fairs, and civic events of all sorts. The funeral procession is a dignified way of transporting the body of the deceased and his mourners to the place of the committal. It also gives a dignity to all men, as did the processions for John and Robert Kennedy and Martin Luther King during the troubled 1960s. The funeral is part of the "passing parade" that gives testimony to the life that has been lived.

What about flowers and other expressions of sympathy?

Many persons wish to express their sympathy by sending flowers or some other memorial in addition to extending their condolences in person. Others do this because they cannot be present at the visitation or service. Those who wish to demonstrate their feelings should be able to do it in the way they prefer and which is most natural for them. Flowers, for example, have a message all their own. They add beauty to the casket setting and to the funeral service. It is considered proper for the family to suggest a certain memorial, but it should not be done in such a manner that any other form of expression is excluded or that implies a tangible solicitation of sympathy.

Are there alternatives to the funeral with the body present? What are they?

Yes. There are two alternatives to the funeral with the body present: (1) immediate disposition of the body with a memorial service some days or perhaps weeks following the death, and (2) immediate disposition of the body without a service of any kind.

What are memorial societies?

The Continental Association of Funeral and Memorial Societies says, "A memorial society is a group of people who have joined together to obtain dignity, simplicity, and economy in funeral arrangements by advanced planning." They recommend immediate disposition of the body to be followed by a memorial service. They also suggest minimum-priced funerals.

Do memorial societies provide funeral and/or memorial services?

No. Memorial societies are not in funeral service. Their officers and staffs are not licensed to conduct funerals or to make funeral arrangements. They have no facilities, services, or merchandise, all or some of which may be desired when death occurs. They prefer to assume no financial liability but instead attempt to "contract for services" with established funeral homes.

Do those who belong to a memorial society still have to deal with a funeral director?

Yes, in all states but California. However, memorial society members generally call the funeral director(s) the society recommends or with whom they have "contracts."

Is there a difference between a "funeral" that follows a death and a "memorial service"?

Yes. Every funeral is a memorial service, but not every memorial service is a funeral. The rites and ceremonies that follow death which are organized, purposeful, time limited, flexible, and group-centered and involve the presence of the body are a *funeral*. Some form of acknowledgment after death without the body present is a *memorial service*.

If a major organ is transplanted from a body, can the body still be present at the funeral?

Yes. Most organs or tissues for transplants must be removed as soon as possible after death; and the basic Uniform Anatomical Gift Act, which is in effect in one form or another in all states and the District of Columbia, says that "After removal of the (anatomical) part, custody of the remainder of the body vests in the surviving spouse, next of kin, or other persons under obligation to dispose of the body."

If a body is given to medical science, does this guarantee that it will be accepted for medical science purposes?

No. State laws permit the rejection of the gift. Many schools have all the bodies required for anatomical study; others still experience a shortage. Some schools accept bodies, if available, for transfer to others reporting a shortage. The condition of the body may also determine whether it will be accepted. For example, some schools cannot use a body which has been autopsied or which has been mutilated by a violent death. If a limb is missing or there has been a transplant of a major organ, the body may have limited value; and if the person was very obese or the body was emaciated, it may be rejected.

Bodies can be stored for limited periods for future use or transported where needed. It is important, however, to realize that an offer by the decedent during his lifetime or by his survivors following his death *does not* guarantee that the body will be accepted for medical purposes. Only at death can a final determination as to acceptance be made. Such acceptance will depend on the place of death, the condition of the body, the school's current needs, and other factors which may change frequently.

What about the gift of a body to medical science? Can a funeral be held with that body before delivery to the medical institution?

Yes. When specified by the deceased or by his survivors, most medical institutions will permit the presence of the body for the purpose of funeralization, after which it is delivered to the donee medical institution for study. When a funeral is requested, the funeral director notifies the medical school and prepares the body as required by the school. Also, interment services may be requested for the residue of the body after research and study are completed by the medical institution. These arrangements and any other conditions or limitations may be made by the funeral director in cooperation with the medical school.

What should one do if death occurs away from home?

The answer depends on whether there will be partial services, such as a visitation where death occurs, or whether the body will be prepared where the death took place but the funeral and final disposition will be at the home or former place of residence of the deceased.

In any event, there will be two funeral directors involved. If the funeral and final disposition are going to be at a place other than where death occurred, the funeral director who will be in charge of such services should be contacted and will counsel the family. If there will be some services at the place of death with duplicating or additional services at the place of final disposition, the funeral director selected at either of the locations will be able to make the necessary arrangements.

Regardless, the family should pay the equivalent of only one complete service plus any additional charges for services incurred because the place of death and the place of final disposition require the services of two funeral homes.

Do funeral practices differ?

Yes! They are different in various sections of the country and even within the same city. A custom in California may seem strange in Vermont. A New Orleans funeral and method of disposition may be hard for a Minnesotan to visualize. Of equal significance is the variance between a Jewish shiva and an Irish wake being held at the same time within a few blocks of each other. There is no one prescribed form of the funeral. The funeral which is arranged should be the one which best meets the needs of those who survive.

Should a funeral be prearranged and maybe even prefinanced?

There are many different reasons for prearranging a funeral. Some persons, especially those who are alone in the world, may want the assurance of a funeral and burial which meet their personal beliefs, standards, or lifestyle. Others feel a responsibility to assist survivors by arranging approximate funeral and burial cost guidelines. Still others have moved to distant places or maintain both summer and winter residences. They may want to make sure that certain recommendations are heeded as to where the funeral and burial or other final dispositions will take place. Actually, there are almost as many explanations for prearranging funerals as there are people requesting them.

What are the important factors to consider in the prearranging and prefinancing of funerals?

- Review the possible effect on survivors.
- Approach realistically the logic and economics of planning now what might not take place for many years.
- Keep in mind that the selection of a funeral director or a funeral firm as well as burial merchandise for use at a future indeterminable time must, of necessity, be on a tentative basis.
- Remember, too, that money paid in advance of need for funeral services and merchandise, including burial vaults, is governed by law in most states

If there are no such laws in the state in which the prearrangement is made, it is recommended that the prepaid funeral agreement include the provision for a trust fund with the person making the payment maintaining control of the account. The fund should include all money paid in advance of need for services and merchandise, including burial vaults. The agreement should also entitle the person in control of the trust to the interest earned with the option of applying it to the principal to offset any increased inflationary costs. Such person making the payment should retain the right to terminate the contract at any time without forfeiture of any of the funds paid or earnings accrued.

Is there a code of professional practices for funeral directors?

Yes. Some of the large national associations have such codes. The following are two pertinent paragraphs of the code of the largest group, the National Funeral Directors Association:

> Because the price of the funeral is related to the casket selection, there should be a card or brochure in each casket in the selection room. Such card or brochure should outline the services offered by the funeral home. Services and merchandise not included where a unit price method is used should be listed on the card or brochure as separate items.
>
> When a family decides on the kind of service desired, the funeral director should provide a memorandum or agreement for the family to approve or sign showing: (1) the price of the service that the family has selected and what is included therein; (2) the price of each of the supplemental items of service and/or merchandise requested; (3) the amount involved for each of the items for which the funeral director will advance monies as an accommodation to the family; and (4) the method of payment agreed upon by the family and the funeral director.

Are there any controls on funeral homes and funeral service licensees other than those of a voluntary organization(s)?

Yes. As indicated previously, all states have some form of individual licensure. Many states license or register the funeral home or mortuary as well. Violation of the laws and regulations governing the licensees and/or their places of business puts such licensee(s) in jeopardy.

What changes will there be in the funeral in the next few years?

As the mobility of our nation's people increases, more deaths will occur at a place other than where the funeral and/or burial will take place. There will be the humanist or secular funeral service for those who do not profess a specific religious belief. A humanist funeral service, arranged at the request of the family, is one in which all of the facets — visitation, viewing, funeral ceremony — are similar to any other funeral rite or ceremony, but there is no religious content or orientation within the service. With a growing number of persons finding organized religion dysfunctional, the humanist funeral becomes a viable option for such people.

On November 1, 1971, the new liturgy for the Catholic funeral rite became mandatory. It is often referred to as the Resurrection or White Mass. The new Catholic rite encourages verbalized participation in the service by those attending the wake and/or church and/or cemetery service. This trend is bound to grow not only among those of the Catholic faith but of other faiths as well, as in those services which are humanistic or secular. Litanies, responsive readings, group singing, and verbal commendation are becoming part of many funeral services, thus allowing those in attendance to be participants rather than just observers.

There are other ways in which there will be greater actual participation by those attending a funeral. There have been members of motorcycle clubs who turned out with their vehicles to act as escorts for the procession of a member of their group who died or was killed. These persons often also participate in the committal ceremony, sometimes by taking off their shoulder patches or other means of identification and placing them on or in the casket or in the open grave. Organizations other than motorcycle clubs, groups of individuals, and sometimes individuals are also doing this as part of an organized activity or as a personal response to the situation.

There have been some groups through the years which have stayed for the complete or partial lowering of the casket into the grave following the committal service. This trend will probably grow in the future. The folk-type funeral service will continue with the accompaniment for the music by guitar or other instrument. Also, whether the music is guitar or organ, or whether there is a capella singing, there is a move toward the use of contemporary music and away from the songs and hymns which have been regarded as more or less standard for funerals over the years.

The impact of youth on the funeral will increase. Most young people are sensitive to the needs and wants of others. They also believe in expressing themselves; and while they may want their needs satisfied differently from other persons, and their forms of expression might vary from that which may be termed traditional, for them the funeral of someone loved can be an experience of value as it meets such needs and provides a proper climate for their expressions.

In the months and years which lie immediately ahead, there will be more seminars and symposia and courses in institutions of higher learning dealing with various facets of death, grief, and bereavement. A funeral functionary — the funeral director — has a very definite place therein because he is the caretaking professional who is involved in the greatest number of situations involving loss by death.

SUGGESTED READINGS

Irion, Paul, *Cremation* (Philadelphia: Fortress Press, 1968).
————, *The Funeral: Vestige or Value?* (Nashville: Abingdon Press, 1966).
————, *A Humanist Funeral Service* (Baltimore: Waverly Press, 1971).
Jackson, Edgar N., *The Christian Funeral* (New York: Channel Press, 1966).
————, *When Someone Dies* (Philadelphia: Fortress Press, 1972).

Pamphlets (available from the National Funeral Directors Association, 135 West Wells Street, Milwaukee, Wisconsin 53203):

"Some Questions and Answers About Your Child and Death"
"The Condolence or Sympathy Visit"

"The Pre-Arranging and Pre-Financing of Funerals"
"Someone You Love Has Died"
"Some Thoughts to Consider When Arranging a Funeral"
"With the Body Present"
"What About Funeral Costs?"
"Code of Professional Practices for Funeral Directors"

12

How to Select a Cemetery

What are the kinds of cemeteries?

*What should you ask before selecting a
particular cemetery?*

How is price determined?

Are vaults or concrete liners necessary?

*When might a body be moved from one
cemetery to another?*

WILLIAM MORGAN

Many people wait until the death of a loved one before
selecting a cemetery. Would it not be wiser to make the choice on a
pre-need basis? What kind of cemetery should one choose? On what
basis? How about price? How many spaces to buy?

William Morgan is the executive vice president of Sharon
Memorial Park in Sharon, Massachusetts.

How to Select a Cemetery

When should one select a cemetery?

For most families in our society there comes a time when they will choose a cemetery in order to establish a family lot. A widely accepted method of making this choice is to do it on a pre-need basis. In this way the people involved, usually husband and wife, can make their decisions under normal emotional circumstances and exercise wise judgment. You can readily see that this is a far more acceptable alternative than the one in which a widow, or a relative, or a friend, makes a hasty decision, pressured by the time factor involved in making final arrangements once a death occurs.

It has been my experience that people who do choose their cemetery property on a pre-need basis, in addition to having all of the obvious advantages of selection and prudent fiscal procedure, make a positive contribution to themselves and their family in terms of their own mental health concerning the acceptance of death. When a man or a woman dies the surviving spouse proceeds, strengthened by the knowledge that they chose their cemetery lots together and that the decision was an acceptable one. Later on there are no sad misgivings or vain regrets.

A recent study was conducted under the direction of Doris R. Poté, an attorney and associate professor of law at Suffolk University Law School in Boston. Professor Poté is a noted activist in the consumer movement, and she investigated the cemetery business. One of her recommendations was: "Pre-need buying of space for burial must be stressed by cemeterians to preclude the problem of overbuying by those under emotional stress because of the death of a loved one." It is interesting to note that Professor Poté's report concludes: "The cemeteries of today are fulfilling their mission. They are serving the community and serving it well."

To most people the cemetery seems to be a forbidding place, with its operation and management shrouded in some kind of mystery. People ask all kinds of questions, out of curiosity or genuine concern, about cemeteries and what they do. Actually what they do and how they do it need not be a mystery. Almost everybody in our society buries their dead in areas specifically set aside for this purpose. This has been an ongoing custom from ancient times. It is, therefore, the responsibility of the cemetery organization to provide a place to carry out this function. People bury their dead with dignity and reverence and usually require that the cemetery be a place of natural beauty, well cared for. This care and concern translates itself into reverence for the memory of the dead.

How is the cemetery developed?

Once a site for a cemetery is selected and the permit from the local authorities is secured, the cemetery must be developed. This means that it must be graded and prepared for its function; roads must be built, the land must be surveyed and laid out into subdivisions or plots. Engineers are required to plan drainage and irrigation. All of this must be engineered in a precise manner, the surveying being done by civil engineers who survey, chart, subdivide, and number the tract of land to be used. Maps must be published for administrative purposes, sales purposes, and for actual use in the digging of graves by the ground crew. Roads must be planned, keeping in mind easy access and egress and traffic patterns. Landscape architects are frequently hired to assure that the cemetery is properly planted to provide beauty and serenity. Having developed a piece of land and properly surveyed it and charted it, the cemetery can then proceed to sell the lots and issue proper deeds marking the specific lots and graves the public will purchase.

Today's modern cemetery ground crews are a far cry from the stereotype gravedigger many people still have visions of. They are men who like to work out of doors and are usually knowledgeable about the care and maintenance of lawns, shrubbery, and trees. The men responsible for the layout of a grave have to be very accurate and employ mechanical as well as mathematical knowledge in order to see that graves are properly and precisely opened. They are, as a general rule, very proud of the appearance of the cemetery they work in and are conscious of the important service they render to the public. This means that there is no hesitation on their part to work frequently under difficult weather conditions and under pressure of time.

What are the various types of cemeteries?

The earliest kind of cemetery in the United States was the church cemetery. Frequently located adjacent to or near the church, it primarily served the congregation and others in the area.

As populations grew and these small churchyard cemeteries could no longer provide the necessary land or service required, mutual cemeteries were formed, usually owned and run by the families who were going to use them. These mutual cemeteries, as a general rule, had no stockholders and were run by boards of trustees.

As municipalities were developed, local governments felt the need and the responsibility for establishing cemeteries for people who dwelt within their jurisdiction, and so municipal cemeteries started to appear.

In some places, especially in the southern part of the country, privately owned cemeteries were developed. These were usually owned by public-spirited citizens whose primary goal was to render a needed service in their community.

Religious and fraternal groups, ethnic groups, and craft organizations soon started to develop cemeteries of their own to take care of their members. The need was increasing, and each group, in turn, felt a special obligation to provide this service.

Because many of the cemeteries with various types of ownership had no provisions for perpetual care or endowments, and did not set up rules and regulations, a new concept in cemetery operation was instituted on the West Coast in the 1920s. The lack of adequate perpetual-care funds or endowment trust funds and the resultant rundown appearance of the older cemeteries gave rise to a demand for more professionally managed property. This new concept was referred to as the memorial park.

The memorial park has all the memorials flush with the ground, making the appearance of the cemetery one vast lawn, with appropriate plantings of shrubbery for beauty. This increased the cemetery's ability to maintain the cemetery with a minimum of expense. Large mowing equipment can be used and some of the costly expenses associated with the trimming and resetting of granite memorials are eliminated.

These cemeteries were usually organized by businessmen. Memorial parks usually have care funds started with the cemetery, and take a percentage of each sale for deposit into the permanent-care fund. There are many variations and combinations of these cemeteries in the United States. Some cemeteries may offer monument sections, flush-lawn sections, mausoleum entombment, aboveground crypts, and columbariums for storing cremated remains.

How does one choose a cemetery?

In making your choice there are some things you should keep in mind. First and foremost, the reputation of the cemetery you are contemplating doing business with should be investigated. Does it render good service to the community? Is it being well maintained? Are there responsible citizens in the community guiding the cemetery and its policies? Is its management readily available to discuss problems that may arise? Of paramount importance is the manner in which its care funds are handled. Is money being set aside on a regular basis for care? Does your purchase agreement stipulate that money is being set aside, and how much? Is the care fund being run by well-known and trusted citizens of the community or a well-known and trusted banking or investment organization? The interest generated by these trust funds should be for the specific purpose of keeping grass cut and shrubbery well cared for. You should visit the cemetery, if you have not already done so, to make sure it is, indeed, the kind of institution in which you want to establish your family lot.

What determines price?

In all cemeteries prices will depend on the individual cemetery itself and the location of the lot. Prices may run from $150 to $850 per grave. Cemeteries frequently charge more for property they feel is esthetically preferable. People have to weigh their own ability to pay against their ideas about appearance, location, and service afforded by various cemeteries in their area. At this point a word of caution may be in order. I have, on numerous occasions, had the opportunity to select with prospective buyers their cemetery property. Very often people will say, "I want the least expensive," or, "What difference does it make after I am gone?" or, "I won't know or care when the time comes." All very understandable comments. The problem is that at a time when the property is used to inter the remains of a family member, there is too often an entirely new attitude. What was heretofore an academic approach becomes an emotional, visceral feeling. A piece of land becomes the final resting place of someone dearly loved. A lot becomes sacred ground which is visited to express respect for the memory of a mother, father, husband, child, etc. Too often those of us in the cemetery profession hear people express regrets about their purchase or selection after the burial is over. Some people feel so strongly about the location, they go through the expense and emotional upheaval of moving a body from one cemetery to another, or even from one location to another within the same cemetery.

I suggest that a person motivate himself to face some sobering facts when cemetery property is chosen. Ask yourself: "Is this where I would want to bury members of my family?" That, after all, is really what we are talking about.

Most cemeteries require that when a purchase is made at the time of need, the space be paid for in cash in full. Some cemeteries require that all spaces being purchased at that time be paid for in full. There are many cemeteries that arrange for installment purchases on pre-need lots. Some of these cemeteries have an interest charge on the purchase price — some do not. It would be wise to investigate what options you have and what terms are offered for the purchase of your cemetery property.

Some cemeteries offer price advantages for undeveloped land. Should the family purchasing lots in an undeveloped garden have the need for making a burial between the time of the purchase and the time the garden is completed, the cemetery will then provide alternative spaces in a developed garden.

If you are contemplating purchase in a privately owned cemetery, it may be well to find out if the cemetery belongs to the National Association of Cemeteries, the American Cemetery Association, or the Pre-Arrangement Interment Association of America. These organizations have very definite codes of ethics, and the NAC and the PIAA have a lot exchange plan whereby a lot owner can exchange lots in participating cemeteries all over the country.

There are, of course, many personal decisions that have to be made in choosing a cemetery.

What questions should you answer before buying?

- What are its rules and regulations *vis à vis* my own religious requirements?
- Do I prefer the monument type of cemetery or the memorial park cemetery with flush lawn markers?
- Do I want a cemetery that is nonsectarian or would I prefer a cemetery specifically devoted to people of my own religious denomination?
- Who owns the cemetery?
- Who manages the cemetery?
- Is there a care fund?
- How much of the purchase price goes into the care fund, and is it stipulated in the purchase agreement?
- Who administers the care fund?
- What are the prices currently being charged in the various cemeteries and which price category do I feel I want to be in?
- Do I care about the esthetics?
  Is it important to be at the top of a hill? Would I like
- the graves located as close as possible to flowers or shrubbery?
- Do I prefer a cemetery that has provision for the interment of cremated remains?
- Are there rules and regulations concerning the placement of flowers and the designated time to visit graves, etc.?
- Is there somebody always in attendance who can help

people find lots or answer questions? This gives the lot owner the opportunity to request improvements should that become necessary.

- Will the cemetery buy the lots back? If so, how much will they give me for them based on my purchase price?
- Can I sell my lots to another person? What are the rules concerning resale?

Are vaults or concrete liners necessary?

Each cemetery has its own rules and regulations and people should know what they are before purchasing. For instance, are vaults or liners required? Many cemeteries require either a vault or a concrete liner for every interment. The vault or concrete liner is placed in the grave and is an underground tomblike receptacle in which the coffin is placed. After the coffin is lowered into the vault or liner, a cover is placed on the top. The reason for this requirement is that it eliminates the problem of sunken graves. After a period of time a coffin will deteriorate in the ground and be compressed by the weight of the earth over it. This is, of course, accompanied by the sinking of the grave area. A vault or a liner will prevent this sinking from taking place. Therefore, the cemeteries can maintain their lawned areas more efficiently without the added expense of filling in unsightly depressions that occur when the casket deteriorates. Since vaults supply a certain amount of protection to the casket, there are many individuals who feel they are desirable whether or not cemeteries require them.

Can a body be moved from one cemetery to another?

Occasionally a family, for personal considerations of their own, will want to know about the details of moving a body from one cemetery to another. The requirements vary with statute from state to state. These arrangements are usually made through a funeral director with the cooperation of the two cemeteries involved. Removals such as this can be made, and one should be very careful to investigate all costs before going ahead with any of the arrangements.

Why an opening charge?

All cemeteries have what is called an "opening charge." This charge is the labor charge for opening and closing the grave, and all other services that are related to the actual interment. This may be paid to the cemetery directly or, very frequently, is billed by the funeral director to the family. The opening charges for a cemetery and what that involves should be a matter of concern to the family. Some of the questions that might be asked in this connection are:

- Are canopies provided? If so, at what additional cost, if any? (Canopies or tents are set up to protect family and friends should the interment take place under adverse weather conditions.)
- Does the cemetery use automatic lowering devices? (Automatic lowering devices are used to lower the casket into the grave slowly and without chance of mishap.)
- Are chairs provided for the immediate family?
  Is there always somebody in attendance from the cemetery to supervise the service to make sure that everything is in order?
  If vaults or liners are required, does the cemetery provide them? If so, at what additional cost?
- Does the cemetery charge for reseeding and resodding of graves?
- Does the cemetery charge in the event their

memorials or markers have to be moved in order to make a burial? If so, how much?

How many spaces should I buy?

This is a decision the family will have to make, based on what they can reasonably project as their need. We live in a highly mobile society and it is not unusual for families to be scattered over the length and breadth of the land. Unless there is a reasonable assurance that all the family will remain in the area, it is my suggestion that buying too many lots is not a wise decision. On the other hand, it is a well-established fact that families prefer, insofar as possible, to be buried together. Frequently people buy too little space and later are sorry when they find space is not available close to the grave of a loved one.

Very recently a young couple in their middle 30s came into my office, intent upon purchasing cemetery property close to the wife's deceased parents. I had sold them two graves when the wife's mother died two years previously. Her father died within the next year and was buried next to his wife. When I told them that we had no available spaces adjacent, or even close by, they became very indignant. I reminded them that at the time we made the initial arrangements, I encouraged them to consider purchasing pre-need spaces for themselves in the same lot. Their answer was that at the time they thought I was capitalizing on their emotional state and trying to oversell them.

Two days after their visit to my office, one of our lot owners dropped by to tell me that his family situation had changed and they no longer felt the need for the eight-space lot that he had purchased twenty years ago. He was anxious to sell two of the eight spaces.

It can readily be seen that I have set up the problem, but it is for the purchaser to supply the solution. As for myself, I have four children ranging from teenage into their early 20s. I have provided for our family protection a twelve-space family lot, two spaces for my wife and myself, and two for each of the children and their future spouses. It is my feeling that should one, or even two, of the children move away, the spaces would still be used by a third generation of our family who probably will be in the area. These spaces may be used for any of my grandchildren, but more importantly, afford my children the added protection of extra spaces should the unfortunate need arise to bury a grandchild.

While I am sure that my own family-protection plan is wise for our situation as far as cemetery planning is concerned, I would hesitate to recommend it to everybody I speak to. I have no doubt that a discussion with an experienced cemeterian, whether he be a clergyman, a sales counselor, or a cemetery manager, will result in the wisest decision possible regarding the number of spaces to be arranged for your family.

Purchasing cemetery property is a personal decision and the amount of spaces purchased must be based on your ability to pay, a reasonable projection of what you think the requirements will be, and your own personal feeling concerning keeping the family together in death.

What if people move away?

In choosing the location of the cemetery *vis à vis* where you live, it is my feeling that this in not an important consideration. There is no guarantee that people will be living in the same community all the time. People move from homes to apartments and from one house to another in the same general area. If a cemetery is in the general vicinity of where you live, I think it is more important that you choose it based on some of the considerations discussed earlier, rather than proximity to your home. A ride to the outskirts of town, or perhaps even a half hour to an hour out of the vicinity, may be well worth it to the family if the cemetery provides the beauty, dignity, and service the family desires.

How should I go about selecting a cemetery? The answer is "carefully." Hopefully, you will do it before the need arises. In any event, investigate the situation and raise the questions that have been discussed here. As in all your other important family decisions, bring your problem to reputable people in the community who have a background of integrity and a record of concern for the public they serve.

13

Choosing a Memorial

How to choose a memorial dealer.

What should a memorial cost?

How to judge differences in quality.

When are flat markers and mausoleums appropriate?

What symbols and inscriptions should be used?

IAN R. WINTERS

When a loved one dies, where do you go for the selection of a memorial? How do you select a dealer? The difference in the qualities of memorials — how to tell them apart? What size should the memorial be and how much should it cost? What about an inscription?

Ian R. Winters is a graduate of the Philadelphia Museum of Art, has served as editorial writer for a government-sponsored Japanese-language monthly, and is now the creative director of the Rock of Ages Corporation in Barre, Vermont.

Choosing a Memorial

Where can memorials be chosen?

Memorial dealers are usually located near a cemetery. Others are located in or near most communities. Your cemetery can give you the name of a reputable dealer or you might look in the yellow pages under "Memorials." Most dealers belong to either the Monument Builders of America or the American Monument Association. Although professional associations, membership alone does not ensure a dealer's reliability — the memorial industry, like any other, has its share of operators, as well as a majority of reputable dealers.

How does one select a dealer?

Your truest indication of quality and value lies in the name of the memorial manufacturer, rather than the name of the dealer. The best of these manufacturers quarry their own granite, produce the finished memorials, including the cutting of the design and lettering, and sell them through franchised dealers. The dealer may sometimes cut the names and inscriptions in the memorial to the same standards as the manufacturer, but his chief responsibility is to properly set the memorial on the plot site.

Reputable and well-established manufacturers guarantee their memorials unconditionally and without time limit to be free from any defects in material and workmanship. Other manufacturers without specific franchised dealers band together into "area associations" and mutually guarantee memorials bearing the association trademark; so even if a specific manufacturer should go out of business, the replacement of a defective memorial is borne by the association.

The best guarantees and the most ironclad, from the consumer's point of view, are the "double protection" guarantees. This means that either the purchaser or the cemetery where the monument is erected can make a claim for repair or replacement, at no cost. *Insist* on this guarantee.

There are few products which carry such complete protection for the consumer, for as long as the manufacturer or guild is in existence. Of course, that's the catch — a fly-by-night memorial manufacturer or dealer can blithely offer all sorts of "perpetual" guarantees — all quite meaningless if he leaves or goes out of business. So: Know the manufacturer.

Your proof of actual guarantee is a *dealer franchise certificate*. Ask to see it, because most memorial dealer franchises are *not* exclusive. A dealer may hold several franchises; he may even buy rough stone and cut his own memorials. Unfortunately, if you assume that all the dealer's monuments are of the high quality implied by the franchise sign, the dealer might "allow" you to buy a poor quality, un-guaranteed memorial that seems to come from a top manufacturer and is offered at a greatly reduced price.

Then you should ask to see the manufacturer's trademark or Guild Seal, which has been sandblasted into the memorial in an unobtrusive place. This seal is mandatory if any claim is to be honored. Further, the dealer should give you a certificate of guarantee issued by the manufacturer regarding the sale of your memorial. However, if the certificate is ever misplaced, don't fret: "double protection" claims will be honored on *any* memorial bearing the sandblasted trademark or seal.

Two words of warning. First, due to the unexclusive franchise system which prevails through most of the memorial industry, manufacturers are not responsible for any fraud or deception practiced by a dealer *except* where the manufacturer's *product* is concerned. Conversely, the dealer is not responsible for any fraud committed by an un-scrupulous manufacturer. Dealers can have their franchises revoked for defrauding you, which ends the manufacturer's involvement in the affair. Scant consolation! Further, losing a franchise does not put a dealer out of business. And your recourse against a fraudulent manufacturer is no easier or speedier (or surer) than any consumer action taken against a manufacturer, say, of a defective auto or washing machine with a weak or deceptive guarantee.

Memorials (even poor ones) are not cheap, and since they are a one-time purchase you owe it to yourself and your family to purchase a fully guaranteed (double protection), reliably manufactured, and reputably sold memorial.

The second warning — no dealer or manufacturer has yet been able to guarantee their product against vandalism, natural disaster, acts of war, or even negligence on the part of the cemetery. If a dealer implies or specifies such a guarantee, run — preferably to your nearest better business bureau, consumer protection agency, or state attorney general.

How does one judge differences in the quality of memorials?

The best memorial stone, in terms of durability, is granite, which like any natural substance is subject to wide latitude in quality. Granites come in black, various shades of gray, pinks, soft reds, and white. Regardless of color, the finest granites are easily distinguished by an absence of any discoloration, seam, crack, or discernible pattern. Put another way, premium granite has a very fine, uniform grain texture and color.

The best memorial manufacturers subject their granite to constant, scrupulous quality checks — a costly and time-consuming process since a flaw is often undiscernible until the final carving or polishing. One premium manufacturer discards over 60 percent of all quarried stone as unsuitable for memorial use — then they reject even more stone due to hidden flaws discovered in manufacturing, or because of carving and workmanship below standards. Ultimately, 80 percent of their stone winds up as mountains of grout (the Scottish word for waste).

In the past, other stones besides granite, such as marble, slate, or sandstone, have been used for memorials, but a visit to a colonial cemetery will quickly reveal how poorly these stones "weather." This is because they are all sedimentary rock, formed by the deposit of various minute mineral particles in water, layer upon layer, and subjected to enormous pressure over long periods of time. But what water hath joined together, water can put asunder. Water and wind erosion ruin exposed sedimentary rocks in a relatively short time.

Granite, on the other hand, is an igneous rock, created from pure minerals in a molten state deep within the earth. Some granite deposits are as old as the earth itself. Only millions of years of sedimentary rock erosion or cataclysmic upthrusting can bring granite near to the surface of the earth. Granite is a combination of three minerals: mica, black and glassy, present even in white granite; quartz, a clear or translucent crystal; and feldspar, an extremely dense and hard mineral which gives the granite its color. The three form a uniquely durable substance.

Obviously, for a granite to have a rich, uniform color, the three minerals must be uniformly minute-sized grains, evenly dispersed. Only the varying *percentages* of these minerals alter the color of granite — the grain and texture must be unvarying.

Poorer granites result when iron ore exists in them, ultimately causing rust stains, or when beds of granite formed at different times melted and intermingled like marble cake, or when the long, delicate cooling process was interrupted and the mineral components separated into uneven masses.

The point behind this is that only the finest granite

can accept fine carving and sandblasting. A quick look at a carved memorial can be quite revealing — if the edges of the inscription lettering are crumbled, or if the carving appears "rounded" or rough, you are looking at an inferior stone.

Of course a fine granite *can* be subjected to inferior carving. In this case, look for cut lines that are of unequal width or depth, curves with flat spots, shaped carving that is shallow and without "depth," poor detail, unpleasing proportions — all danger signs, all reducing the value of even the most premium granite.

While memorials are machine cut to size and machine polished, the actual production of a memorial is still largely a hand craft. Master designs, often specially created for you, are traced onto rubber sheets cemented to the granite. The rubber is hand cut with knives to expose the granite. The memorial is then placed in a booth where an air hose fires a fierce jet of tiny steel shot which bounces off the rubber but cuts into the granite. This is called sandblasting.

It sounds simple, but it isn't. The rubber is thick and resistant, and the granite below dulls cutting knives quickly. Intricate designs, particularly floral motifs, tax the cutter's stamina and skill. Even a simple straight line must be cut twice so that the rubber can be peeled away in an even, parallel strip. Indeed, all outlines must be cut twice.

The sandblaster, while hampered by heavy protective clothing and a helmet like a deep sea diver's, must wield the awkward air hose with ease to ensure uniform depth of his cuttings and avoid "burning" the rubber away, which could ruin the clarity of the cut — while all the time he is being bombarded by thousands of ricochetting steel shot and the screaming noise of compressed air and steel colliding with stone. In order to shape a simple leaf, the sandblaster must first blast the overall form of the leaf — a delicate S-curve. The memorial is removed from the sandblast booth and the rubber shape of the leaf is recemented into place. Then the outline of the leaf and the central vein are cut out of rubber. Once again, into the sandblast booth. The leaf shape, protected by rubber, is again blasted to carve the exposed deep outline and vein. Multiply this by a half-dozen roses, petals, leaves, stems, and a family name, given names, dates — or add hand carving requiring a skilled artisan-sculptor, using a variety of pneumatic chisels and drills, carving from a clay half-size model or his own experience and genius, and you have a complex, demanding, and skillful piece of work. This is why a beautiful granite memorial, exquisitely carved, is expensive.

Polishing granite, like polishing any gem, deepens the color, adds luster, and also exposes flaws. All carving or sandblasting in granite, however, removes the polish. For esthetic reasons, many people now prefer a completely unpolished memorial where the carving and sandblasting blend harmoniously with the whole memorial, the granite having a warm, light, matte appearance. Indicative of how granite men themselves feel about polish versus matte-finished memorials are the cemeteries in the vicinity of Barre, Vermont, where the finest gray granite is quarried: most memorials are matte finished, or "memo" or "axed," as the surface is variously termed in the area. There has been the belief that polishing granite seals the surface against moisture and other climatic rigors. This is true only when the granite is a lower quality, porous stone.

Quality granite is the most moisture resistant, and the extremes of climate have little or no effect on matte-finished granite. To be sure, rain will darken the stone as it fills the surface pores, but the granite dries quickly and uniformly to its original color. The one drawback to a matte finish is its susceptibility to organic stains present in soil or carried by polluted air. Yet these stains are generally easily removed from premium granite. On the other hand, the chief drawbacks to polished stone are its reflective properties: seen at a short distance, the mirror-smooth surface will reflect sky, grass or you, when light conditions are right; but then, that is really a matter of esthetics: some people simply enjoy a smooth, polished surface; others like the soft texture of velvet.

How long will granite last?

There are Egyptian granite carvings that show little or no wear after 5,000 years. In the harsher climate of Northern Europe, granite used in the construction of Gothic edifices is still untouched by time after 1,000 years. But then you can also find granite only a century old that has chipped, cracked or flaked, stained or discolored. Here, as in everything else, quality is the determining factor. By quality, of course, we mean the knowledge, experience, and skill of the quarrier/manufacturer, combined with ethics and honesty. Add to all this an ironclad guarantee, and you can be assured that your memorial will last indefinitely barring unpreventable disaster.

How much will a memorial cost?

Prices of memorials seem to fluctuate wildly from dealer to dealer, yet, given the criteria for judgment detailed earlier, it is actually quality which varies — and price only reflects quality. In general, it is wiser to buy a smaller, better-quality memorial than a big, cheaper one.

Of course, the type and amount of carving and sandblasting you want will influence the cost of a memorial, as will size, color of granite, and shipping costs. A fact that is easily overlooked by the average consumer is the cubic weight of granite. For instance, a standard memorial measuring 3' x 8" x 2' with a base measuring 4' x 1'2" x 8" contains 7.15 cubic feet of granite, which weighs 1,285 pounds. Increase the memorial 6" in width and 2" in height, enlarging the base proportionally, and an additional 1.47 cubic feet have been added to memorial and base. This means that the whole memorial weighs 265 additional pounds.

Some recent costs of memorials by reputable manufacturers range from $400 and up for flat, flush-to-the-ground markers and $590 and up for an upright family memorial. This does not include installation. Of course, it is that "and up" which really counts. Large, complex memorials can cost several thousand dollars. However, of all the expenses involved in a funeral and interment, the memorial is the only one which remains visible — permanently visible — over the years.

What size memorial is appropriate?

Practically every cemetery has restrictions on the size of memorials. These are dictated by the lot size, and a height-to-width ratio is usually established. Unfortunately, there is little uniformity nationwide. However, your memorial dealer or the cemetery management can inform you of size limitations, as well as any other restrictions. Such restrictions usually exist to protect and preserve the appearance of the cemetery, and facilitate perpetual care, while preventing bad taste from detracting from the mood of the cemetery.

Whether a memorial is a flush-to-the-ground (or "crypt top"), a slant, or a family upright, a memorial dealer can be relied upon to give the best proportioned shape to meet cemetery restrictions. The upright memorial can be designed in several ways — narrow and tall, low and wide, curved concavely or convexly, and with a variety of curved tops or sides. Within the limits of outside dimensions, there are round memorials, diamond-shaped ones, and even memorials that are rhomboidal or trapezoidal instead of the conventional rectangular shape.

There is also a whole category of special memorials which require the purchase of several burial lots in order to provide ample space for them. The family mausoleum is the most familiar of this category, providing from one to eight crypt spaces. Family mausoleums range in style from the purely classical to modern. The colonnade, or the smaller balustrade, consists of two, four, or more columns set on a base and, possibly, topped with a capstone. The sarcophagus is an elaborate aboveground crypt, while the exedra is an alcove, or wall with a bench attached, often set off by a fountain and flowers or shrubs. Then there are unique memorials such as a bench, a sundial, a fountain, or a statue. Such memorials are quite appropriate in the case of cremation or when interment is not possible — of course, a memorial can mark a memory as well as a grave.

What is appropriate for children's graves?

Children buried in special children's sections of cemeteries are usually memorialized by small flush-to-the-ground markers or slanted markers. Still, there is no reason why a child cannot be interred in a family plot and commemorated in the usual manner.

When does one erect a memorial?

Aside from specific religous practice, there are no hard and fast rules about when to erect a memorial. The spring, particularly around Memorial Day, has proved a popular time.

What about flat markers? Mausoleums?

Flat markers are the only memorials allowed in memorial parks; either in granite or bronze or the two combined. They are generally less expensive than upright memorials — also less obtrusive. Bronze markers have the disadvantages of tarnish and discoloration which can only be retarded, but never stopped, by protective coatings, and the number of designs available are few indeed. Flat granite markers can easily trap dirt or grass clippings in the sandblast carving, and require careful maintenance. The chief advantage to flat markers, low cost aside, is in their appeal to park owners. Maintenance costs are low since lawn mowers can be driven back and forth over the markers, cutting work time to a minimum. Also, some people find some appeal in the relative anonymity and conformity of flat markers and memorial parks.

The family mausoleum, as previously discussed, can hold from one to eight caskets — some are even larger. Even with the advent of predesigned and precut mausoleums ready for assembly, the family mausoleum is an expensive proposition. Yet the cost of construction has to be balanced against the cost of six or eight separate interments. The family mausoleum is the logical extension of the family plot and the cost can be apportioned in the same way.

Often in the past, family mausoleums have been built of marble, but the already mentioned weaknesses of marble have resulted in marble being prohibited as an exterior building material by most cemeteries in the U.S. and Canada.

The leading granite manufacturers provide free design service for proposed mausoleums or other unique memorials. All of them maintain libraries of designs created over the years which can be modified to suit individual tastes.

Are inscriptions appropriate?

As recently as the last century, inscriptions ranging from the ridiculous to the sublime were quite common on memorials. One old cemetery had a restriction against "advertising on tombstones," which gives you an idea of what extremes have been resorted to. Other epitaphs, in prose or poetry, are quite touching and beautiful. Perhaps the decline of the epitaph as an art form is due in part to our declining sentimentality; perhaps it's just a matter of economics — memorial lettering costs money. Still, there is no real reason why you cannot have an epitaph more personal and less banal than "together forever" or "in God's care." The Psalms, for instance, provide ample material.

What symbols are appropriate?

Over the centuries, an elaborate and vast symbology has developed in our culture based on elements as diverse as ancient Egypt and the near East, Greece, Rome, Scandinavia, Central Europe, Byzantium, and the Orient. Many plants and animals—common or rare—have some assigned characteristic relating to human emotion or experience. All of these have been represented in natural form or stylized in as many ways as there have been human cultures, and the process of modification and redesign goes on. Then there are the "pure" symbols, such as the cross in all its multiplicity of form, the Star of David, or the 5,000-year-old Egyptian "Ankh" symbol of life, recently revived. Heraldic crests and coats-of-arms, professional or organizational symbols, such as the doctor's caduceus or the Masonic emblem, further enrich our symbology.

Symbols have had and will no doubt continue to have a deep influence on memorial art. Presently, flowers and religous symbols, generally represented realistically, are the most popular. Still, unique and elegantly designed symbols often find their way into memorial art, which is all to the good. Perhaps what we say at the end should have been said at the beginning: a memorial in its truest and best sense is a permanent statement that an individual, unique in all of history, once came this way, to leave some sort of imprint on this world; and then returned to that unknowable and unknown place from which life came.

SUGGESTED READINGS

Beable, William H., *Epitaphs: Graveyard Humor and Eulogy* (New York: Thomas Y. Crowell, 1925).

Bliss, Harry A., *Modern Tablets and Sarcophogi* (Buffalo: H. A. Bliss, 1923).

Brindly, William, and Samuel Weatherly, *Ancient Sepulchral Monuments* (London: Brooks, Day, and Son, 1937).

Deacy, William H., *Memorials Today for Tommorow* (Tate, Georgia: Georgia Marble Co., 1928).

Laas, William, *Monuments In Your History* (New York: Popular Library, 1972).

14

To Cremate or Not

What is the process of cremation?

Whom to call for cremation.

Is cremation always cheaper than burial?

How widespread is the practice of cremation?

What are the psychological advantages and disadvantages?

PAUL IRION

Archeological evidence points to the origin of cremation during the Stone Age in Eastern Europe or the Near East. In England, the current percentage of cremations is 57; in the United States, less than 5 percent of the total number of deaths annually. As a mode of bodily disposition, is cremation cheaper than burial? What are the psychological advantages and disadvantages? How about the religious and legal questions?

The Reverend Paul Irion authored *Cremation* in 1968 with the hope that the volume would foster a more favorable climate in which individuals and families would have a freer choice in their selection of funeral practices. As professor of pastoral theology at Lancaster (Pennsylvania) Theological Seminary since 1959, Mr. Irion has written extensively in the pastoral psychology field, especially in relation to ministry to the bereaved. His books include: *The Funeral: Vestige or Value?*, *The Funeral and Mourners*, and *A Manual and Guide for Those Who Conduct a Humanist Funeral*.

To Cremate or Not

Novel and unfamiliar customs readily raise quesions. Cremation has not been widely practiced in many parts of America, so openminded individuals often pose questions about the psychological, the religious, the economic, the practical implications of this practice.

What is cremation?

It is a mode of disposition in which the body of one who has died is quickly reduced by intense heat to its component elements. It is one of the means in our society by which the body of someone who has died is separated from the community of the living. In this sense it is an alternative to burial in the earth or in a mausoleum.

What is the process?

The body of the deceased is taken to the crematory in a casket or other suitable container. Here, usually in a chapel setting, the casket is placed into the crematory, much as if it were being rolled into a mausoleum crypt.

The crematory is a specially designed furnace, fired by oil, gas, or electricity. It is capable of creating extremely high temperatures and is designed so that all smoke and gases are recirculated through heat chambers so that there is very little discharge into a chimney.

In an hour or two the body and the casket are reduced to several pounds of ashes. The lighter ash from a wooden casket has largely been broken down by the heat, so that the residue is largely the ashes from the bony structure of the body. When a metal casket has been selected, the cremation takes place within the casket. After the ashes of the body are removed, the casket is suitably disposed of.

Each body is cremated separately and the ashes removed from the cremator before the next cremation. Crematories are scrupulously careful with identification. In some countries, especially in England, ashes are routinely pulverized by machine into a fine powder. In the United States such pulverization is less common, but if the ashes are to be scattered, the few remaining larger pieces of calcified bone are easily crushed. The ashes are then disposed of according to the wishes of the family.

What disposition is made of the ashes?

There are several options available to the family. Inurnment — placing the ashes in a small metallic or stone container — is fairly common. This urn is then usually placed in a niche which is purchased, much as a grave is purchased, in a columbarium. Very often there are columbariums in connection with the crematory. These facilities range from the simple to the elaborate. There are usually perpetual care agreements in force and certain regulations about the placing of memorial flowers at the niche.

A second option involves placing the ashes in the simple cannister in which they are delivered from the crematory into an earth grave. Some burials of ashes take place in family plots in regular cemeteries; others are in special burial plots which are available in connection with some crematories. This burial of the ashes usually takes place several days following the cremation.

The third option is strewing or scattering the ashes. This requires some pulverization. The ashes are then distributed on the surface of the ground or into a flowing stream or ocean. In England the crematories are surrounded by lovely gardens in which the ashes are strewn. Most crematories in the United States would be willing to scatter the ashes on their grounds. Other families may wish to strew the ashes in some place of particular sentimental attachment. A few states in the far west have legal prohibitions against scattering the ashes in any places other than those specifically designated for that purpose, so families should check the legality of their proposals before carrying out their intentions.

When the ashes are strewn, some focused memorialization is often desired. With this practice, there is no particular place to which a family turns as the final resting place of the body of the deceased. Sometimes memorial plaques are used to indicate the general location of the ashes. Sometimes a tree or shrub is dedicated to the memory of the deceased as a tangible memorial. Some crematories have Books of Remembrance in which the names of the deceased are suitably inscribed and displayed.

Sometimes a final committal service is held with the family when the ashes are finally disposed of by any of these modes. This is helpful because the family thus completes the process of separation.

How does one locate a crematory? What facilities are available?

The funeral director who serves your family can tell

you the location of crematories. In nonurban areas it may be necessary to go to a large city for cremation.

In the United States most crematories are owned and operated by private corporations or individuals, unlike England where they are most commonly operated by municipal authorities. Here some are operated also by cemetery managements and by funeral directors.

Usually the crematory will offer three facilities: a chapel where funeral service and/or committal services may be conducted, the cremating equipment, and a columbarium for the preservation of the ashes or a garden in which they may be buried or strewn.

Whom does one call if he wishes to have a deceased person cremated?

In the division of labor operative in our society the funeral director normally has the responsibility for caring for the bodies of the dead and making the necessary funeral arrangements. Since cremation is one of the options in such arrangements, the funeral director will provide information, make the necessary contacts, and carry out the funeral and cremation.

Is cremation relatively new?

Cremation is a very old custom reinstituted in Western culture during the last century. There is archeological evidence that cremation was widely practiced since prehistoric times. It was generally practiced among the upper social classes in ancient Greece and Rome.

The Judeo-Christian tradition, which has had a major impact on Western culture, generally favored earth burial. When the early Christian church was under persecution, the Roman authorities often cremated the bodies of the martyrs as a way of precluding, according to their literal understanding, their victims' resurrection from the dead. So cremation came to connote paganism. For nearly fifteen centuries in Western culture cremation was used only in emergency situations: plague, massive battlefield casualties, natural disasters. In other sections of the world, particularly in the East, cremation has continuously been widely employed.

In the second half of the nineteenth century, in various countries in western Europe, the modern cremation movement began. In part this new interest in cremation grew out of improved technology that made possible design for a cremating furnace which could incinerate a body quickly and completely and without noxious by-products. But the new cremation movement was literally a movement because it also had an ideological base, a base which varied from place to place. In Italy, where the movement had its birth in 1872, there was an antiecclesiastical and anticlerical disposition among the proponents of cremation. Some of them were Freemasons who were reacting to the monopoly which the Church exercised over Italian burial places. But a far larger group of people became advocates of cremation because of concerns for public health. It was not coincidence that many of the strongest voices favoring cremation at this time were physicians. In England, particularly, the practice of mass graves created serious pollution problems and the scarcity of land caused popular opposition to devoting large tracts for cemeteries.

The practice of cremation has only very slowly replaced the customary earth burial of most Western societies. Only since World War II has there been a rapid acceleration in the number of cremations each year, particularly in nations of high population density, such as England and Japan.

How extensive is the practice of cremation today?

The latest statistics compiled by the International Cremation Federation (1971) indicate that Japan has the largest number of cremations. Seventy-five percent of the people who die in Japan each year are cremated. In England the percentage of cremations is 57 percent. Sweden, Denmark, Switzerland, and Czechoslovakia also use cremation widely.

In the United States the percentage is much smaller, under 5 percent, although the actual number of cremations has grown slowly through the years. In 1971 there were 92,-251 cremations in the United States. The largest number of these take place on the West Coast, in Florida, and in large metropolitan areas. This would indicate that cremation gains in popularity in areas where population density increases drastically or where large numbers of people die far away from their family home towns.

Is cremation cheaper than burial?

Cost depends very much on the way in which cremation is used. In terms of the actual process itself, cremation involves roughly the same costs as burial. Although the price of cremation is established locally by the operator of the crematory, in many communities it would be about the equivalent of the cost of opening a grave at the cemetery, assuming the family already owned a burial plot.

All other costs would depend upon the arrangements made by each family. Whether these costs were higher or lower than average would depend not on whether the body was cremated or buried but on the family's overall plans for the funeral.

What are the economic implications in cremation?

Costs are related to the way cremation is utilized.

There are several alternative patterns. If economic considerations are the only basis on which one decides what will be done after death, cremation can be made relatively cheap. This is normally called simple disposition. The funeral director takes the body of the deceased; with no preparation the body is placed in a simple wooden box, taken to the cremator, cremated, and the ashes are disposed of by the crematory with no ritual of any kind. It is impossible to estimate the actual dollar cost because it would vary from city to city, but this type of simple disposition would be the most economical arrangement in almost any locale.

A second pattern in which cremation may be used is commonly called the memorial service. In this case the body is usually cremated soon after death. At a later date a public service is held in which the deceased is remembered and family and friends have the opportunity to express their response to that loss. If there are lower costs in this arrangement, it is due to the decision of the family to minimize preparation of the body and to select a casket of minimal cost.

Yet another pattern employs cremation as an alternative to burial, with all other funeral customs carried out as normally observed in the community. The only important variation is that instead of going to the cemetery for burial, the family goes with the body to the crematory for committal and their ultimate separation from the body. In this kind of arrangement the cost is roughly the same as regular funeral costs, if one assumes that a grave plot is already owned by the family or that there will not be extensive columbarium expense.

It should be pointed out, however, that shaping the pattern of marking the ending of a life solely on economic grounds may result in the exchange of low cost for a number of psychological and social values which are more available in some patterns than others. Many mourners are helped by having the opportunity to reinforce the reality of their loss by viewing the body of the person who has died. They are supported by a structured pattern in which with family and friends they can dramatize their loss. They are not helped if they are guided by a desire to avoid facing up to the fact of death, including their own mortality, by minimizing opportunities for reflection upon the relationship of life and death, by getting the deceased out of sight and out of mind as quickly as possible.

Granted that the economic aspect of funerals and alternate practices should not be ignored, one must raise the question of value. The essential question in any transaction is: Is sufficient value received to justify the cost one pays? Within the limits of our means we are usually willing to pay for what we feel is of value to us. Thus it may be unwise economic judgment to lose important values by keeping costs as low as possible without regard for those values.

What are the psychological advantages of cremation?

If cremation is not being employed to circumvent the pain of the mourning process by trying very quickly to get the body of the deceased out of sight and mind, it can have some helpful psychological benefits. Cremation can facilitate the psychological process of mourning by which one recovers from significant loss. A crucial element in this process involves coming to the realization, both intellectually and emotionally, that the relationship which one has had with the deceased has now ended and that life must go on without the presence of the deceased. Cremation very effectively symbolizes this finality. The dissolution of the body which has been the medium of that relationship helps in the understanding that the relationship does not continue as it has been experienced. Mourners are assisted by this realization in the process of adjusting or reorienting their lives without the presence of the person who has died.

For others there is a psychological advantage that is seen largely in esthetic terms. They prefer to think of the quick, clean incineration of the body rather than of the slow process of decomposition which follows burial. Some like to think of the way in which the body is quickly broken down into its chemical components and then mixed with the elements of the earth, symbolizing oneness with nature.

Are there also psychological disadvantages to cremation?

It is quite possible that for some people the choice of cremation would be psychologically counterproductive. The way in which it is possible to employ cremation as a supposedly quick way out of the grief process has already been mentioned. When this is done, it can result in a delayed grief reaction or confirmed patterns of neurotic escapism. Mourners who are seeking to avoid facing death and the pain of loss by getting rid of the body quickly often work to their own disadvantage.

The person who has a strong feeling against being cremated himself may well have psychological reservations about having a loved one cremated. Only if a mourner would be willing to be cremated (whether he actually plans to be cremated or not), should he arrange the cremation of another. If there is any personal reluctance of this sort, the bereaved would be well advised not to have the body of a loved one cremated. By the same token a person who wishes to be cremated when he dies should always permit his closest survivors to change that plan if they have deep personal reservations about being cremated.

It should also be recognized that where there has been a strong negative relationship between the deceased and the mourners cremation may create additional problems. For example, where there has been hostility, mourners may actually come to interpret their participation, even passive participation, in the obvious destruction of the body of the deceased as a symbolic acting out of their negative feeling.

In looking at both the psychological advantages and disadvantages of cremation, then, it becomes apparent that individuals and families should think very seriously of the symbolic meanings cremation may have for them before making the final decision.

What are the religious or theological considerations involved in cremation?

Various religious groups view cremation in different ways. In a limited space all of the variations cannot be discussed, so we can deal only in general terms, limiting discussion to the Judeo-Christian traditions.

Ancient Judaism practiced earth burial and used cremation only in exceptional circumstances. There is no biblical prohibition against cremation but it clearly was not regular practice. In Old Testament times cremation was used only to dispose of large numbers of bodies after battles or catastrophe and to burn the bodies of executed criminals.

The three modern branches of Judaism have somewhat differing views. The Orthodox tradition is most explicit in its opposition to cremation, basing it upon ancient scriptural precedent and talmudic teaching. In general this resistance is shared by Conservative Jewish congregations. Reform Judaism does not necessarily regard burial as normative practice and has no opposition to cremation.

The early Christian church followed the traditional Jewish practice of earth burial. Cremation, which had been widely used in Graeco-Roman culture, came to be defined as a pagan custom. This position was further strengthened, as we have mentioned, when in the Roman persecution the bodies of the martyrs were burned by the authorities in the belief that they would thus deny the Christians resurrection. So historically Christianity did not practice cremation, although its opposition was not based on theological teaching.

This position has continued until very recently in Roman Catholic practice. When the modern cremation movement began in Italy in the 1870s, its early advocates were fighting against the Church's monopoly on burial arrangement. This caused the Church to see cremation not merely as a nontraditional practice, but also as an act of rebellion against its authority. So canon laws were enacted which forbade cremation and any cooperation with the practice under pain of excommunication. The Church repeatedly pointed out that its objection was not theological opposition but was a matter of church discipline.

The Second Vatican Council, recognizing that cremation was being widely employed in some countries like Japan and England, authorized priests to participate in cremation services when requested to do so. The Church now permits cremation, although it still points out that burial is the preferred practice.

Many Protestant denominations are totally permissive on this point, acknowledging either burial or cremation according to the wishes to the mourners. Only extremely conservative Protestant groups resist cremation, usually on the basis of a very literal interpretation of the resurrection of the body or because of the lack of scriptural precedent.

This objection is not unlike that made during the last century when many voices were raised in the Church of England against cremation because destruction of the body by fire was thought to deny hope for the resurrection. To this Lord Shaftesbury responded, "What would in such a case become of the blessed martyrs?"

Are there legal issues involved in cremation?

Since the early days of modern cremation there has been the concern that this practice might be used to cover up foul play. Because of the total dissolution of the body there is no possibility of investigating suspected causes of death, as would be the case with exhumation following burial. So in all countries there are carefully established procedures which must be followed to secure certification of death and approval for cremation. If an inquest is required or if there is any serious question about the cause of death, cremation cannot take place until the authorities are satisfied that the circumstances of the death are clearly known.

Another kind of legal issue emerged in the efforts of some persons to assure that they would be cremated following death. Some of the early advocates of cremation felt that their families were unsympathetic with their wishes and therefore arranged their wills so that all inheritance was contingent upon the carrying out of their wishes. Such practice, which fortunately has become less common as cremation advocacy became more practical and less ideological, is psychologically undesirable. Funeral practices should always center upon the needs of the bereaved rather than becoming avenues for imposing arbitrary decisions of the deceased.

Under common law the body of the deceased is regarded as being in the control of the next of kin. If one assumes close emotional attachment, there is psychological value in this as well, because the body has played a part in the relationship, and the way in which mourners separate from the body is important. Thus the mourners' wishes are of primary significance.

What are helpful bases for making the decision

252 / Concerning Death

to be cremated or to have the body of a loved one cremated?

Simply put, the following are the conditions that should be met before the decision to cremate is made: One should be sufficiently secure to be willing to follow practices that may not have total acceptance in the community, to innovate.

One should be convinced of the necessity for facing the reality of death and loss and be alert to tempting easy ways of avoidance and escape.

One should not feel the need of a tangible focus for remembering the deceased.

One should be willing to be cremated himself, although it is not essential that he actually plan to do so.

One should freely acknowledge that the relationship with the deceased has ended as it has been known, and that life must go on without the presence of the deceased.

SUGGESTED READINGS

Cremation in Great Britain, revised edition. The Cremation Society, 47 Nottingham Place, London W1M 4BH, England.

Irion, Paul, *Cremation* (Philadelphia: Fortress Press, 1968).

Polson, C. J., R. P. Brittain, and T. K. Marshall, *The Disposal of the Dead* (New York: Philosophical Library, 1953).

15

Organ Donation and Transplantation

What is transplantation and what is a donor?

Is there an urgent need for organ donors?

Medically, how is the organ transfer accomplished?

How does an organ donor legally grant permission?

Does transplantation eliminate the funeral?

BENJAMIN A. BARNES

One of the most remarkable advances in medicine today is the development of methods to transfer a healthy organ from one individual to another. It is no longer uncommon to hear of the kidney, liver, heart, cornea of the eye, and even skin being transplanted in order to bring sick people back to health. How great is this need for organ transplantation? What is the rate of success? In what ways are the living donors selected? How to give permission for an organ donation?

Dr. Benjamin A. Barnes is secretary of the Interhospital Organ Bank Committee, which serves as a regional clearinghouse for procurement, preservation, and distribution of tissues and organs for transplantation. Dr. Barnes is a surgeon at the Massachusetts General Hospital, assistant clinical professor of surgery at Harvard Medical School, and a frequent contributor to medical journals.

Organ Donation and Transplantation

In this chapter we consider some of the most urgent and pressing issues that may confront a family at the time of death. This confrontation is the consequence of today's medical knowledge, providing a unique opportunity to help others in need, and of the moral imperative urging such action. The act of donating an organ from a living donor may be reviewed deliberately and occur after reflection on the part of the donor. Contrariwise, giving permission for an organ donation from an incapacitated dying member of the family is an urgent decision and is inevitably associated with all the emotions understandably present at the time of a death.

At such times do medical knowledge and moral imperatives seem less relevant or at least less obvious? Of course this is true; but knowledge in advance about organ donations and transplantations may provide an understanding and broader perspective that is needed by everyone meeting a death to avoid the possibly destructive consequences of fear and indecision at the moment when an organ donation for transplantation could be arranged. What are the basic concepts?

What is a transplantation and what is a donor?

A transplantation in medicine today refers to a transfer of an organ such as skin or a kidney from one person, called the *donor*, to a second person, called the *patient*. The patient is suffering from some illness involving the function of a vital organ requiring replacement by transplantation. Severe thermal burns destroy skin, which needs replacement in restoring health. Longstanding kidney infections destroy kidney function, which needs to be replaced to return a patient to normal health. Inflammation of the eye may destroy the transparency of the lens system, which needs replacement to permit restoration of sight.

The donor obviously plays a key role in transplantation, and where an organ may be spared without permanent loss of health to any significant degree the donor may be alive. Such is often the case when a parent or brother or sister gives one of two healthy kidneys to a member of his or her family with fatal kidney disease. The transplantation of skin from a healthy member of a family to a severely burned member is another example where a living person can donate the expendable outer layers of skin to help someone survive a severe and extensive burn. The outer layers rapidly re-form in the donor.

However, extraordinary as it may seem, a donor need not be alive. Where organs are transplanted that are essential for life such as the heart, liver, or lungs, it would be impossible to use a living donor. Such organs must be removed promptly after death in good condition if they are to be transplanted at all. With skin and kidneys, although living donors are entirely possible as noted above, the nonliving donor is also an important source. Indeed for those patients without a family donor the nonliving donor is the only source for a transplantation that could be the only means for the restoration of their health and for the rejuvenation of the quality of their lives.

Transplantation is a broad term and covers three major activities:

- Selection and preparation of a patient for an organ replacement by transplantation because of some organ disease leading inevitably to death because of impaired function.
- Selection and preparation of a donor for giving the appropriate organ.
- Transfer of the organ from donor to patient, which requires a standard, sterile operation in a hospital completed by a team of surgeons, anesthetists, and nurses.

Has medical science advanced to the stage where physicians can successfully transfer a healthy organ from one individual to another?

This is a fundamental question and can be answered, astonishing as it may seem, by an unqualified "Yes." It may not seem so astonishing, however, if it is realized that extensive experimental work has preceded any attempts to apply transplantation to the treatment of disease in man.

In the pre-Christian era, writings from Egypt, India, and Syria stated clearly the use of skin transplants, but these were always limited to transfer from one part of a patient's body to another and were not between individuals. The experimental evidence for transplantation was largely developed in studies on the growth of transplanted tumors in mice fifty years ago. Another advance was made in the 1940s when the British investigator Sir Peter Medawar studied exhaustively skin grafting in rabbits and mice. He established rules for the growth of transplants of normal organs between individuals and defined methods for promoting successful function of the transplant by the use of various treatments. Ultimately the fundamental importance of his work was acknowledged when he received the Nobel Prize.

Finally, in Boston, Massachusetts, where most of the early contributions to transplantation were made in its application to man, a large number of kidney transplants were carried out in dogs whereby knowledge and confidence were gained that could justify the treatment of disease in man by essentially similar techniques.

So success today is a fact, and it is in large part due to intensive animal experimentation in a twenty-year period before the first successful kidney transplantation in Boston in 1954.

What organs can be transplanted?

Patients have benefited from many different kinds of organ transplantations. The most numerous and successful are kidney transplants, of which over 10,000 have been done in the entire world, to date. They are of great significance since these transplants are the oldest reported and have provided a model in many ways for subsequent organ transplants. The earliest kidney transplants are still functioning after twenty years.

Skin is the second most common, with over 5,000 transplants. Many of these transplants were done under circumstances where the use of the skin was life-saving, but did not necessarily lead to a permanent skin transplant as with the kidneys.

Third, 200 heart transplants have been completed, using in every case a deceased donor. However, the results have been satisfactory in only one or two specialized centers, but with considerable promise for the future. A comparable number of liver transplants have also been done. Other organs including bone marrow, pancreas, and lung have been so infrequently performed that it is too early to define exactly their role in the treatment of disease. The beginnings are very promising, and today the question is no longer, "Can we?" but rather, "When do we?"

The outer lens or cornea of the eye has been replaced in over 10,000 patients with an unusual degree of success since parts of the eye are far more easily transplanted than other organs. The earliest corneal transplants were done almost one hundred years ago before all the complexities of transplantation were appreciated, but fortunately the special site — the eye — permitted an unusual degree of success with the restoration of vision for many people otherwise confined to the life of the blind.

Is there an urgent need for organ donors?

There *is* an urgent need for organ donors, since at the present time several thousand individuals treated in the United States alone are waiting for a kidney from a cadaveric donor and hundreds of individuals needing a corneal graft to restore their eyesight are likewise waiting. Skin transplants are in great demand for treating burned individuals who have had large areas of their skin destroyed. Such skin is most helpful in the care of children where the use of skin transplants is recognized as life-saving therapy. The urgent need for all organs is greatly *under*appreciated by the public.

How is a living donor selected?

A living donor in a sense selects himself, having been

convinced that a donation is something that he wishes to do to fulfill his own conscience or ethical standards for helping others. However, more than the donor's interests must be considered since organs can only be accepted from healthy individuals and must be obtained from donors that are *compatible* with the patient to receive the transplant. *Compatibility* for organs is very similar to compatibility for blood transfusions, and just as there are individual blood groups that control the proper selection of a donor for a patient to receive a blood transfusion, there are also similar considerations in transplantation.

Living donors may be selected for kidney transplants since the removal of one of two healthy kidneys results in no impairment of the donor's health, and indeed some individuals are born with just one kidney and are never aware of this fact. However, the advantages of obtaining a kidney from a living donor are limited to a patient within the family of the donor. Therefore, donations of organs from living individuals are restricted to their helping members of their immediate family. The donor being a blood relative as close as a parent or brother or sister favors the successful function of the transplanted organ.

When are donations of organs from people after death used?

If a donor and a patient are not in the same family, equally good success in function may be obtained from an organ removed from an unrelated donor immediately after death. Such donations are used when a patient requiring an organ transplant does not have a medically qualified or willing related donor. Also organs essential to life (heart and liver) and not present in pairs (kidneys) are obtained from nonliving donors. Organs procured from a donor immediately after death (a cadaveric donor) function just as well as those from a living donor unrelated to the patient.

How is the transfer of an organ accomplished from donor to patient?

The transfer of an organ is a remarkable consequence of modern immunology and surgery. In a surgical operation the organ is removed from the donor and placed in the patient. The major artery and vein supplying and draining the organ are connected to the patient's blood vessels. In the procedure precautions are taken by a team of surgeons and nurses to avoid infection, just the way they are for any other surgical procedure. The postoperative course of such patients is unusual in that they are given special medicines which reduce the tendency of the patient's system to react against the new organ until he becomes adjusted to it. These medicines are potent and are used in large doses during the first few weeks following transplantation. During this time patients must be in a hospital for close observation, although after four to eight weeks they are discharged on much lower doses of these drugs to start their new life.

How many medical centers are there in the United States engaged in transplantation?

At the present time there are approximately 120 medical centers engaged in major transplantation programs in the United States.

What is the record of success with kidney transplantation?

A standard way to answer this is to give the percentage of kidneys functioning at one and two years after transplantation.

KIDNEY FUNCTION

Donor Group	Percent Functioning for at Least 1 Year after Operation	2 Years after Operation
Identical twin	100%	100%
Brother or sister	80	75
Parent	70	68
Cadaver	50	45

These figures for function of the kidney are lower than patient survival because when a transplant fails the patient generally resumes treatments with the artificial kidney and awaits a second transplant. Equally important as transplant survival is that 60 to 90 percent, depending on donor group, of the patients with a functioning transplant have been fully restored to normal, active lives after years of contending with the incapacities of chronic kidney failure. Many patients are alive and well fifteen to twenty years after receiving a kidney transplant.

What is the Interhospital Organ Bank?

In response to the need for a central agency to serve the interests of both patient and donor, the Interhospital Organ Bank was incorporated in 1968 through the collaboration of transplantation centers in New England. The bank promotes the procurement, preservation, and distribution of tissues and organs for transplantation principally in the six New England states and eastern United States. The matching of a donor to a patient by special tests is known to increase the likelihood of success of the transplant, and the performance of these tests and their interpretation at any time on a 24-hour service coverage are the responsibility of the bank. On the basis of this information the proper patient is identified for a particular organ that might become available at any moment, day or night, due to an unexpected death.

How does one give permission for an organ donation from oneself at the time of death?

Such permission must be available for reference by attending physicians in the event of an accident or medical emergency that could make it impossible for one to volunteer the needed permission. A serious automobile accident or spontaneous brain hemorrhage could lead to unconsciousness and death in a hospital; therefore, many persons carry in their wallet at all times a standard, well-known permission card. These are obtained from many agencies in your community such as the Kidney Foundation or the National Kidney Foundation. Write and request the donation form. Additional questions about donation will be answered, and a small card will be issued, which you can carry in your wallet. This card identifies the bearer as a willing, potential donor for organs, and instructs medical personnel caring for you, should you become incapacitated in an emergency, to designate you as a donor of organs for transplantation in the event of your death. The state of death is, of course, only determined by the patient's physician without any regard to the possibilities of transplantation. This is the simplest procedure for organ-donation permission when an individual is in good health and wishes to assign his organs after death for transplantation to benefit others. Such an assignment need not be repeated in one's will and has the significant advantage of being immediately available for reference in a hospital at the moment decisions critical for a successful donation must be made.

How does one give permission for an organ

*donation by an incapacitated relative in the event
of his or her death?*

Many families consider the arrangements for an
organ donation in the event of death of a relative suffering
from an incapacitating and fatal illness. Such a donation
may be desirable because of known opinions held by the
relative in regard to helping others. In addition it may be a
particularly appropriate expression of the generous and
charitable character of the relative. It is possible for families
in advance of death to give permission for an organ donation
should death occur. Distressing as it may be, it is necessary to
discuss these possible arrangements in advance of death to
ensure a successful transplantation because of the time needed to prepare a patient to receive the organ promptly. It has
been observed repeatedly that, in the sad and tragic circumstances where an unexpected emergency and illness have
led to an untimely death, families derive great consolation
and comfort from the act of donation thus making a
transplantation possible. They are permitting a donation that
at once helps another patient to return to good health and
symbolizes in one magnanimous act values firmly upheld by
their relative during life.

*Is there a conflict between organ donation and
one's religious faith?*

Virtually all religions in the United States have no
restrictions in regard to the donation of organs to help
another patient regain his health. Clergymen of all
denominations are ready and willing to advise and assist
families in understanding these matters. Their experience
and sympathetic views have been most helpful. Often, where
religious scruples appear to be in conflict, careful review of
the principles involved by a member of the clergy will reveal
a misunderstanding.

Does the removal or an organ from a cadaver limit the funeral arrangements?

The removal of an organ for transplantation in no way modifies the funeral arrangements. It is similar to a post-mortem examination except that the removal of the organ is carried out in an operating room by a team of surgeons and nurses for transplantation to the patient. Following removal of the organ a brief post-mortem examination is carried out since it is important to be certain that no disease is unwittingly transmitted with the organ to the patient as might occasionally occur if a post-mortem examination was not done. No additional expenses are incurred by the family or estate of the donor.

The answers presented to these questions commonly asked concerning donations of organs and transplantation provide facts. Yet knowledge of these facts, or of their fuller review by a clergyman or a physician, will not alone lead to decisions. Moral and ethical considerations are paramount. The personal involvement is great indeed whether one is deciding to be a donor or not or whether one is fulfilling appropriately a relationship of trust and of love in authorizing a donation from an incapacitated relative in the event of death. These are issues born of medical triumphs and of our interpretation of our duties and obligations to others. Every reader must take his own stand.

SUGGESTED REFERENCES

Moore, F. D., *Give and Take: The Development of Tissue Transplantation* (Philadelphia and London: Saunders, 1964).

Film: *A Part of Yourself.* Produced in 1971 by Public Television, WGBH, Channel 2, Boston, under sponsorship of the Interhospital Organ Bank, Inc. P.O. Box 306, Bosto Massachusetts 02114.

16

The Condolence or Sympathy Call

*Should mourners be left alone after
death?*

*What is, and why, the condolence or
sympathy call?*

*How do the bereaved feel about these
calls?*

*What should or shouldn't one talk
about?*

How long should the caller stay?

Should honest emotions be hidden?

REGINA FLESCH

When a friend's relative has died, to visit or not to visit is
an important question. Do the bereaved prefer to be alone? What
does one say to the mourners? What should *not* be talked about?
How long should you stay?

Dr. Regina Flesch is a medical research scientist at the Eastern Pennsylvania Psychiatric Institute in Philadelphia. She received her Ph.D. at Bryn Mawr College and has worked extensively in the field of bereavement and mental health.

The Condolence or Sympathy Call

What is a condolence call?[1]

A condolence call is a personal home visit made to a bereaved person or persons by family members, friends, associates, neighbors, or by acquaintances soon after they have learned of the death. It is distinct from attendance at the viewing or funeral — customarily somewhat formal services, usually conducted at a funeral home or religious chapel, for a number of mourners.

The condolence call has several purposes. Its immediate and overt purpose is to express the caller's sympathy to the mourner and to offer help. This conveys to the mourner that he is not alone in his grief, that there are people who care about and understand his sorrow. Implicitly, a condolence call also conveys to the mourner that, despite his loss, individuals in society are maintaining their ties to him. In effect, the call says, "You may feel that your heart is in the grave, but *you* are not. Through this call, we bind you to the living."

Who makes condolence calls?

Because it is not easy to make condolence calls, there seems to be a widespread impression that not everyone should make them. It is true that in a few rural areas condolence calls are made only by immediate family members, but this is the exception rather than the rule. Among the

Jews, condolence calls formerly were made by any member of the bereaved member's synagogue. It was the duty of the entire congregation to express sympathy and concern to the mourner. Our social customs suggest that anyone may call on the bereaved, to express sympathy. One needs no invitation to make a condolence call, just as one needs no invitation to a funeral. The following case provides illustration:

A young mother lost her only child under severely painful conditions for the child. Members of her church decided against calling at the home immediately after the death, because they assumed that the large family would be with the grieving parents. One member of the church, however, had not been on speaking terms with the bereaved mother for some time. When informed of the decision by the church members against visiting, she alone decided to go for only a few moments to extend her sympathy. At the house the door was opened by the mother, who flung her arms around the caller, clinging to her and pulling her inside. Since the child's death not a soul had come to the house. The five-minute call stretched on for hours; old quarrels were forgotten. All that mattered was that someone had cared enough to call.

Are condolence calls a duty?

Some books on etiquette indicate that when one hears of a death, one must go immediately to the home of the mourner to offer help and condolences. This suggests that calls are a duty, but this orientation contributes to the difficulty in making them. It is preferable to think of the sympathy call as a privilege. The mourner carries a heavy load which expressions of concern and sympathy lighten as much as possible.

When are condolence calls made?

Books on etiquette suggest that condolence calls be made as soon as possible after the news of a death is received. The example quoted above would indicate this is a sound dictum. However, having made the call, the caller should not assume that he is not to come again. The individual who fails to go early to the bereaved home also need not assume that he may not go later. Condolence calls may be made at any time, before the funeral or after, during the early weeks following the funeral, and also during the first year after the death. This first year formerly was set aside as a period of withdrawal and "ritual mourning," but now is less so, although still tacitly acknowledged as the "year of mourning."

THE MOURNER

How do the bereaved feel about sympathy calls?

One cannot predict precisely what the response to a condolence call will be at a specific time. The caller must remember that the bereaved person usually is not in a normal frame of mind. Often the bereaved person himself does not know how he feels, or indeed, if he feels at all. It is not unusual for a bereaved individual to say that he had no feeling whatsoever about a death at the time he learned of it. Thus, the mourner also may not know how he feels about receiving callers. However, it is safe to assume that the call will be appreciated even if not acknowledged gratefully or even received graciously, at the time.

How do the bereaved feel when the community is indifferent?

There is a tendency on the part of individuals who have suffered a great loss to feel that no one understands and that no one cares as they care. In the deepest sense, this probably is an accurate assessment of their bereavement, for no one can actually enter into the grief of a parent, a child, or a spouse. When this feeling of private suffering and isolation is augmented by actual indifference on the part of the community, it increases the mourner's inclination to withdrawal and bitterness. It becomes more difficult for the mourner to feel those social ties which he must feel if he is to remain bound to the living.

Are mourners really aware of who calls after a death?

Even if in a state of shock, the bereaved person usually is very much aware of what goes on around him. Indeed, he probably has a heightened perception of events and individuals. One bereaved husband told this author that he was aware of everybody who came into the room when his wife died, of what these people were wearing, and of what they said. Although he felt that his memory was not good, he remembered equally well *those who failed to come.* A young widow also interviewed by the author stated that she remembered every detail of the viewing and of the funeral for her husband. She recalled who came, what they wore, what they said, how they acted. She had absolutely no recollection of her own conduct, but the details of the conduct of the others present were engraved on her memory forever.

Should mourners be left alone after a death?

This question is sometimes raised because instances have been known where mourners themselves would not receive callers, but asked friends or family members to assume this obligation for them. Also, mourners have been known to withdraw from all social contacts, some even becoming unable to leave their homes for necessary tasks. In this author's opinion, these sad instances should not influence individual decisions about making a condolence call. A mourner who does not wish to receive callers will find a way to make that known. However, in most instances, an instinct for self-preservation and a sense of discipline and politeness persuade the bereaved to try to take the hands that reach out to them.

The majority of mourners feel a need for human ties and human support. Because the burden of grief must be carried alone, most mourners value the moments of human companionship that come through calls from supportive individuals.

THE CALLER

How does the caller feel about making the call?

Many people find it awkward to visit a household soon after a death. Some also feel timid and sorrowful. It is not unusual for callers to have a sense of uneasiness and even hesitation, as though intruding upon sorrow. This is understandable because the mourner psychologically is partially withdrawn from the contact. Also, we all have a natural tendency to avoid painful situations. We should accept such feelings as completely understandable, a concomitant of a painful situation. Having accepted these feelings for what they are, one simply goes on with the call.

Is there any way to make condolence calls easier?

The best way to make the calls easier is to have a clear idea of their purpose. Also, it is helpful to know what to wear, what to say and what not to say, and how to act.

There are a few general rules that may be followed. With regard to clothing, one should try to dress appropriately for the occasion. If the caller has had some time to prepare for the call, in other words has been able to plan, then it is appropriate to come neatly dressed, perhaps not in the deep mourning of black, but in unostentatious, simple garb. On the other hand, if one has heard the news of a death and has rushed directly to the house, one's attire is secondary. The author knows of a beautiful call paid in a swimming suit, which was what the caller was wearing when she heard of the death. This caller went immediately to the house, thinking only of helping and expressing sympathy, not of her personal appearance. In the same way, one's demeanor should be simple and direct, with the focus on the bereaved person, not on the self.

THE CONTENT OF THE CALL

What does one say upon entering?

There is no prescribed ritual in our country, but the natural approach is to state the purpose of the visit, "I have come to express my sympathy on your loss." One may vary this remark according to one's sentiments and style, in your own way conveying to the mourner that you feel for his· bereavement.

A friend of the author related that in her home community in Nova Scotia, the custom is for visitors to give a firm handclasp and say, "I'm sorry about your father." Little else is added but that is enough.

The custom of speaking only good of the decedent also is sensible. The decedent and his loss are uppermost in the mind of the mourner, who will welcome the sharing of good memories, particularly at this time.

What should one not talk about?

There are some don'ts which seem too obvious to require mention, but they are mentioned because they are actual experiences taken from the author's clinical observation. It is well to avoid mention of one's own problems when making a condolence call. In this author's opinion, that prohibition includes discussion of one's personal losses. The purpose of the call is to express understanding and sympathy for the bereaved, who cannot be expected to understand or appreciate similarities of experience. The author has been told of callers who have said such things as, "I've been through this myself." Almost without exception these comments were offensive to the mourners, who found circumstances that made the analogies inapplicable. It is wise also to avoid comments about others who have had similar or worse losses. Such comparisons are not healthy and should not be encouraged by the caller.

If the decedent was old and ill for a long period, one may indicate that the mourner also must have suffered during the illness, without adding, "Death was a mercy." Immediately following the loss, the person who has loved the decedent cannot think of death as a mercy. Such an orientation can come only later. It is also best to refrain from such comments as, "It was all for the best," or, "It was God's will." Whether or not a loss was for the best is not for the caller to judge; nor is God's will his domain. Advice about specific problems also should be avoided. Often the mourner is beset by problems regarding the burial, insurance, etc., but is not then able to manage these problems and to consider the advice offered. If one wishes to be helpful, one may offer to make oneself available at a later time.

The caller should not undertake predictions about the length of the grief process, as in the examples cited below. This author has heard of more than one call in which such comments were made as: "You're young, you have your life ahead of you. There will be time for you to re-marry," or "to have other children," or "to get over this loss," as the case may be. One well-educated woman actually remarked: "You know, you're going to feel worse before you feel better." It is difficult to conceive of circumstances in which such a remark would be helpful.

It is also best not to tell mourners that they will feel better after a certain period of time, a few weeks or a few months. They may or may not feel better, and in any event they are so concerned with problems and feelings of the moment that such comments can mean little. The standard comment that the mourner will feel better after the first year also may not necessarily apply, and later may even be recalled with resentment.

One minister advised a mourner in his church: "Don't cry about it; pray about it." Prohibitions on the shedding of tears are painful and often are ill-advised at the time. The mourner senses that such remarks are made not out of concern for him, but because the caller has a problem in seeing tears shed.

Should honest emotions of grief be expressed?

In answering this question, much depends on what is meant by "expressed." This author believes that there are many different forms of expression, and that words represent merely one form. Feelings also are expressed nonverbally. Genuine grief is hard to conceal. Compassion and empathy can be conveyed with a handclasp or quick embrace. If the caller has difficulty restraining his tears, this form of expression is too sincere to be overlooked. However, if by "expression of grief" one means copious weeping, wailing, and lamentation, such expressions may be burdensome to the bereaved. Some callers are affected so visibly that the bereaved feels obligated to comfort them. These callers show small consideration for the individual who really bears the major burden of the loss.

How long should you stay?

When making a condolence call it seems sensible to plan on no longer a call than one plans on for a hospital visit — that is, not more than fifteen minutes. It takes no longer to express condolences, to speak a few words of comfort and commendation of the decedent, to offer help, and to say good-bye. However, one can tell from the mourner's demeanor whether or not there is a wish for a longer visit. If the mourner appears to wish a longer visit, and if it is possible for the caller to remain longer, that may be the kind thing to do. If the caller cannot remain longer, but a longer visit seems desired, an assurance should be given of a return call, and that call should be made.

While conducting research interviews with the bereaved, the author has visited households where there was a very recent loss. On occasion she has been received ungraciously, at first. However, as the visit went on, it often became apparent that the mourner wished the discussion continued. The alert caller will take his cue from the mourner, and will be guided by his wishes.

What do you do if you are turned away?

If you are told that no callers are being received, simply leave your name with a message of sympathy and indicate that you will stop by again, at a later time. One may express regret at not having the chance to see the bereaved individual, but the refusal must be accepted with a word of sympathy.

In this author's opinion, a direct refusal is rather unusual. It is more likely that the individual who does not wish to receive callers will indicate that other duties are pressing, or that he has too much to do to stop for a visit. It is best to accept these excuses, simply saying that you could not pass by without an expression of sympathy and an offer of help. If the caller feels that a return call would be received differently, he may indicate that after the immediate crisis he will try another visit.

When do you use the telephone to express condolence?

One uses the telephone only if distance prevents a personal visit. Many individuals think that it is appropriate to telephone condolences when they first learn of a death. Chances are that the bereaved person will be inundated with calls from persons who are far away, from monument salespeople, and from persons who have a direct interest in the funeral arrangements. The jangle of a telephone bell can be one more annoyance to a person under tension. It is safe to assume that the mourner will not regard a telephone call as a substitute for personal contact.

What should you do when you meet people on the street after they have had a loss?

What one does and says depends on whether or not one has been to see the person after the death. If one actually has paid a condolence call, and there has been a direct expression of sympathy, one may do what would be natural under any other circumstances. One may express interest in how the individual is getting along, ask how things are going, and then ask if there is any way to be helpful during this time.

If no condolence call has been paid, one may feel an impulse to make a condoling comment. The tactful person will manage to convey sympathy without saying much about the loss. Comments on the death and loss may elicit tears, which, on a public street, could be peculiarly painful to the mourner as well as to the condoler. The author is reminded of a bereaved father whose chief recreation had been his stopping for a beer at the end of a day's work. After the death of his only child, the father gave up his visits to the neighborhood taproom. His reason was that friends meeting him there expressed their sympathy to him, usually with some such statement as, "I'm sorry about your boy." These comments annoyed the father, who told the author that he assumed people were sorry. He "just didn't want to hear about it." In effect, the condolences in public served to deprive him of the companionship of neighbors when he most needed them.

If one has not seen or spoken with the bereaved since the death, a warm, firm clasp of the hand can convey support. This may be accompanied by some comment as, "I hear that these have been hard days for you." "I understand that you have had a loss; let me know if I can be of help." If you wish to visit, simply ask if the person is seeing callers at home. If the answer is yes, try to set a convenient time to stop in. When making the call, a tangible and practical expression of sympathy may be in bringing substantial foods, that is, not merely confections but, if possible, even a complete meal. Similarly, if you meet on the street a bereaved person to whom no call has been paid, an expression of sympathy is implied in an invitation to share a dinner or lunch at a definite, specified time.

SOME COMMON QUESTIONS
What can you say when anger is expressed?

Like sympathy, anger may be expressed in many ways, but here we shall assume that any anger about the death will find open, verbal expression. When anger is verbalized directly, one may listen supportively, even to an emotion that appears unreasonable or irrational. It is questionable if the listener then should say anything about the irrational component of the anger. Anger immediately after a bereavement generally is understandable, and individuals who vent anger usually are not just then in a position to examine any irrationality. If, shortly after a bereavement, his irrationality is pointed out to him, the mourner usually does not perceive this as a kindness. A murmur of "I understand" may be the most effective way of helping the bereaved develop his own understanding.

What can you say when the question is asked, "Why did this happen to me?"

This question is raised by many mourners who have been deeply hurt through a death. If one works to any great extent with bereaved individuals, one realizes this question is almost universal. Probably the anguished mourner who cries out "Why?" really has neither the expectation nor even the wish for a reasonable reply. And it is likely that any explanations and answers a caller may attempt would be found by the mourner to be distasteful, if not actually presumptuous.

This author believes that although one cannot provide a list of helpful words or suggested activities, there is a point of view or orientation which the mourner may perceive as consolatory; in other words, as an adequate response to his outcry. That point of view involves acceptance of the tragedy in life as an essential element in our earthly existence. The following examples will help to clarify this orientation:

In one of her beautiful short stories. "The Immortal Story," Isak Dinesen deals with the very question raised above. In her story the heroine, who has been a rich, petted,

spoiled daughter in a wealthy home, has fallen on evil days
and is asked to take part in a procedure or drama which is
peculiarly painful to her. She raises the question of why she
should do so, angrily asking the answer of a young man
whose fate has been worse then her own, although she has no
knowledge of that. His answer bears repeating here.

> "Listen, Miss Virginie," said Elishama. "In the shawls
> . . . that I brought you, there was a pattern. You told your
> friend . . . that you liked one pattern better than another.
> But there was a pattern in all of them."
>   Virginie had a taste for patterns. . . . She frowned a lit-
> tle, but let Elishama go on. "Only," he went on,
> "sometimes the lines of a pattern will run the other way of
> what you expect. As in a looking-glass." "As in a looking-
> glass," she repeated slowly. "Yes," he said, "but for all
> that, it is still a pattern." This time she looked at him in
> silence. ". . . only in this pattern, it is reversed." From
> behind her veil of hair Virginie said: "Reversed?" "Yes,"
> said Elishama. "Reversed. In this pattern the road runs the
> other way. And runs on. . . . And why not, Miss Virginie?"[2]

In an interview with this author, a bereaved mother
gave substantially the same answer after the death of her
teenaged daughter. She said, "I asked myself why this should
happen to me." The interviewer asked, in turn, "What
answer could you give?" She replied: "I asked what made me
think I was better than other people. Why shouldn't it
happen to me?"

The distinguished Danish novelist and the meagerly
educated American mother had come to the same conclusion, that the pattern in many lives "runs the wrong way"
from what we expect, but that there is no discernible reason
why this should not be so. Prior to his loss, the mourner
himself may have given little thought to the tragic dimension

in life, and may not even have accepted it: but in his bereaved state he is certain to be especially sensitive to the presence or absence of such acceptance in the individuals with whom he raises the question. The caller who himself gives assent to the dangerous conditions of life also will be able to convey compassion for its inevitable pain, conveying that compassion palpably, without words, and without teleological explanations. Nothing more is needed.

What do you say when the bereaved person rails against God?

In general, here too there is little one can say. In interviews with bereaved persons, this author often has heard complaints against the Almighty, as well as against mortals who were held responsible for the loss. I have never attempted to discuss theological issues or to "justify God's ways to man." Sympathetic listening has seemed the safest way, and indeed has proved to be so.

BIBLIOGRAPHY

Dinesen, Isak, *Anecdotes of Destiny* (New York: Random House, 1953).
Flesch, Regina, "The Condolence Call." In *Death and Bereavement*, edited by Austin Kutscher (Springfield, Ill.: C. C. Thomas, 1969).
Gorer, Geoffrey, *Death, Grief and Mourning* (Garden City, N.Y.: Doubleday, 1965).
Post, Emily, *Etiquette: The Blue Book of Social Usage* (New York: Funk and Wagnalls, 1960).

NOTES

1. To the best of the author's information, there is little written on condolence or sympathy calls. The interested reader may wish to refer to an earlier article by this author, "The Condolence Call" in *Death and Bereavement, edited by Austin Kutscher. Emily Post writes helpfully about customs and conduct following bereavement in The Blue Book of Social Usage.* However, nothing is said specifically about sympathy calls.
2. Isak Dinesen, *Anecdotes of Destiny* (New York: Random House, 1953), pp. 189 - 191.

The work on which this paper is based was supported by the Commonwealth of Pennsylvania, Department of Public Welfare, and by the United States Public Health Service, National Institute of Mental Health, Research Grants MH15063 - 01, 15063 - 02, and 15063 - 03. The author expresses appreciation for this support and also for the cooperation of the interviewees who participated in the study.

17

The Condolence Letter

Why are expressions of concern really important?

How does the condolence letter help the bereaved?

How may you say what you really feel?

Should the condolence letter be answered?

When are sympathy cards effective?

EDGAR N. JACKSON

Besides the sympathy call, how else can we effectively communicate with the bereaved? A meaningful way is the condolence letter. But how to write it? How long should it be? For if properly written, this expression of friendship could be treasured by the mourners for years to come.

Dr. Jackson has combined his thirty years in the pastorate and his extensive experience in psychotheropy to write this significant pioneering chapter.

The Condolence Letter

Often death comes to those we love and are concerned about when we are a long way off. How can the miles be bridged so that we can express our feelings and give support in time of crisis to those we cannot be with in person?

We all know that the condolence letter is hard to write. It seems that the things we would say are beyond words. What we would communicate is so charged with deep feelings that words seem a futile vehicle to carry our real meaning. In a way the words frame a painful reality that we would rather avoid, so we tend to retreat from the task of writing and withhold from others what they need as well as what we need. That is, we tend to run away from the reality we have to live with from this day on.

Yet we know that the condolence communication is important for on occasion we have known its value. There must be some ways for making it less threatening. How can we develop some simple guidelines that can be helpful? The following suggestions may be useful.

What do we wish to say, and how?

First, we would consider the motive. We need to communicate because human beings are social beings who protect themselves from the intolerable burdens of life by sharing them. The condolence letter is like Shakespeare's concept of mercy, for "it blesses him that gives and him that takes." It verifies the supportive relationship that exists with those who care even at a distance. At the same time it verifies the need to confront the facts of life that are unalterable. To deny reality would be to create the illusions that are unsafe to live with. So the communications we make are good for us as well as those who receive them.

Second, it seems wise to do it right away. The strong emotional impulse you feel when you first hear the sad news should be acted on as soon as possible. When you delay you find it becomes more difficult, for the excuses and the defenses begin to build up. You hear yourself saying, "My note probably won't make much difference anyway" or, "What can I say?" or, "They will have more things to do than read a letter from me." These excuses are a natural way of trying to get away from the task that is unpleasant, but they are misleading denials of what is important.

Perhaps a phone call or telegram?

Third, consider the alternatives. If the letter seems too hard for you to write, you may pick up the telephone and in a few moments be speaking to the bereaved person. This direct and personal communication gives a chance for an immediate response and makes it possible for you to assess the state of mind of the person to whom you speak. Or you may send a telegram which has an immediate and personal message. In both instances this immediate response may be a prelude to the letter that may come along a few days later. It will usually make it easier to write the letter if you have already talked directly to a person by telephone.

Fourth, symbolic communication has special meaning. We know that words are important but there are times when it is possible to send messages without words. A gift, a floral piece, or a message in book form may well bring you into the presence of those for whom you feel concern in a way that is different and yet doubly meaningful, for the message keeps restating itself every time it is seen or read.

Fifth, be as personal as possible. Sympathy cards may have their value as an expression of concern, but a poem or a verse with only a signature seems to say that the sender was afraid to be personal when being personal is so very important. If a sympathy card is used, it makes a great difference if a few personal words of love and shared feeling are added in one's own characteristic handwriting.

Finally, in most instances it is wise to be brief. This is probably not the time for long letters filled with philosophical or theological references. These may come later when there is need for mental readjustment and adequate time for doing it. But the briefer form of reassurance with genuine expressions of love and friendship, written by hand rather than typewritten, seems to go more directly toward the acute need for love, support, and empathy. It is not a matter of how long the letter is as much as how warm, tender, and loving is its expression.

Should we expect an answer from the bereaved?

Be considerate of the bereaved. Each human situation has its unique characteristics. These may well be recognized in simple and honest terms. It may also be an act of concern to say, "While we would love to hear from you, please know that we understand how burdened you must be right now, so do not feel that this note requires an answer." A simple statement of this kind may ease the burden of correspondence at a time when a response would be difficult.

Is your expression of concern important?

The resolution of grief and aid in the mourning process come at least in part through the fabric of human relationship and the active ingredient in this relationship is communication. Though it may be difficult, it is important. Friendship and expressions of love can undergird faith and help the bereaved to face the future knowing there are many who care. This is so important it cannot be overemphasized. Many persons treasure and reread these letters of loving interest and keep them for years. The tributes to the person who has died become important to the survivor in verifying his love and resolving the almost universal feelings of guilt that accompany death.

While each person would want to make his communication his own personal expression, the following illustrations may be of help to those who are called upon to write letters of condolence.

To be added to a sympathy card:
"To these words we would add our love and concern. Our prayers cover the miles."

"You are constantly in our thoughts and prayers and we want you to know you are surrounded by our love and sympathy through these sad days."

"No words can express adequately our sympathy and concern but we want you to know we are with you in spirit with our love."

For the personal note or letter perhaps nothing surpasses the model for real feeling and completeness with brevity that is contained in the letter Abraham Lincoln wrote to a mother concerning the loss of her sons in the Civil War. While no one would violate good taste by copying so famous a historical document, it may be studied as a model for brevity and clarity. It is honest and direct. Yet it is rich in its inspiration and its personal tribute.

Executive Mansion, Washington, November 21, 1864

Mrs. Bixby, Boston, Massachusetts:
Dear Madam: I have been shown in the files of the War Department a statement of the Adjutant-General of Massachusetts that you are the mother of five sons who have died gloriously on the field of battle. I feel how weak

and fruitless must be any words of mine which would attempt to beguile you from the grief of a loss so overwhelming. But I cannot refrain from tendering to you the consolation that may be found in the thanks of the Republic they died to save. I pray that our heavenly Father may assuage the anguish of your bereavement, and leave you only the cherished memory of the loved and lost, and the solemn pride that must be yours to have laid so costly a sacrifice upon the altar of freedom.

Yours very sincerely and respectfully,

Abraham Lincoln

How often might you send a note?

A final suggestion would be to send a note every few days for a while. Continuity of concern can be important to keep a bereaved person from feeling abandoned. At first he may be flooded with expressions of love and good will. But when the difficult days of adjustment come his needs for communication may be even greater. Letters and friendly notes during this time or reorganization of life are deeply valued and may be doubly important.

18

The Widow and Widower

How to deal with loneliness.

What are the problems with children, in-laws, and friends?

When should one date and contemplate remarriage?

Where to turn for assistance.

ROBERT L. BUCHANAN

To the average husband and wife with a growing family, death often seems a remote possibility. Medical research shows that an average individual can expect to achieve age seventy or beyond. But there are many thousands whose mates die unexpectedly and prematurely. After death — what?

How to adjust to a new life with children, in-laws, friends, job, daily routine? What about ways of handling property, insurance money, and investments? How to become part of society without feeling unwanted or useless? Should the person remarry? How long to wait?

The Reverend Robert L. Buchanan has devoted much of his ministry to helping the widow and widower, those "who feel barely whole." He is a member with supervisor status in the

American Association of Marriage and Family Counselors and is a counselor at the Presbyterian Counseling Service in Seattle.

The Widow and Widower

In the past eleven years I have had the privilege of working and associating with nearly 3,000 persons who have been widowed. With that background, I thought it would be easy to share conclusions found in the basic problem areas. Instead I found great diversity. *There is just no stereotype for widowhood.* This is logical once you accept the fact that death does not discriminate because of race, color, creed, wealth, health, or intelligence. Death is the common denominator of us all.

However, there are basic problem areas that the widow and widower face which should be examined. Please keep in mind that the illustrations and reactions I share may not be your own since *you are a unique person.* However, they do represent the feelings of many.

What are the initial feelings after a husband or wife has died?

No matter how drawn out the suffering of your mate may have been, the actuality of death comes as a shock because death is so final and irrevocable. Even though you may be glad that your mate no longer has to suffer, there is the feeling that "If only I could have had a few more hours or days with him. There are things I would like to have done and said."

Usually a state of shock takes over and continues for days, weeks, and on occasion, months. The degree of shock is modified somewhat by your own emotional strengths and the comfort given you by relatives and close friends. Your belief in life after death will also have a major influence on your reactions during this period. However, the emotional reactions are as if you had been suddenly struck a hard blow. Sometimes your feelings become numbed, and you just go through motions. When you look back later, you wonder how or when you accomplished the things you did.

A flood of different emotions is likely to come. "Why did she leave me?" "If I had only taken better care of him." "God, why did you take him first and leave me alone?" "How can I go on without her?" "God, are you punishing me for some sin?" "It isn't fair; we were just getting ready to enjoy a well-earned retirement." Or, it could be something like this: "It isn't fair; I need her to help me raise the children." "What a relief he is dead; I thought I would go stir-crazy sitting there day after day watching him slowly die." "I'm so lonely. Just having him alive, no matter how sick, seemed to help hold me together somehow." These are but a sample of the complex feelings that run through a widow or widower's mind.

How can the funeral director be of assistance?

I would say one of the most misunderstood professions in our society today is that of the funeral director. Granted there are funeral directors who are not what they should be, but the large majority of funeral directors I've known are capable, concerned, and well equipped to handle most of the immediate emotional needs of a newly bereaved person. I would say that if you are not widowed, it would be well to be aware of a funeral director whom friends have recommended. When a crisis comes, it is important that you don't have to think twice about whom to call on. There are several ways of finding a good director. Your clergyman or trusted friends are usually reliable sources.

A funeral director is of immediate help. He helps you locate all of the necessary legal papers that are needed such as V.A., life insurance, Social Security, welfare, etc. The directors I have known are compassionate professionals, aware of your grief and the fact that most likely you will be irrational about many decisions you must make during the first few days. They will try to honor your decision as to what type of funeral you want, where it shall be, and who is to officiate. It is important that you make clear to the director your financial situation, so that he can structure the cost of the funeral to meet your needs. Lavish spending certainly does not prove the depth of your love for your mate.

A survey made of several hundred widowed persons found that of the three major helping professions — doctors, clergy, and funeral directors — the latter was considered the most helpful unless the doctor or clergyman was a personal friend.

What of the insurance agent?

It is good to get hold of your insurance agent immediately. He can be helpful in expediting policies, the will, etc. It is important to realize that some policies may not be immediately cashable. You may be short of funds for a period of time. It is important that you have liquid assets for living expenses for three months. Know where your policies are. Keep them in a safe place.

What immediate matters must be considered before the funeral?

One of the *good* parts of preparing for the funeral is the fact that you are forced to be active. You are forced to notify friends and relatives of your mate's death. You are forced to contact a funeral director and look into the immediate circumstances. You are forced to decide whether you want to have an autopsy held. You are forced to share your feelings with your clergyman. You are forced to give comfort to and seek comfort from your friends, relatives, children, parents.

Don't be surprised if the decisions you must make come at you too fast. It is nice if there is a trusted friend or relative who can help you make decisions. Some of these decisions include the following: what day to have the funeral, what hour, what location; whether the friends should send flowers or send money for a particular charity; what type of coffin; where the interment will be; what type of service — funeral or memorial.

The funeral is over: how to work with your grief over the loss of your mate?

The answer to working through your grief over the loss of your mate is different for everyone concerned. One thing is certain; grief is a painful experience. Many express it as a physical hurt. Years ago I recall hearing Edgar Jackson give an illustration from the time when he was a chaplain in the service. He was walking through one of the wards of a hospital when a young soldier with his leg in a cast up on a pulley said, "Chaplain, would you scratch my toes?" The Chaplain responded, "Sure," and proceeded to scratch the toes when the man said, "No, the other leg." The Chaplain looked down and saw there was no other leg. It has been amputated, but the sensory feelings for that leg were still there.

I believe it is very much the same in widowhood in that even though the mate is gone, the emotional feeling for him/her is still very much alive. The death of a loved one is like an amputation and will be painful for days, weeks, or, as I said earlier, sometimes months. The thing I would suggest is to accept the help of friends. This can be especially helpful in those early days. As a whole, friends try to be very helpful, providing food, comfort, encouragement, sympathy, and, hopefully, some empathy. However, you need to face the fact that death is real. One of the values of a funeral, I believe, is to bring about the reality that your mate is dead.

I would not try to make a lot of decisions at the beginning. Tend to go slowly, especially on any kind of important decision. One mistake that is often made is that you feel the house is too big for you, and you say, "I will move into something smaller and less expensive." Generally I would recommend that you remain in your home for at least a year, if it is at all possible, so that you can make a more mature, rational decision. The emotional support your home can provide may outweigh any additional financial expenditures during the first year.

It is good to be able to talk about your feelings to friends or relatives whom you can trust. I used to think that when a person had to retell the story of the events of the death over and over again to people who came to the funeral home, it must be hard or even cruel for them. I have since changed my mind and believe it can be therapeutic to repeat the story again and again. It helps to keep from repressing feelings that need to be aired, as well as helping to validate the reality of the situation.

Again, your religious faith will be a large factor here as to whether you are able to communicate with your God, asking for guidance in this period of grief and new-found loneliness. One of the things you are going to discover is that within a matter of three or four weeks, your friends who were considerate and helpful the first few days are now starting to be less noticeable. In many cases, by the end of the month, you are pretty much left on your own. This often comes as a shock to the widowed, but remember this is common. There are exceptions, of course, and some people do stay around and care for months and months, but I would not count on it.

Edgar Jackson's book *You and Your Grief* is excellent for helping one deal with grief. Be sure to read his chapter in this book on dealing with grief.

What are the psychological stages in the aftermath of death?

It is difficult to define the stages for everyone, since we are all unique. One of the first stages we find ourselves in is grieving for ourself. We are painfully deprived of someone we loved very much. A lot of our unspoken anger is that we are left alone. A second factor that often comes to us is the feeling of fear. Every time our life is changed there are things to face in a changed world in which everything will be different. If we have been dependent on our mate for one, twenty, thirty, or more years, we have been used to accepting the security given by him or her. Now there is the fear of the unknown. Where do I go? What will I do? How will I get along without my mate, raising the children, earning a living, and just existing in a world that is so complex? It is normal to feel insecure, almost as if the earth beneath you is crumbling. Order has turned to disorder.

Another phase is some form of bitterness and anger. It is not uncommon for the widowed to be bitter or angry with God. Perhaps they feel that their mate was killed by a particular person because of neglect. Sometimes the anger is misplaced. Sometimes it is aimed at the doctor, as if somehow he didn't do a good enough job, or was careless. You could be angry at yourself because you didn't take care of your mate properly, or you could feel anger at God because he is the giver and taker of life. I would suggest giving vent to your anger or bitterness. I have known many who contained this anger for indefinite periods of time, and it has usually had negative aftereffects for both the widowed and their families.

Your whole life is going to have to be restructured: how you spend the money available, how you react with your in-laws, how you discipline your children, how you handle work and leisure, how you handle your relationship to God.

One word about sexual feelings. In the early stages the sexual feelings are often blunted. In fact for many the drive seems to dry up for periods of time. Some people are bound to assume you are desperate and offer you sexual assistance. Often the individual is the last person you would have thought of, sometimes a close friend of your deceased mate. Women under forty often find themselves in this situation. I would caution you not to be bitter toward persons making such overtures. Just give a firm negative response and let time take care of the matter. Remember that you are the one it will bother most. Your "friend" usually can quickly forget the incident and not be embarrassed. Weeks or months later the sexual drives return, occasionally like a flood. I know of one woman who had been widowed nearly ten months. One night she woke up and felt wild with sexual passion. She reached for her husband who wasn't there, and found herself wanting relations with a man, any man. Later, when she was sharing these thoughts with me, she said she felt that she had become a nymphomaniac. It was most comforting to her when she was able to share this fear with other persons in our THEOS group (THEOS stands for They Help Each Other Spiritually — a group for widows and widowers) who could understand. Emotions seem to be partially frozen during these early stages, and they thaw at different rates.

How do you readjust your life with your children?

The answer depends upon age. If you are a widow under the age of thirty, chances are that you have small children to care for. You are faced with the immediate problem of how you are going to finance the family, as well as that of being both mother and father. Will you have to go to work, and if so, who will you get for a babysitter? Will it be someone you can trust? Will it be an in-law? If you do have a babysitter throughout the day, is it someone you can count on to teach the ethical values you believe in? It is discouraging for a mother working all day to discover that the housekeeper has not been teaching values she'd like or enforcing discipline.

It is hard to adjust to being both hard and soft. In other words, one nice thing about being a couple is that when one is the disciplinarian, the other can be a little sympathetic. It makes it much more difficult when one person has to be both. There are some good chapters in the Egleson book, *Parents Without Partners*, on this subject. I would also recommend books explaining death to your children by Earl Grollman and Edgar Jackson (these books are listed in the bibliography at the end of this chapter).

If your children are older, of course, there are different kinds of problems that have to be faced. There are going to be some real adjustments to make. There is danger, for example, for a woman to say to her son, who may range in age anywhere from six up, "Okay, you are now the man of the house." This just may be a load that the young man is unable to handle, and it may have some bad psychological effects. Children also need to have an opportunity to share their negative feelings and to have an outlet for their frustrations. Teenagers can actually be of real assistance to their parent, but the fact remains that *they are still adolescents and are going through the normal adolescent changes*. They may be even more difficult to handle because there is only one parent.

A big adjustment for grown children will involve whether they feel responsible for taking care of you financially or physically. Some older children immediately panic, thinking, "Oh no, mother or father may want to move in with us." This may be a traumatic time for both. The widowed person may not want to move in with the children, or it may be just the opposite. These areas must be carefully looked into, so that both parents and grown children have a common understanding. It is an area that may have to be reevaluated often.

How do you adjust to your in-laws?

Your in-laws can be of real help to you in a supportive way, but on the other hand it isn't easy for them to adjust to the new situation either. Sometimes the in-laws may be angry at you because your mate is dead. Logical or illogical, occasionally members of the immediate family feel that the death of your mate was somehow partly your fault, and may be angry with you. Your own parents may suddenly see you as a child again and may treat you as such.

The problem of in-laws comes up immediately in the area of child-raising. Will they be involved in rearing the children? This can be an important decision to make as you may not agree with the method they used on your mate and fear they may do the same to your youngsters. Some in-laws may feel that you should become a recluse; that you should always live in the memory of your mate. They may feel you should never remarry. Others will believe just the opposite. They will feel compelled to become a matchmaker, thinking that you should remarry for the children's welfare or because of your own loneliness. In-laws can be one of your most supportive groups of people or the biggest "pains."

What advice do you need to handle your property and insurance?

This question will vary according to each person's financial ability and resources, but I would encourage the widowed to immediately contact a trusted person in the financial world. Often widows find themselves going through their money too quickly partly because their husbands have always controlled the outflow. They find themselves spending much faster than they anticipated. Many, regardless of how much money they are left with, are practically devoid of money within three or four years, unless they have good advice on using available funds. I would like to suggest to any person not widowed reading this, that you have insurance or some form of savings that would allow your mate to live comfortably for three years without having to leave home, especially if there are small children involved.

Is there a way of stretching your money and making wise investments?

There are many ways of doing this, and again I would refer you to a trusted financial expert. Most church congregations have one in their own midst. There are some very simple things like learning to shop more effectively. Most widowers will spend far too much on food unless they are given good counsel. It would be an excellent idea if the widower would find a trusted housewife friend with good shopping knowledge to go with him several times to the supermarket. She can give valuable clues on how to buy sensibly and economically. Widows need help when it comes to the family automobile. Some widows complain that they get cheated by the automobile mechanics because they are unable to question what is being done to their car. A trusted male friend can be of real assistance if he will take the time to go with you the first few times. One of the values of our THEOS group is that we have persons in many walks of life to help each other.

If you don't have a trusted financial advisor, most banks have trust departments geared to help you with your particular income. I would caution you not to be suckered into get-rich-quick plans. This, unfortunately, is a common ploy used by many persons to the newly widowed. They promise to make quick profits on your money. These schemes are more likely to take what funds you do have and lose them. For those who have a little extra money, there are several ways of making wise investments that will help give you annuities for the balance of your life.

For those not widowed who are homeowners I would like to suggest that you consider mortgage life insurance. It is relatively inexpensive and it is good to know that if the breadwinner dies the house will be fully paid for.

How do you again become a part of society without feeling like a fifth wheel, unwanted, or useless?

This question has to be dealt with individually. For most of us, when we lose a mate, we realize that our whole social structure is going to be tilted. I often use the following example for illustration. Let us say that you are a woman, your name is Sally, and you belong to a couples' bowling league. Your husband dies. A week or two has gone by, and your friends call and say, "Sally, please come to the bowling league. We miss you and want you here with us." They encourage you to come, everybody is friendly, you bowl your game, and your score is probably atrocious. People are understanding because they know you are grieving. It may make you feel warm all over that even though you are different — that is, your mate is gone — they still love you and want you around. Later on, unless your score increases and you develop a thicker skin upon hearing jokes about married couples, you may find that your friends are getting increasingly self-conscious around you. You start finding excuses for not going . . . developing headaches . . . having to take the children somewhere . . . or simply being too busy.

It is important to recognize that you *do* have a different relationship with many married friends. Some couples you will be able to continue friendship with on a fairly normal pattern, but most of your married couple friends will gradually change their life pattern with you. Unless you have a partner with you they will tend to feel uneasy with you. Married women are prone to be uncomfortable around a widow if their marriages are a bit rocky. It seems to be true that both widowed and divorced women have kind of a sixth sense when it comes to unhappiness in other people. This is partly because, being alone, they may be more tuned in to loneliness, pain, and hurt. Another factor is that a widow may see the wife treating the husband in what she feels is an unfair manner, and she may make some sort of comment. "Look, your husband is alive; take good care of him. At least you have a husband; I don't!" Even if these words are not spoken, the feelings may come across this way.

One of the best ways I have discovered to deal with a fifth wheel is to have a common group for people who are widowed so they can come together and share their feelings. We meet once a month in a standard meeting. We also have smaller groups meeting throughout the month on a weekly basis for those who have special needs. The purpose for this is to help one another. One of the valuable things about this group is that then you can move out into society, into other organizations, with the knowledge that there is one person or group of persons who understands you. I suppose the one common ingredient that all of us have is that we want to be understood. One of our biggest fears is rejection. It is wonderful to be in a group that accepts you as you are; where you do not have to perform or be other than what you are to be accepted.

Another way of dealing with being a fifth wheel is to get involved with hobbies or activities that you individually enjoy, that do not require a couple. In some respects a widowed person finds himself freer to do things that he had felt hampered from doing when married. Even in the best of marriages the mate sometimes did not like to do some activities that the other enjoyed. You now have the opportunity to follow through on these particular activities if you desire. Sometimes people don't because they feel guilty, as if somehow that wouldn't be fair to the deceased spouse. However, this just isn't the case. This is an opportunity for you to express a part of you that perhaps had not been expressed in your married life.

Should you date? Should you remarry?

The first thing I would say about dating is this: it depends on your age and your own need for companionship. To be brutally honest, it must be pointed out that there are roughly four to five widows for every widower. Therefore, if you are a widow, your chances of remarrying a widower are one in four. The reason I jumped immediately from dating to marriage is that the ultimate result of dating, in the minds of many of us, is that it will eventually end in marriage. Therefore, when you decide whether you want to date or not, you need to recognize that finding a mate will depend a lot on the numbers available. The widower, on the other hand, finds himself with many opportunities. As a matter of fact, sometimes so many are on hand that he is somewhat panicked because he has difficulty knowing who would be the right person.

As a marriage counselor I feel that a second marriage on the part of a widow or widower must be examined every bit as carefully, if not more carefully, than the first marriage. Again, a whole chapter could be written on dealing with the problem of remarriage for a widowed person. Briefly, I would say this: when you do date, as much as possible the date should be someone that you are comfortable with. The danger for a widow dating a single or divorced person is that should it eventually develop into closer feelings and marriage be considered, she may discover that the single person has too many apron strings to his mother, or other complications which make marriage for him not too satisfying and for her extremely painful. The problem with a divorced person could be worse, because many have not worked through the original problems in their first marriage. Several people I have known personally married a divorced person, and within a matter of months, they found themselves divorced because they found the situation intolerable. Some then act as if the marriage never took place, it was so distasteful to them.

How soon should you date?

I have known couples to date within a matter of weeks after the death, and others to wait years. There is no best time. I would say it is up to the individual; when he or she feels the need for companionship and can feel comfortable going out with another person would be the appropriate time. I mentioned earlier that often dating ends in marriage. Dating, however, can be a very rewarding experience without marriage.

How would your children react to your dating or remarriage?

This of course will depend on their ages and their maturity. Small children, expecially preschoolers, are usually very warm to the idea of having a new daddy or mother. Children in the primary and junior ages are a little more discriminating, more likely to express the opinion that they don't like him or her. In the adolescent stage, this will become even more pronounced. For example, a teenaged daughter may be pointedly antagonistic toward any women her father dates, just as a teenaged boy might be equally surly to any men dating his mother. Married children often encourage a parent to remarry unless they are afraid that their mother or father might be bilked financially.

What are the constant demands and frustrations in being both a mother and a father to your children?

One of the problems of being both a father and a mother is the fact that it is a twenty-four-hour-a-day job. There just is no relief. You may have your mother or father taking care of them, you may have babysitters, you may have a housekeeper, *but the ultimate responsibility is yours.*

Up till now you have been able to share the responsibility with your mate. For a man this total responsibility is particularly frustrating because prior to his wife's death, he has been able to be at work from ten to twelve hours a day with full confidence that his wife was taking good care of the children. Now all of a sudden he not only has his job, but he must be aware during those working hours that he is ultimately responsible and cannot expect someone else to be responsible for him. Hence, when problems come up — decisions about how a child is treated, being bullied by other children, bad grades, clothing styles, morals, attending worship services — the list could go on indefinitely — he realizes he is the one who must make the ultimate decision. He cannot bounce it off to his partner. Even though he may check with his relatives, his friends, his clergyman, he must be the last court of appeal. Making the ultimate decision constantly is a lonely and frustrating feeling.

How to handle your loneliness?

Loneliness is certainly not unique to widowed persons. Single persons, divorced persons, and married persons young and old all share in common the feeling of loneliness to some degree. If you have made your mate your whole life, you are going to have a much more difficult time than persons who have been able to have a more open relationship with other people. The people that I find have the most difficult time adjusting to widowhood are those who have spent their whole lives trying to please their mates or to make their mates the important person. When this person disappears, they are at a loss to know how to handle themselves, since they have depended so heavily upon the now deceased spouse.

To those who are not widowed now, I would heartily recommend that you broaden your base of fellowship to persons outside your immediate family — perhaps in your own church, your own business, in social groups — so that you will have good relationships that can be supporting to you. This in no way means to diminish the relationship you have with your spouse, but don't put the total dependency upon your partner or your children. However, should you be one who has put heavy dependence upon your mate, it is important that you accept the fact and set about trying to change the situation for the future.

The common denominator in loneliness is the fear that you will be rejected if you try to involve yourself with another person. When you are married, there is a certain amount of security in knowing that somebody likes you. Even if the world hates you, you have one person who will stick by you for better or for worse, but after you have lost your mate, there is not even that one person. It is very helpful if you have a good relationship with God, that you be able to commune with Him. Value can be found in reading the Psalms and other sacred literature.

It is important, though, that you start developing relationships outside the home. This is where your own church or social group can be of help; here there are often readymade organizations in which you can participate. In addition, I would like to recommend groups like our own THEOS for the widowed, because they provide a splendid opportunity for widowed people to meet others who have similar lonely feelings. We are able to give help to each other, and we find ourselves mutually sustained. One of the things that we have in our own particular group is a twenty-four-hour answering service so that if a person is lonely or depressed at any time of the day, he or she can pick up the phone and call one of our designated members who will respond, even if only to listen.

It is important to feel that another human being really cares about us. Of course, the other side of the coin is also important. It is important that *you start to care about other people.* Do not be so tied up in your own problems that you cannot appreciate the problems of another person or persons. I would say that one of the best ways to beat the loneliness trap is to become concerned about other people in a real helping fashion, and again the opportunities here are many — being a hospital aide, a church visitor, a school volunteer, visiting the aged, helping in groups like Scouts or Big Brothers or Sisters, being a volunteer librarian, and many, many others.

If you remarry, what role should your children have in choosing the mate?

This question has to be answered individually, according to circumstances. For example, if you are a relatively young person and your children are preschoolers, I would say that the major decision would be up to you. The biggest adjustment usually takes place with children between the ages of six and twelve. They are old enough to remember their deceased parent, and will have as many as twelve years to live at home with your new mate. The potential father or mother should be given ample exposure to the children in a variety of circumstances. If the children are strongly negative, proceed with caution. I would suggest that you and your fiancé go for pre-marriage counseling from a qualified marriage counselor.

Teenagers will usually respond with strong feelings pro or con. Girls will often be very hard on a new mother (and boys on a new father). It is important that the relationship be clarified. Teenagers may balk at calling the new mate Mother or Father, and prefer using their new parent's first name instead. Count on a lot of ambivalent feelings. Again, a marriage counselor would be a good idea. I would suggest taking your teenagers with you for at least some of the sessions. This preventive method may be one of the wisest investments of your life.

What role does the religious community have?

In my opinion the religious community is sadly lacking in ways to help integrate the widowed into their new lifestyles. Historically, the widow is to be cared for by the church. Since there are over eleven million widowed in the United States, and their numbers are increasing rapidly each year, immediate attention needs to be given to this matter.

Though clergymen are helpful during the first week or two, in the weeks that follow, the burden of adjusting to widowhood is placed squarely in the widow or widower's lap. Many are just not prepared to deal adequately with their new life, and specific help from the religious leadership is often lacking. Though many have found a spiritual renewal in the church, a large number have become embittered and feel estranged. I strongly recommend a training program to prepare the religious community to serve the widowed person's need more effectively. If there are clergymen and other involved leaders reading this chapter, please give consideration to getting clinical training in this essential ministry.

What organizations might you turn to for help in solving the problems that confront you?

In the past decade, several organizations have been started in different sections of the country. However, only three groups serve a large geographic area. They are Naim, Parents Without Partners, and THEOS.

The earliest organization of any consequence is the Naim conference, started in 1957 in Chicago. The founders were Jean and Bill Delaney, who had the cooperation of Father Timothy Sullivan. It has had excellent success in the greater Chicago area, with about thirty chapters now formed.

They have well-planned monthly programs covering educational, spiritual, and social needs of the widowed. During the year several conferences are held in which they have a widow and widower speak on the problems of adjustment. This is followed by a lawyer who talks on financial and legal problems. A priest then leads a discussion period, which takes in the spiritual aspects of widowhood. The present director is Father Corcoran. Any further information on this organization may be obtained by writing to him at the St. Patrick's Roman Catholic Church in Chicago.

Parents Without Partners, Inc., is an international, nonprofit, nonsectarian, educational organization. It is devoted to the welfare and interests of single parents and their children. In 1971 they had 60,000 single-parent families become a part of the program. They now have 500 chapters across the United States and Canada. The chief value of this rapidly growing organization lies in its educational and social aspects for young and middle-aged parents. The founders, Jim and Janet Egleson, wrote a book based on personal experience and acquired knowledge, *Parents Without Partners,* in 1961. It contains a fine chapter written especially for the widowed.

A word of caution for the widowed: since the large majority of the membership is divorced or separated, their angry attitude toward their former spouses often upsets or irritates the widowed. Divorced persons tend to see the worst in their former mates, while the widowed often eulogize theirs. Also, newly widowed women often find the male aggressiveness encountered difficult to deal with.

In Pittsburgh, a national, nondenominational organization called THEOS (They Help Each Other Spiritually) was founded by Bea Decker in 1962. When her husband died, she realized the necessity to learn how to cope with the many problems that came her way. THEOS has been geared primarily to the needs of the recently bereaved and to the young and middle-aged who need to work through this major transition period in their lives. Mrs. Decker is co-authoring a book called *After The Flowers Are Gone* that will give specific information about THEOS. It should be published in 1973. Monthly meetings are held dealing with eight basic problem areas:

- Reorganizing your life.
- Working through grief and loneliness.
- Dealing with the "fifth-wheel syndrome."
- Raising children alone.
- Handling finances.
- Discussing dating and remarriage.
- Learning to express such emotions as bitterness, anger, and fear in a healthy fashion.
- Coming to grips with feelings about God and the religious community.

Several retreats are held each year dealing with specific problem areas. The Seattle chapter of THEOS also has small therapy groups meeting weekly to deal with individual problems a widow or widower might have.

Here is a listing of groups relevant to the needs of widowed persons:

- Carmel Club, North Shore Shopping Center, Peabody, Mass. 01960
- Catholic Widow and Widowers Club, Hamilton, Ohio
- Eschaton Club, 100 Arch St., Boston, Mass.
- Jewish Widows and Widowers, Beth El Temple Center, Belmont, Mass. 02178
- Naim, St. Patrick's Roman Catholic Church, Chicago, Ill., Fr. Corcoran, Director
- Parents Without Partners, 44 Wood Ave., E. Longmeadow, Mass., Patricia Devine, Director
- Post Cana, sponsored by the Catholic Archdiocese of Washington, D.C.
- The Widowed to Widowed Program, 13133 Julian Ave., Lakeside, Calif. 92040
- THEOS for the Widowed, 125 Veronica, Pittsburgh, Pa. 15235, Bea Decker, Director
- Vistas Club, Central Y.W.C.A., Hamilton, 10, Ontario, Canada
- Widow's Consultation Center, Inc., 136 E. 57th St., New York, N.Y. 10022
- Widow-to-Widow Program, now under the auspices of Action for Independent Maturity, 1225 Connecticut Ave., Washington, D.C. 20036
- Widows and Widowers Associated, Bridgeport, Conn.
- Widowed, Inc., 1111 Lovett Blvd., Houston, Texas 77006, Shirley Wolfe, Director
- Women's Fellowship Group, Church of the Ascension, Rochester, N.Y.

Has there been any major research done for the widowed on a clinical basis?

Yes. By far the most ambitious program in the area was the recently completed five-year Widow-to-Widow program. The program, headed by Dr. Phyllis Silverman under a grant from the National Institute of Mental Health, researched the needs of over two hundred widows in a section of Boston. Widow-aides were hired to personally contact and work with the newly bereaved widows. They found three basic periods that each widow seemed to go through: the initial period of adjustment, the recoil phase, and the recovery period.

The program worked on the assumption that a widow was the best-qualified person to help another widow. This theory proved to be valid. One of the values of the widow-aides was that they could share common experiences. The chief problem with the program in my eyes was not its theory, but its cost factor. To do the job well would mean the cost would have to be assumed by a large, continuous grant. If you desire more information about this program, I refer you to the articles written by Dr. Silverman mentioned in the following bibliography.

BIBLIOGRAPHY

Beck, Frances, *Diary of a Widow* (Boston: Beacon Press, 1965).

Champagne, Marion, *Facing Life Alone* (Indianapolis: Bobbs-Merrill, 1964).

Egleson, Jim, and Janet Egleson, *Parents Without Partners* (New York: Ace Star Books, 1961).

Feifel, Herman, "Death." In *Encyclopedia of Mental Health*, Vol. II, p. 427ff.

Feifel, Herman (Ed.), *The Meaning of Death* (New York: McGraw-Hill, 1965).

Gorer, Geoffrey, *Death, Grief, and Mourning* (Garden City, N.Y.: Doubleday, 1967).

Grollman, Earl (Ed.), *Explaining Death to Children* (Boston: Beacon Press, 1967).

Jackson, Edgar, *For the Living* (New York: Channel Press, 1963).

_____, *Telling a Child About Death* (New York: Channel Press, 1965).

_____, *You and Your Grief* (New York: Channel Press, 1966).

Johnson, Mildred, *The Smiles and the Tears* (Old Tappan, N.J.: Fleming Revell, 1969).

Kooiman, Gladys, *When Death Takes a Father* (Grand Rapids, Mich: Baker Book House, 1968).

Kooiman, Gladys, and Bea Decker, *After the Flowers Are Gone* (Michigan: Zondervan, 1973).

Kreis, Bernadine, and Alice Pattie, *Up from Grief: Patterns of Recovery* (New York: Seabury Press, 1969).

Kubler-Ross, Elisabeth, *On Death and Dying* (New York: Macmillan, 1969).

Kutscher, Austin H. (Ed.), *Death and Bereavement* (Springfield, Ill.: C. C. Thomas, 1969).

Langer, Marion, *Learning to Live as a Widow* (New York: Julian Messner, 1957).

_____, "Widowhood and Mental Health." In *Encyclopedia of Mental Health*, Vol. VI, p. 2013ff., 1965.

Lewis, C. S., *A Grief Observed* (New York: Seabury Press, 1961)

Marshall. Catherine, *Beyond Our Selves* (New York: McGraw-Hill, 1961).

_____, *To Live Again* (New York: McGraw-Hill, 1957).

Pastoral Psychology. Issue devoted to "The Widow, The Divorcee, and The Single Woman," XVII, December, 1969.

Shultz, Gladys, *Widows Wise and Otherwise* (New York: Lippincott, 1949).

Silverman, Phyllis, "The Widow as a Caregiver in a Program of Preventive Intervention with other Widows," *Mental Hygiene*, 1970.

_____, "The Widow-to-Widow Program." *Mental Hygiene*, Vol. 53, No. 3, July, 1969.

_____, "Factor Involved in Accepting an Offer of Help." *Archives of Foundation of Thanatology*, Vol. 3, Fall, 1971, p. 161ff.

_____, *Proceedings of a Workshop for Widows and Widowers*, sponsored by Widow-to-Widow Program: Harvard Medical School, Boston, Mass. (mimeograph copies only), June, 1971.

Start, Clarissa, *When You're a Widow* (St. Louis: Concordia, 1968).

Streib, Gordon, and W. E. Thompson, "The Older Person in a Family Context." In *Handbook of Social Gerontology* (Chicago: University of Chicago Press, 1960), pp. 447-488.

Switzer, David K., *The Dynamics of Grief* (Nashville, Tenn.: Abingdon Press, 1970).

Taves, Isabetta, *Women Alone* (New York: Funk and Wagnalls, 1968).

Thomas, John R., "Marguerite and Me." *Pilgrimage*, Vol. 1, Fall-Winter, 1972, p. 35ff.

Torre, Marie, "How I Survived," as told by Edie Adams. *Redbook*, September 1962, pp. 94-97.

Torrie, Margaret, *Begin Again: A Book for Women Alone* (London: J. M. Dent, 1970).

"When Your Wife Is a Widow What Then." *Changing Times*, 25:6 - 9, June, 1971.

19

What You Should Know About Suicide

How do you know if a person may take his life?

What to do for the suicidal person.

How to approach the grieving family after suicide is committed.

Is a public funeral recommended for the suicide victim?

Whom to contact for help.

EARL A. GROLLMAN

Once every minute someone tries to kill himself with conscious intent. Sixty or seventy times a day these attempts succeed. How can we understand the suicidal person's inner world, his interpersonal conflicts, and societal pressures? Since research has proved that the potential suicide often gives indications of his intent, how best can we meaningfully intervene during the crisis? And when a suicide is committed, what can we do for the family and friends of the victim?

Dr. Grollman is the author of *Suicide: Prevention, Intervention, and Postvention*, and a member of the American Association of Suicidology.

What You Should Know About Suicide

Suicide is a topic that few wish to talk about. The thought of self-destruction arouses anxiety-provoking emotions. Self-imposed death is generally considered a form of insane, bizarre, unconventional behavior. Suicide is a subject that stigmatizes not only the victim but the survivor as well. Yet the iron curtain of silence must be lifted.

Who would possibly attempt to take his own life?

Almost everybody at one time or another contemplates suicide. Death-oriented behavior is one of the choices open to human beings. Suicide has been known in all times and committed by all manner of people, from Saul, Sappho, and Seneca to Virginia Woolf, James Forrestal, and Ernest Hemingway. Every person is a potential suicide.

What is the incidence of suicide?

In America the problem has reached somewhere between twenty-two and twenty-five thousand annually or one suicide every twenty-six minutes. If unreported and mis-reported deaths by self-execution were added, the true number could easily be doubled or tripled. Suicide, which once ranked twenty-second on the list of causes of death in the United States, now rates tenth, and in some states, sixth. And for everyone who succeeds in committing suicide, fifteen will have tried and failed. This statistic does not even include indirect forms of self-destruction.

What are indirect forms of self-destruction?

To be classified a suicide a person must intend to kill himself and must actually do so. There are those who are suicidal and yet are not recognized as such. They find life intolerable and unmanageable and participate in death-oriented behavior. Their entire lifestyle involves a movement toward the brink of self-annihilation. This could include overeating, overworking, and heavy smoking.

The car also serves as an ideal instrument of self-execution, since auto accidents are particularly resistant to later observation, statistics, and analysis. Alcoholism is a form of life-shortening activity in which a physical disease such as cirrhosis is then listed as the cause of death. By drinking to excess the alcoholic plays an unconscious and indirect role in his own demise.

Accident types of suicides are another form of self-inflicted death. The accident-prone individual may believe that he is careful, yet he behaves in curiously self-destructive ways, such as stabbing himself with a knife or "accidentally" taking too many sleeping pills. Social scientists refer to this behavior as either an indirect, partial, slow, installment plan, subintentioned, submeditated suicide equivalent. Yet whatever the terminology, self-imposed death — direct or indirect — is the Number One cause of unnecessary deaths.

Is there a relationship between suicide and environment?

Suicide reflects the relationship of the person not only to himself but to his community. Actuarial data provide additional information about individual behavior as contrasted to one's surroundings and cultural milieu.

Two males commit suicide for every female. Yet more women attempt self-execution than men. The male is more skillful with lethal weapons and uses the gun as his chief instrument of self-imposed death, while women mostly use barbiturates as their method of self-destruction.

Married people have a lower suicide rate than single, widowed, or divorced persons. Divorced men and women have a higher percentage than the undivorced of the same sex. For the very poor as well as for the rich, the rate of self-inflicted deaths soars during periods of economic depression. Although there are exceptions, the percentages are highest in the professional/managerial categories.

Caucasians have a higher suicide rate than any other race. When black people migrate to northern industrial centers, their rate of suicide rises markedly. There is an increase of suicide among middle- and upper-class blacks which is rapidly becoming comparable to the white groups. Among the American Indian, there is a virtual suicide epidemic among those between the ages of fifteen and twenty.

More suicides occur in April, when there is a sharp contrast between the smiling spring world and one's despairing state of mind. Because many people are alone and lonely, the Christmas period also has an uncommonly elevated rate of suicide. Of all the religions, Protestants have the highest suicide rates. Catholics are second, and Jews are third.

Statistically, city dwellers are more likely to attempt suicide than those of the rural population; countries which are urbanized and industrialized have more suicides than where the economy is farming and nontechnological; military personnel more than civilians; and those people having no offspring tend to be more prone to suicide than those who do have children.

Suicide rates generally go up with age and are higher with the elderly than with any other age group. Youth is a special case.

What about suicide and youth?

Suicide rates among young people have risen dramatically. While suicide is listed as the tenth leading cause of death in the United States, it is third now among youths fifteen to nineteen years, and second among college students.

Pressures starting from early childhood are the one important motivation of this self-destructiveness. Attempts by youths to end their lives are based on depressed feelings of being unable to meet competition. A terrifying concern of the student is the inability to compete successfully in school. Failure brings not only disappointment and disapproval from parents but a shattering of personal confidence. Many young people also have difficulty with interpersonal relationships, and if a romance is broken there is often more than just disappointment, but the tumultuous feeling of being rejected and abandoned. Eighty-eight percent of the suicides occur at home; very often with the parents in the next room.

How can a parent help his suicidal child?

Lack of communication between parent and child is a significant factor in the period preceding suicide. It becomes obvious that much can be done to bring about a happier relationship between adult and youth.

Don't substitute authority for honest answers to your child's questions. Spend more time listening, trying to comprehend what he is really saying and thinking. You need not agree on all issues in order to communicate with one another. Demonstrate in word and touch that even though there are differences, there is still love and respect.

When serious problems arise, a professional should be consulted. If suicide is attempted, it is often recommended that the youth be hospitalized, if only briefly, and placed in a ward where other adolescent patients might offer warmth, support, and understanding. When the young people are first brought to the hospital they are shaken, anxious, insecure, depressed, guilty, and apprehensive. The therapist can ask them to try to understand the precipitating events, such as their parents' refusal to let them go out, or a broken romance, or a feeling that no one cares. He guides them to cope better with their conflicts and to communicate more effectively with their family and peers.

What about the elderly and death-oriented behavior?

The suicide rate is highest among the older citizens. Year in and year out the elderly rank at the bottom of the list for suicide threats and attempts, but they top the statistics of those whose suicides have been completed. Although they make up only 9 percent of the population, men and women over sixty-five years of age commit over 25 percent of the reported suicides.

Life-shortening behavior could include the following danger signals: self-starvation, refusal to follow physicians' prescriptions, hazardous activity, voluntary seclusion, previous suicidal behavior, psychiatric disorders, putting effects in order (although this may be merely appropriate behavior and must be so evaluated in the light of other events), and threats of suicide. The final cause may be a crisis during which the elderly person who lives outside a group is deprived of the community's emotional support. Such an event may be the death of close friends and relatives, loss of employment, economic insecurity, and feelings of rejection and uselessness. Serious physical sickness is a most significant contributory factor. Many older people appear to prefer death by their own hand rather than waiting for it passively. ·

Admittedly, treatment of a depressed elderly individual is difficult. Not only may he have lost confidence in his own ability to cope with his problems, but he may believe (and often he is correct) that no one is really interested in him. First, try to turn such a person back to life by reassuring him that people *do* care and that someone knows what must be done and will do it. Medical and psychotherapeutic support could be enlisted to ascertain both the physical and psychological implications. A church or social agency might be contacted to determine the community's recreational and social resources for its senior citizens. Other persons, particularly friends, colleagues, and relatives, might be notified to comfort and assist the troubled person.

Feelings vital to the morale of people of *all* ages — love, caring, and understanding — are so often forgotten when elderly people are concerned.

How do you know if a person is suicide prone?

Suicide does not occur suddenly, or unpredictably, or inevitably. The final act is the result of many, many overt failures of adaptation. This is why it is so important to be aware of the clues signaled by those who willfully end their lives.

The following warnings may be communicated by the suicidal person.

The Suicide Attempt. The surest sign of intent is the attempt. Do not dismiss the incident with the exasperated comment: "He was only trying to get attention." Any suicide effort must be taken with the greatest seriousness. Twelve percent of those who attempt self-execution will make a second try and succeed within two years. After an abortive try, many resolve: "I'll do a better job the next time." And they mean it.

The Suicidal Threat. The myth that those who talk about taking their life seldom do it has proved both dangerous and erroneous. Thus, the verbal intimidation must be viewed with utmost concern. Initially, the threat could be an unconscious appeal for protection and intervention: "I am tired of life." "My family would be better off without me." "I won't be around much longer for you to put up with." "I just can't go on any longer." And, "If I were to die now my parents would feel sorry for their meanness." Later, if no one is really concerned, the person may set the time and determine the method for the self-imposed death. Sometimes the coded indications are nonverbal. The member of a group abruptly resigns under the guise of moving to another location. The parsimonious man suddenly makes outright, generous grants of cash to relatives and friends. The youth gives away all his valued books and prized phonograph albums. Once an individual has decided to kill himself his behavior is a bit different than before the suicidal preoccupation.

The Situational Hint. Something is happening both *within* the person and *around* him. Suicide often occurs when status is destroyed or shaken. A person may destroy himself because he is driven by guilt of the past, or he may take his life because he cannot accept the alarming prospects of the future. Common precipitating factors in order of frequency are: poor health, economic distress, divorce, domestic difficulties, and the death of a loved one.

The Family Hint. The suicidal person could mirror

his own family's emotional stress. He might be neurotically tied to a depressed parent and reflect the elder's throes of despair. He may feel accountable for the problems of those whom he loves, or may even be held responsible by them for the difficulties involved. Often families unconsciously select one member to become the object of their accumulated aggression. Unfortunately, this one does not know how to cope with their malice; he cannot retaliate and respond appropriately. When he finally decides to kill himself, he is really acting out the antisocial impulses that are covertly present in the other family members.

Emotional Hint. Any sudden change in a person's personality is always a perilous warning. The majority of potential suicides suffer from depression, usually beginning insidiously, with feelings of apprehension and despondency. A person may not even remember when it all began. All he knows is that lately he has been feeling sad, blue, "down in the dumps." The future looks bleak and he sees no way to change it. He imagines that he has cancer, insanity, or some other dread malady. Ordinary tasks and simple decisions become difficult. There is a lassitude and lack of energy; there may be a falling off of sexual activity (the disturbed person may think that he is sterile or impotent). Physical complaints are frequent among suicidally depressed people. The melancholy person prefers more and more to be alone. The preoccupation with self usually is in a negative, self-reproachful, self-deprecating way. He neglects his personal hygiene and appearance. There is a marked decline in his job performance. Unable to perceive alternatives, he assumes there is no choice but death.

Mental Illness. It is difficult to define "mental illness" but an apt description is: "Functional changes in which there is less achievement than usual of life-preserving and other valuable goals." As a result of a new overwhelming responsibility, a person loses some of his ability to function, organize, and maintain life.

To be mentally ill does not mean to be psychotic. The great majority of suicides are in touch with reality, can care for themselves, and on the basis of their symptoms need not be committed to a mental hospital. The patient who, from a statistical point of view, is most likely to commit suicide in a general hospital is an individual who is suffering from an organic brain syndrome. This disorder is manifested by confusion, disorientation, and agitated depression.

Psychotically depressed people often become suicidal either when entering or leaving a totally depressed state. When encapsulated within it, they are often too immobilized to kill themselves.

Who are those most susceptible to self-destruction?

These are the clues to those with the greatest suicidal predisposition:

- Previous suicide attempt
- Suicide threat — direct or disguised
- Chronic illness or isolation
- Recent death
- Financial stress — bankruptcy, joblessness
- Domestic difficulties — divorce, separation, broken home
- Severe depression
- Psychosis — withdrawal, confusion, depersonalization
- Alcoholism — uncontrolled drinking for a period of years
- Chronic use of bromides, barbiturates, or

hallucinogenic agents
- Family history of suicide

Is there a composite picture of a suicidal person?

- Male
- Caucasian
- Protestant
- Adolescent, or over 65 years of age
- Unemployed, retired, or with recent trouble
- Widowed or divorced
- Living alone and feeling unwanted and unneeded
- Depression with feelings of hopelessness, guilt, and shame
- Previous suicide attempt
- Alcoholic and/or drug addict
- Somatic (physical) disease — delusions or real
- Psychiatric disorder
- Unable to cope with both normal and stressful situations

How do you help the potential suicide?

Fortunately, no one is 100 percent suicidal. Notes often reveal mingled emotions: "Dear Mary, I have to kill myself. I hate you. All my love, Sumner." Since the most ardent death wish is tentative, there is much that you can do for the distressed individual.

First, be aware of the warning signals. Many people shut themselves out from the reality situation because the very mention of the word "suicide" makes them uncomfortable. Others suppress communications because they simply do not wish to become involved.

Form a relationship based on an unshakable attitude of acceptance toward the perturbed person. The friendship should not be only of words, but a nonverbal mutuality of empathy. This is not the moment for moralizing but for loving support. Make the individual feel at ease and understood. Caring and concern are great sources of encouragement.

When an individual has a disgust of life, he needs desperately to ventilate his burdensome feelings. He needs responsive listening and full attention from you, his friend. Concentrate not only on his words but his actions: how he looks, acts, his appetite, his changing moods and outlook, his irregular sleep pattern, and his impulsiveness in the face of an acute situational problem.

Identify the source of distress. This might prove difficult; suicide thrives on secrecy. Relevant questions to stimulate discussion are: "What's been happening to you lately?" "When did you begin to feel worse?" "What's new in your life?" "What persons have been involved?" The potential suicide should be encouraged to diagnose his problem in his own words and to define as precisely as possible the precipitating stresses. Assure him that he can express his true feelings with impunity, including negative emotions of hostility, hate, anxiety, grief, resentment, bitterness, and even a desire for revenge. If he is reluctant to share innermost emotions, his affective responses might be expedited by observations: "You seem to be quite sad." "You appear to be ready to cry." "You seem so troubled. Perhaps if you told me how you feel, I might understand." Keep the troubles and feelings in view.

Inventory his problem-solving resources. Clarify how he has handled similar situations prior to this time. Listen for references to experiences in the individual's past which are analogous to the present scene.

Discover his values. What still matters to him? Watch for signs of animation when the "best things" are touched on (noting especially his eyes). What is still available that has meaning? Who are those persons who continue to touch his life? Now that his life's situation is reexamined, are there not alternative solutions? Is there not some ray of optimism? The element of realistic hope should be communicated in a loving and convincing manner.

Don't try to handle the problem alone. Seek other sources of help such as a physician or therapist. Keep the physician or therapist informed of any changes in the suicidal person's mental and physical condition. Never undermine the competence of the professional's expertise.

Remove from the premises all weapons and potentially dangerous medications. Make sure that the person takes the correct amount of any prescribed medicines on schedule. In case of emergency call the suicide prevention clinic in your area or the nearest hospital.

Whom do I contact for help?

The family as helper. Whenever feasible, the cooperation of the family should be enlisted. Relatives might give information that may have been "accidentally" overlooked by the troubled individual. Occasionally the appearance of a loved one will cause the person with suicidal preoccupation to reconsider. Unfortunately, it may be that no one really does care if the person takes his life or not. Sometimes a self-inflicted death represents the fulfillment of the subtle and unspoken wish of others. Occasionally families are not always helpful and may unconsciously wish that the miserable individual was not around.

The church and synagogue. Houses of worship often substitute for a missing family. The clergyman may pose spiritual alternatives to ultimate anxieties, i.e., death, guilt, suffering, and failure. The pastor could be most effective in his role as the surrogate of the God of Forgiveness.

The professional. Friends may be well intentioned but often lacking in knowledge and experience, besides being emotionally involved. Many ministers are superb pastoral counselors — understanding, sensitive, supportive; but there are others who are completely untrained in crisis intervention. Whenever in doubt, the family physician is a fine resource. He usually knows the intimate background of the patient and would be most helpful in both evaluation and referral. Meanwhile, he might suggest some effective antidepressant to tide the person over until comprehensive help is forthcoming.

The psychiatrist or clinical psychologist could be of invaluable assistance. Mental health care is not just a luxury of the affluent. There are private as well as public agencies, supported by national, state, and county funds, which offer a wide range of services at low cost. By his acquired basic knowledge, skills, and attitudes a therapist has a disciplined capability to understand the suicidal person's innermost feelings, demands, and expectations.

The suicide prevention center. Available in many American cities, such centers were established to afford the perturbed individual both emergency counsel as well as an effective sanctuary until the self-destructive impulse has passed.

Community resources. There is also a variety of recreational, social, and educational activities that can give the suicide-prone a feeling of identity by active participation with the larger community.

What happens after the suicide attempt, and the

person seems to be on the way to recovery?

Since the initial emergency is past, no one — professional or family — can relax completely. The worst may not be over. Improvement is often confused with the person's increase of psychomotor energy and exuberance. Do not merely breathe a sigh of relief and let down your guard. This phase may reflect only an inner resolve to wipe the slate clean and *now* to do away with himself.

Ironically, many regard the person who attempts suicide and survives as a failure. He earns the double contempt of being so deranged that he wanted to die and so incompetent that he couldn't even do it properly. The emotional problems which led to suicidal crisis are seldom resolved even when the extremity has seemingly passed. The emergency is not over until the would-be suicide is ᵃt home with life.

How do I approach the grieving family who just sustained a suicide?

Natural death has its share of emotional overtones: disbelief, hostility, depression, panic, guilt, and loneliness. But death by self-execution brings the greatest of affronts to those who remain. The act of suicide raises the inevitable questions: "Why?" and "What could I have done to prevent it?" The survivor is anxious and grief-stricken and wonders, "How can I face my friends?"

As a friend, give your best self — neither prejudiced by taboos, nor judgmental of the actions of the deceased or the remaining family. Neither justify nor censor. Offer your concern and love. Conversation should be natural. Interest should be genuine and sincere. One should not try too hard. Oversolicitation only engenders further suspicion and guilt. Listen responsively to what the other experiences from his internal agonizing frame of reference. Although suicide is often viewed as insane behavior, to inform the family that the person who killed himself was crazy only brings fear of an inherited mental illness.

Should there be a public funeral for the person who took his life?

A first impulse is to hold the service as quickly and quietly as possible. Yet the relative just cannot hide from reality. A private funeral seems to say that the family is unable to bear the disgrace and therefore want to keep it "secret." But a public worship service offers the opportunity for friends to comfort the mourners. The funeral where no one is invited but all may attend affords a sharing occasion for supportive love at a time when it is so desperately needed.

What about the guilt of the bereaved family?

The "living victims" are the survivors who bear the burden of guilt and the stigma of having a loved one who has willfully taken his life. The widowed spouse will never know if some act of unkindness on his or her part was the spark that inflamed the mate with the urge for self-execution. Parents blame themselves for negligence, and the children of a suicide are haunted by the fact that they perhaps did something to expedite their parent's death.

It is of no help to say, "Don't talk about it." The bereaved is going through an intense emotional crisis and needs to articulate and act out reactions — loud denial, turning slowly to bewilderment, and finally to weeping, despairing confrontation with the truth of his loss. Review the memories of the deceased and as pain is felt at the recall of these experiences, the individual begins to slowly dissolve himself of his emotional ties to the dead person. After the funeral, self-recrimination may still be present, but the most meaningful way to relieve guilt is by transforming any errors of the past into more noble behavior in the future.

How can you tell if the survivor's reactions are unusual?

In general, one is able to distinguish normal from pathological grief not by the latter's being abnormal per se, but rather by emotional reactions being so intensive and prolonged that the physical and mental well-being are jeopardized.

When grief work is not done, the survivor may suffer morbid distress characterized by delayed responses. He may show great fortitude at the funeral but later develop symptoms of agitated depression and bodily affliction. He may complain of such psychosomatic illnesses as ulcerative colitis, rheumatoid arthritis, asthma, and hypochondriasis (imaginary ills). Symptoms of a tension headache may lead to the conclusion by the bereaved that he has a brain tumor; arthritic pain is interpreted as heart disease; constipation becomes a symptom of a malignancy.

Obsessive-compulsive behavior may manifest itself. One may try to appease his guilt through extreme cleanliness. Or he may be unwilling to terminate the atmosphere of the funeral service, i.e., "Tell me the eulogy again." There may be self-destructive behavior detrimental to social and economic existence. If there are any doubts as to a person's emotional health, professional help should be consulted.

There may be moments when I don't want to live. What should I do?

If you are considering a self-imposed death, make sure you follow these rules before you finally elect to die.

First, pick up the telephone and call somebody — a hot line, a suicide prevention center, a hospital, a clergyman, a neighbor, a relative, a friend, the police station. If you do not have the number, the telephone operator will be of assistance in reaching the designated individual.

Tell the person of your plans for suicide — how, when, where, why. If you are contacting a stranger, give your complete name, address, and telephone number. Just say whatever comes into your mind — your current crisis, your diminishing reasons for wanting to live, your unexpressed anger, your inability to cope with stressful situations.

Give information as to the other members of your family and close friends. As soon as possible, arrange to visit a professional counselor. This may be the person whom you just called or someone just suggested. Don't give up hope. Remember, once you die, you *cannot* be brought back to life. At the moment, everything may look bleak; but darkness and light, joy and anguish are strands in the texture of life. Try to hold out for a little bit longer. A cry for help is a summons for rescue.

SUGGESTED READINGS

Bibliography on Suicide and Suicide Prevention, 1897 - 1957, 1958 - 1967 (Chevy Chase: National Institute of Mental Health, 1969).

Blaine, Graham B., Jr., *Youth and the Hazards of Affluence* (New York: Harper & Row, 1966).

Dublin, Louis I., *Suicide: A Sociological and Statistical Study* (New York: Ronald Press, 1963).

Durkheim, Emile, *Suicide: A Study in Sociology* (Glencoe, Ill.: Free Press, 1951).

Ellis, E. R. and G. N. Allen, *Within Our Suicide Problem* (Garden City, N.Y.: Doubleday, 1961).

Farber, Maurice L., *Theory of Suicide* (New York: Funk and Wagnalls, 1968).

Farberow, N. L., and E. S. Schneidman (Eds.), *The Cry for Help* (New York: McGraw-Hill, 1961).

Freud, Sigmund, *Civilization and Its Discontents*, translated and edited by James Strachey (New York: W. W. Norton, 1962). "Mourning and Melancholia." In *Collected Papers*, Vol. IV. (London: The Hogarth Press, 1949).

Grollman, Earl A., *Suicide: Prevention, Intervention, Postvention* (Boston: Beacon Press, 1971).

Henry, Andrew F., and James F. Short, Jr., *Suicide and Homicide* (Glencoe, Ill.: Free Press, 1954).

Kiev, Ari, "The Early Recognition and Treatment of Potentially Suicidal Persons." In *Identifying Suicide Potential* (New York: Behavioral Publications, 1971).

Meerloo, Joost A., *Suicide and Mass Suicide* (New York: Grune and Stratton, 1962).

Menninger, Karl A., *Man Against Himself* (New York: Harcourt, Brace, 1938).

Oates, Wayne E., and Kirk H. Neely, *Where To Go For Help* (Philadelphia: Westminster Press, 1972).

Pretzel, Paul W., *Understanding the Suicidal Person* (Nashville: Abingdon Press, 1972).

Resnik, H. L. P., "Center Comments." *Bulletin of Suicidology*, National Institute of Mental Health, Spring, 1970.

Resnik, H. L. P. (Ed.), *The Diagnosis and Management of the Suicidal Individual* (Boston: Little, Brown, 1967).

Resnik, H. L. P.. and Joel M. Cantor, "Suicide and Aging." *Journal of the American Geriatric Society*, February, 1970.

Richman, Joseph and Milton Rosenbaum, "The Family Doctor and the Suicidal Family." *Psychiatry in Medicine*, January, 1970.

St. John-Stevas, Norman, *Life, Death and the Law* (Bloomington: Indiana University Press, 1961).

Schneidman, E. S. (Ed.), *Essays in Self-Destruction* (New York: International Science Press, 1967).

Schneidman, E. S., and N. L. Farberow (Eds.), *Clues to Suicide* (New York: McGraw-Hill, 1957).

Schneidman, E. S., and Philip Mandelkorn, "How to Prevent Suicide." Public Affairs Pamphlet No. 406, 1967.

Seiden, Richard H.. *Campus Tragedy: A Study of Student Suicide* (Grant #5T. MH-8104, National Institute of Mental Health).

Sprott, S. E. *The English Debate on Suicide from Donne to Hume*, (LaSalle, Ill.: Open Court, 1961).

Stengel, Erwin, *Suicide and Attempted Suicide* (Baltimore: Penguin Books, 1964).

Teicher, Joseph D., "Why Adolescents Kill Themselves." *National Health Program Reports*, January, 1970.

Williams, Glanville, *The Sanctity of Life and the Criminal Law* (New York: Knopf, 1957).

20

Death Education in the Face of a Taboo

When should death education begin?

How should it be introduced in the schools?

What are the best available books and materials?

Teachers, parents, and others often ask: "Aren't you afraid you will unleash a flood of heavy emotions?" Are they right?

What about death education in the community?

SANDRA L. BERTMAN

Schools are increasingly concerned about social consciousness. Subjects like sex education, peace education, environmental education, and consumer education have evolved in curriculums from coast to coast. The quest for "relevance," which has spawned mini-courses on every subject imaginable, virtually dictates that discussions of death, the most universal of all natural phenomena, be considered.

Sandra L. Bertman, Ed.M., has spoken before hundreds of children, youth, and adults about the taboo subject of death. She is a teacher, media programmer, and educational director of Equinox Institute, Brookline, Massachusetts. She has developed courses on death for the Adult Education Program in Cambridge, Harvard University School of Public Health, and the elementary and secondary public schools of Boston, Belmont, and Newton, Massachusetts.

Death Education in the Face of a Taboo

When does death education begin?

With the first lullaby a mother sings to her child, death education begins. In a soft, soothing voice a mother lulls her little one to sleep:

Rock-a-bye baby, on the tree top,
When the wind blows, the cradle will rock;
When the bough breaks, the cradle will fall.
Down will come baby, cradle and all.

What are we telling our youngsters? Are we suggesting that death is a trick? Never listen (to the words). Never think about what the lullaby means. Are we assuming they're not aware of the contradiction between the tone of such an innocuous verse and its meaning?

One five-year-old's response to what the nursery rhyme was all about was, "Well, it's about a baby what was hanged up in a tree in a carriage. His mother put him up there cause um . . . I think it was a wicked mother." (Why?) "Cause she putted him up there. The baby fell, hurted itself." The abandonment by the mother — the baby's being "by alone" was immediately apparent to this little girl. When asked to clarify further, when asked directly what happened to the baby, the youngster replied, "He hurted hisself. He cried. Baby and all . . . no, he didn't die. He just fell down." She's not seeing death. Because she's too young to have a concept of death? Because the thought of death (finality — irreversibility) is too scary?

As a matter of fact, there's something lovely in beginning "death education" this way — mother and child singing together about death, snug in each other's arms. What a warm and secure vantage point from which to peer out at such harsh realities as cruelty, separation, loneliness.

So many of the early fairy tales — the first children's literature — treat anxious concerns such as abandonment and death ("Hansel and Gretel," "Snow White," "Little Red Riding Hood"). The "snug arms," as it were, are written in; i.e., the wicked abandoning mother is never the *real* mother but a "step mother," and death is not the end: rescue, and living happily-ever-after is.

Older youngsters have a marvelous time reviewing the nursery rhymes and children's literature of their youth. Sixth-grade youngsters' first response to "down will come baby, cradle and all" is that the baby is immediately killed. One group of youngsters listened with delight to the taped responses of a kindergarten class. The group concluded that either the five-year-olds didn't want to talk about death or (more probably) couldn't believe death could happen.

Five-year-old responses to "Humpty Dumpty" were, "It really was an egg, so what's so bad about it?" Or, "It's really a person inside. It's good if the egg breaks, he can get his legs out." "Oh . . . if the men can't fix him . . . I mean the person inside can go to the hospital or to a doctor." (What if he couldn't be fixed?) "Well then he would die." (What about that?) "Then that would be sad. Why are the crayons on the drum?"

The sixth graders called attention to the youngsters' evasions — to the person in the egg getting better, to how long it took the kindergarten group to handle the death question at all, and that when pushed to do so, to the quick change of subject.

The fitting climax to this sixth-grade class is *Space Child's Mother Goose*, published in 1968, which happily removes death considerations from the nursery rhyme altogether:

> Humpty Dumpty sat on a wall.
> At three o'clock he had his great fall.
> The King set the Time Machine back to two.
> Now Humpty's unscrambled and good as new.[1]

Contrasting the original rhymes and tales with some of their modern variations is an exciting project for students or for one's own youngsters. Speculating on the reasons for the ending revisions to the "Little Red Riding Hood" story, for example, graphically illustrates our society's growing squeamishness in exposing the idea of death to our young:

. . . Whatever Really Happened to "Little Red Riding Hood"?

"Put the custard and the little pot of butter upon the stool, and come and lie down with me."
Little Red Riding Hood climbed into the bed where, being greatly amazed to see how her grandmother looked in her nightclothes, she said to her:

"Grandmamma, what great arms you have!"

"That is the better to hug you, my dear."

"Grandmamma, what great teeth you have!"

"That is to eat you up."

And saying these words, this wicked wolf fell upon Little Red Riding Hood, and ate her up, too.

— Original story by Charles Perrault (1628 - 1703), *The Blue Fairy Book*, Edited by Andrew Lang (New York: Longman's, Green & Co., 1904).

"The better to EAT you with," said the wolf. And he sprang from the bed and ate Litle Red Riding Hood up.

A passing woodsman stepped into the house to see how Little Red Riding Hood's grandmother was feeling. And when he saw the wolf, he said, "Ah ha! I've found you at last, you wicked old rascal!" He lifted his ax, and with one blow, killed him. Then he cut the wolf open and out stepped Little Red Riding Hood and her grandmother.

They thanked the woodsman for what he had done. Then all three sat down and ate the cake and the butter and drank of the grape juice which Little Red Riding Hood had brought.

— *Little Red Riding Hood*, E. O. Jones (New York: Golden Press, 1948).

"THE BETTER TO EAT YOU WITH, MY DEAR," cried the wolf. He pushed back the covers, and jumped out of the bed. Then Little Red Riding Hood saw that it was the big wolf pretending to be her grandmother!

At that moment a hunter passed the house. He heard the wolf's wicked voice and Little Red Riding Hood's frightened scream. He burst open the door. Before the wolf could reach Little Red Riding Hood, the hunter lifted his gun to his shoulder, and killed the wicked wolf. Little Red Riding Hood was very happy and she thanked the kind hunter.

Grandmother unlocked the door and came out of the closet, where she had been hiding. She kissed Little Red Riding Hood again and again. And she thanked the hunter for saving them both from the big wolf. They were all so happy that they decided to have a party right then and there. Grandmother gave the hunter and Little Red Riding Hood a big glass of fresh milk, and took one herself. They ate up all the cake and fruit that Little Red Riding Hood had brought to her grandmother. And they all lived happily ever after.

— *Read-Aloud Nursery Tales* (New York: Wonder, 1957).

And with these words, the wicked wolf sprang upon Little Red Riding Hood, and swallowed her.

A hunter passing the house had heard Little Red Riding Hood scream. Opening the door he saw the wolf with the grandmother's nightcap on, and raised his gun to shoot. Then he remembered the scream. Drawing his knife before the wolf could spring at him, he cut open the wicked creature. What was his surprise when Little Red Riding Hood jumped out, crying, "How frightened I was! It was so dark inside."

The grandmother was pulled out next, a little out of breath but still alive.

The huntsman skinned the wolf and gave the skin to the grandmother for a winter coat. Then they all sat down to eat the cake and the little pot of butter. And Little Red Riding Hood said, "I will never again forget what my mother told me. Never again will I talk to strangers."

— *Big and Little Creatures*, Untermeyers, Eds. (New York: Golden Press, 1961).

The pros and cons of putting the death question quite out of sight are carefully probed. Is it too terrifying for death to be the absolute end to Little Red? Must we unscramble Humpty Dumpty? Is the happiest of all endings always necessary? Does one flush a younger brother's or son's dead goldfish down the toilet and hurry post haste to the pet store to replace it before he comes home? Who is being protected — from what — and why? Does putting the death question out of sight have anything to do with putting the question out of mind? In another context Mister Rogers sings, "What do you do with the mad that you feel when you feel so mad you could bite?" What do kids do with their secret thoughts of death if there's no place that these thoughts are acknow ledged or allowed to seep through?

From the lesson Little Red Riding Good (!) learned ("I will never again forget what my mother told me. Never again will I talk to strangers"), we look to other uses of death in children's literature. The intent of Puritan children's literature seems to be to scare one into good behavior. But death as threat or punishment occurs not only in Puritan times; it occurs in "The Story of Augustus Who Would Not Have Any Soup" and "The Dreadful Story of Harriet and the Matches," both published in 1844, and again in a modernized version of the boy-who-cried-wolf tale, "Matilda Who Told Lies and Was Burned to Death," published in 1941.

Against the backdrop of squeamishness and tension associated with death, society's changing ideas are reflected in the more contemporary literature which emphasizes death as a natural part of the life cycle, as a reality to be faced, ex- perienced, and accepted. Exposure to death ought to provide a creative experience through which one can grow, as beautifully put forth in E. B. White's *Charlotte's Web* (1952), Carl Sandburg's *Blue Silver* (1922), Pearl Buck's *Big Wave* (1947), S. S. Warburg's *Growing Time* (1969), and John Coburn's *Annie and the Sand Dobbies* (1964).

Youngsters can handle, enjoy, and learn from any

material at any age. Focusing on the younger child's concepts of death becomes the pivotal point for exploring one's own beliefs and ideas. In the class (or home) setting, close attention to the themes and craft of the traditional rhymes and stories stimulates youngsters to experiment with their own photographic essays, stories, and myths. A proper homage to the original Mother Goose is one eleven-year-old's latest revision of the revised "Humpty Dumpty":

> Humpty Dumpty sat on a wall,
> Humpty sat to see if he'd fall.
> When he did fall, off rolled his head
> And Humpty Dumpty was dead.[2]

When should one introduce death education to the children in the classroom and how might a teacher do so?

The techniques or considerations involved in introducing death education to the classroom would probably be the same as those a parent would use in introducing the subject to his own child.

When It Happens. Certainly the occasion of the death of a pet, neighbor or stranger, national figure, relative or friend, teacher or classmate must be faced. The death of a pet, personal or classroom, offers the opportunity for discussing death and for providing a real-life model for coping with painful realities.

In the classroom as well as at home it seems important to consider the following:

- Find out what exactly the youngsters are worrying about. What is their understanding of the circumstances of the death? Are they wondering where the body or "being" actually is?

- Let them talk about their feelings. Let them give vent to them (cry or not) and acknowledge the appropriateness of the different responses. Be willing to share your feelings with them.
- Let them go through the forms of funeral and good-bye. Help them participate in burial, eulogy, or other ritual which seems meaningful to them.
- Let the youngsters experience the pleasure and satisfaction of having lived through it all . . . of feeling more nearly "growned" members of the human race.

When It Doesn't Happen. Immersion in a real-life situation is not the only way a youngster learns about life. Vicarious experience allows him — from a safe distance — to view others coping with crises. His own death and separation fears are exposed when uttered by other characters in different yet similar circumstances. Hearing his very thoughts and anxieties voiced by another ("Why did he have to die?") — voiced and worked through — is doubly reassuring; he realizes he shares kindred feelings with the person in the story or film and that these feelings can be resolved.

Let's stick with the death of a pet. With the very young the teacher might use the filmstrip *My Turtle Died Today*,[3] in which a sick turtle (hard protective shell notwithstanding) dies despite the efforts of the boy's father, teacher, and the pet store owner to save it. Billy is the youngsters' stand-in. He and his friends question one another about the realities of death, bury the turtle, and then find (a bit too quickly?)* a litter of kittens on whom to transfer their love and concern.

The Dead Bird by M.W. Brown (New York: Scott, 1958) goes further in having the youngsters continue to visit the grave even after the burial. . . "and every day, until they forgot, they went and sang to their little dead bird and put fresh flowers on his grave."
The Old Dog by S. Abbott (New York: McCann, 1972) introduces the sense

Small doses of drama allow third- through fifth-grade youngsters to examine their feelings and to test their ideas against those of fictional characters and their classmates. *The Yearling*,[4] a feature-length film that deals directly with life-death or crisis issues on many levels — animal and human — is an excellent instrument for such discussion. Amid the rhythmic cycles of nature — animals birthing, seasons changing — the protagonist, Jody, relates to all forms of harsh realities.

In touching scenes Jody and his crippled friend, Fodderwing, discuss what heaven must be like. When Fodderwing dies, the youngsters cry their eyes out* and with Jody attend his funeral, face his mother, and try to understand her belief that death is a freedom — an end to physical suffering for this young crippled lad. The picture of Fodderwing all straightened out, somewhere caring for the animals he loved, makes a kind of sense in light of that previous heaven conversation. Naming the yearling Flag, Fodderwing's suggested name, is a living memorial to the lad, to his love of animals, and to the two boys' friendship.

Living through extraordinarily difficult circumstances as seeing his best friend die, having to kill an animal to save his father's life, having finally to give up a

---

of the old dog's not being there to share in the experience of the new young (replacement) pup.

Not handled in either of these picture books, however, is the idea of a necessary time lapse before replacement can be tolerated and not seen as betrayal or not caring. This necessary time lapse as a factor in working through one's grief is illustrated in *Growing Time* by S.S. Warburg (Boston, Houghton Mifflin, 1969) and in *Annie and the Sand Dobbies* by J. Coburn (New York: Seabury, 1964).

*We'd talked about being brave, "stiff upper lip," and its being all right to cry; yet this class presented a living example of "boys don't cry." The boys held back their tears and even called attention ("gross," "mushy") to ours (the girls, regular classroom teacher, and myself). In the discussion which followed, the girls had much to say about teasing, "bullying," and other ways of expressing feelings when tears aren't possible.

beloved pet yearling, and running away as a solution to a problem, Jody slowly becomes initiated into manhood.

But he is not the only one who is changed. His father has to learn that protection can be crippling; a body — however young — has to experience disappointment, sadness, and loss in order to grow. His mother, whose "meanness" is her way of warding off the impact of losses, is put in touch with her feelings and ultimately able to show her son the love she feels.

Though the boy is of a different era and lifestyle than a class of suburban youngsters, they understand his sufferings and empathize with him. At the end of the film, Jody, too, is no longer a yearling. And is a slight though significant way, neither are the youngsters in the class.

Granted it's important to get one's questions and feelings out. How does one do so?

Children's drawings are a marvelous entree into the world of their thoughts and fantasies. A teacher (or parent) might have the youngsters draw pictures of themselves now and of themselves as old persons, of their first day in a new school, of a funeral, of the classroom gerbil last month when he was alive, now when he is dead, and three months from now.

Youngsters like to "explain" their pictures and talk about one another's. What happens to the body is of great concern to one six-year-old (figure 1). Not only is the body itself carried, held overhead ("They don't want to drag her"), it is buried directly in the ground (no concept of casket). The figure in the lower left is checking "to see if they already wrote her. There are names in this first big box and these [below] are where they're already *planted!*" It makes perfect sense. It's all so natural — body replanted directly in the earth — and all so personal — the exact spot where she's

"planted" must be recorded. "They feel very very sorry. . . He couldn't make her alive because when you're dead your body gets very old and your heart stops beating." The class discussed whether death is only for the old and whether a body ages at the instant of death. And they uniformly agreed to the existence of some master plan of all-rightness in which death and "afterdeath" comfortably fit.

One eight-year-old's drawing focuses on the survivors (figure 2). The body itself is not seen, though it is carefully protected by the neatly constructed box in which it's buried and the antenna-like lightning rod on top of the stone marker. As explained, "The little boy is asking, 'Why did he have to die?' and the mother replies, 'Well, everyone has to die.' The father is crying and the uncle is crying and praying." Note the clouds (one is low and almost a part of the group) and the expression of the sun. The youngsters in this class might construct a puppet show around this picture, which would begin via expanding this graveside conversation.

The same assignment in an inner-city third grade revealed this group's preoccupation with violence. Three-

Fig. 1

fourths of the class drew pictures of stabbings, hangings, etc. One youngster's picture, entitled *Mugging in the Streets,* shows a lone man lying in the gutter with a knife in his chest. Blood is flowing out of his body onto the street. This youngster was concerned with the ghost of the dead man (his uncle) haunting him. His explanation was the cue for the deluge of classmates' confessions of their own ghosts and devils. Through role-playing, this uncle's ghost excused the boy's bad behavior and forgave him from the other side of the grave, the assumption being one is as understanding and forgiving in death as he would have been in life.

Role-playing is another way to become aware of youngsters' tucked-away concerns and beliefs. The younger

Fig. 2

child is continually "playing out"; but for the older one, specific scenes or situations must be set. Suggested by a fifth-grade group were the following:

- An older brother tells his younger brother of their grandfather's death.
- A babysitter must deal with the six-year-old's dead dog who was just run over in front of the house.
- Later that evening, after a dreadful argument with her grandparents, a twelve-year-old girl learns her grandmother has been hospitalized with a heart attack.
- A young boy visits his terminally ill grandfather in the hospital.
- Two girls pay a condolence call to a friend whose father died.
- A twelve-year-old girl is asked what her father's job is by her classmates, who don't know she has no father.

Playing out as a way of expressing one's feelings is visualized in two scenes of *In My Memory*,[5] a 21 Inch Classroom Television production which portrays a young girl's response to the death of her grandmother. In the first scene, Linda's play with dolls allows her to expose her guilty feelings ("I didn't always do what grandmother said") and her interpretation that grandmother's death is a punishment ("Grandma left me alone; she didn't want to be with me anymore"). In the second scene, Linda and her cousins are playing "Bang, Bang You're Dead." The youngsters in the class talk about playing dead to see what it's like (they all have) or confess sheepishly to having pulled the wings off an insect and watched it die just to see what death is all about.*

Though a bit soap-opera-y for some adult tastes, this television presentation *(In My Memory)* is most useful for classroom purposes. Third- and fourth-grade youngsters identify with Linda's confusions and with her sad and guilty feelings. They call out the questions she wants to ask her parents *before* she asks them. They understand the parents' not talking to Linda — afraid of breaking down in front of her — because that's the way it is in their own lives, although they're quick to dispel her parents' rationalizations: "Linda isn't sleeping." . . . "She doesn't need her rest." . . . "She's worrying anyhow and her parents should talk to her *now*." When a younger cousin asks the whereabouts of Grandma and is told to go play by an older cousin, the class is critical of the mishandling. One should talk to the little boy, explain what has happened, and answer his questions. (They proceed to do so through role play.)

*Whether such behavior is "inhumane" and whether inhumanity as well as humanity is innate in the human species might be an appropriate insert in such a unit. Golding's *Lord of the Flies* is an extremely pessimistic view of childhood savagery. "In the Day of the Robin," a short story by T. Cennamo, two nine-year-olds kill a lame bird and then react to the incident. A nineteen-minute film, *Wargames* (Brandon) visually narrates an innocent tug of war which results in the killing of a goat by a group of young boys on a beach in Tokyo. In another film (thirteen minutes, Sterling, *The Magician*), the question of conditioning is raised as a group of youngsters are introduced to shooting games by a magician in military garb.

The class accompanies Linda to the funeral and identifies the point at which she understands what her grandmother's death really means. When Linda's mother finds her
crying in bed that night, mother and daughter talk about the
continuity of life ("I was her little girl. You're my little girl.
Someday you'll have a little girl of your own") and affirm the
value of tears: "It's all right to cry — especially together."
The youngsters don't all like the ending (mother tucking her
in) because they don't want the mother to leave Linda alone
at this time.

As a matter of fact, they'd add another scene to the
film: Linda, three months later. They want to see if she's still
so deep in her sadness ("Will she always feel this way?") or if
she has worked it through. Seeing a parent break down is
viewed the same way. They understand that strong expression of grief shows one cares deeply.

The Day Grandfather Died[6] is a short film (thirteen
minutes, King Productions) also appropriate for classroom
use. David, the boy of this story, is not as articulate as Linda;
he does not mouth the questions or verbalize his concerns.
Unlike Linda, David shows anger. When he learns of his
grandfather's death he rushes from the room yelling, "No! I
don't want him dead!" Youngsters have much to say about
the way his parents try to draw him out of his sullenness or
isolation ("You're not the only one. . . . You lost a grandfather and friend; I lost my father"). The last scene of the
film shows David a few months after the death, reveling in a
pleasant memory of his grandfather. When his friend asks,
"What's wrong?" David smiles to himself, choosing to keep
his thoughts private, and continues to play with his friend
without explanation or discussion.

Neither the videotape nor the film presents a perfect
model (whatever that would be). Perhaps their value is what
they don't handle well and the way they treat the mishandling of these situations because that's so like it is for most of
these youngsters! Death *isn't* natural and comfortable to talk

about; people *are* concerned about breaking down.

A comparative study of the two is valuable for appreciating different modes of behavior and different ways of handling feelings. One youngster (Linda) is able to talk to her friends and parents and ask the questions ("What's a heart attack?" "What happens when you die?" "Will you die?"); the other (David) is not ("What's bothering you, David?" "Aw, nothing"). Different religious styles are also exposed: the videotape is in Protestant context, the film, in Jewish setting.

Both Linda and David try to visualize the moment of death of their grandparent, and both do attend the funeral. Before viewing these materials, discussion of funerals was punctuated by nervous laughter and, in general, the class felt it was probably best not to attend funerals. After their discussion of the tape and film — after seeing what a funeral was like and knowing what to expect — the thought was not so frightening. The nervous laughter disappeared and the youngsters felt strongly that one ought to be given the choice about his own participation in these rites.

Teachers, parents, and other adults often ask, "Aren't you afraid you'll unleash a flood of heavy emotions?"

Yes, of course. After class a little third-grade girl couldn't stop crying. We talked at length about the fact that she had been excluded from the rest of her family during the days of her grandfather's death and funeral. Her mother's concern (later explained to me by the parent) with sparing her the sadness of the event was extended to forbidding any signs of grief or mourning in their home. The little girl missed her grandmother, who was not allowed to visit their house until she could stop mentioning Grandpa and could stop her eyes from filling up with tears. What's the use of uncorking these tortured feelings if nothing "positive" can come out of it? After all, a teacher can't control or undo a home situation.

What's the alternative? Not to discuss a burning though not visible problem can be a kind of conspiracy to keep these very unhappy thoughts submerged. Allowing a child to share feelings encourages the child to believe he is not singularly abnormal or peculiar. Certainly repression of feeling is a theoretical root of adult psychiatric disease. I asked this youngster after we'd talked if she didn't feel much better and she answered, "No," still with tears in her eyes. I realized simply opening a discussion cannot be the end of the need. The person this little girl needed to talk to was her parent. Might not unburdening her heart to her mother be something else "positive" from this upsetting reaction? Or perhaps the teacher would inform the parents of this experience and share her ideas and resources with them; in this case, suggesting stories mother and child might read *together*, such as Pearl Buck's *The Beech Tree*, Max Lundgren's *Matt's Grandfather*, Audrey Harris's *Why Did He Die?*, or Earl A. Grollman's *Talking About Death*.*

I'm surprised how near the surface these emotions and concerns are. The third graders don't want to stop talking in detail about their loss experiences. Just because they read signals correctly ("I can't talk to Mommy about Papa's death because he was her father; I know not to mention Uncle Harry to Daddy because he was his brother") doesn't

---

Talking About Death (Boston: Beacon Press, 1971) is subtitled "a dialogue between parent and child," the parent's words supplied, the child's, those responses to be his at the time of the reading. The book is beautifully illustrated with soft washes over simple nature phenomena suggestive of the fullness and variedness of the life cycle. The drawings quite subtly place the very personal death of the child's grandfather in the comfortable context of the naturalness of death for all living things. As the author states in his preface to parents, *how* the book is read with the child is as important as *what* is said. "The pace should be slow, quiet, and leisurely. The tone of voice — warm, sympathetic, calm. . . Pause from time to time to give the child an opportunity to express what *he* feels about death, what he thinks, and what he wants to know."

mean the youngsters aren't ready to explode with their anxieties and preoccupations, and, given licence to do so, do. Somehow, in the clear light of the classroom the grotesqueries and devils of the mind lose their potency. Being able to get it said (or resaid and resaid, even if it *was* encouraged to be said at home) is a release from tensions, unhappy or joyous — however temporary.

My anxiety at the tears of a lovely ninth grade girl during and after one of our sessions was relieved by her gratefulness for them. She was proud to know she could still be moved — proud to still "hurt" for her father, who had died almost three years previously.

And what words would you use to describe your feeling when a third-grade boy caught up with you in the corridor after the class, asking out of breath but in all seriousness, "Do you make house calls"?

Shouldn't the teacher leave such issues to the parent or "professional"?

Written in a patient's orders are the doctor's instructions not to discuss the diagnosis with the patient. What a dilemma for the nurse who sees a person struggling to make sense of what's happening to him. The nurse who senses her patient's needs is more than a pill dispenser; she sees her role more broadly than tending strictly to the physical needs of her patient. It is the nurse who is at the bedside continually, even at 2 a.m. when the patient can't sleep and wants to talk. Shall she be trained to detach herself on the dotted line which separates the person from the professional?' Is professionalism learning how *not* to respond to human suffering and anguish?

The teacher is in the classroom when a pet dies; when a grandmother, teacher, parent, or sibling becomes ill; when a divorce is happening; when a president is assassinated. She cannot avoid the issue. All she can avoid by detaching herself on the dotted line is being there for her students when they are confused and in need of help.

What about parent education in the community?

For the parents, it might make sense to have a few workshop sessions which review the resources and materials used in classrooms. Quite recently we held such a "Helping Children Cope" session.[8]

One parent felt we were exaggerating children's ability to grieve. He told anecdotes which raised the question of youngsters' "callousness." We viewed parallel anecdotes of aloofness in film, television, and classroom materials. Quite suddenly in the middle of a heady religious discussion in which Mary is trying to prepare her five-year-old son for the death of his grandfather (*All the Way Home*, Paramount), Rufus asks, "Do I have to wear my hat?" While being told of an assassination by Mister Rogers, owl asks if they can have a picnic ("Mister Rogers' Neighborhood," NET Television). Is it really callousness that's illustrated by the children's active play or their being hungry while the relatives are soberly reminiscing about grandmother just before her funeral in the 21 Inch Classroom production, *In My Memory*? Indeed, active play may be *the* way of dealing with tension. In this particular case, the "play" was "Bang, Bang You're Dead!" For us adults such scenes legitimately suggest denial and "short sadness span." Youngsters can take a little sadness in at a time; they don't "mourn" as mini-adults (or as adults have learned to do); and such behavior is neither, therefore, inappropriate nor as a proof of the youngster's lack of concern.

Some adults were horrified at the visual images of the grandmother struggling for breath or the grandfather clutching at his heart in two of our classroom materials.[9] Why did the film maker include these shots? How gross and sadistic. We discussed the necessity of including such shots if this is in fact what the youngsters are wondering about, because only by their inclusion are we affirming the youngster's right to wonder about such (gross) details and allowing him to see that he's not alone. He is so relieved to discover that other kids, too, wonder if blood gushes out at the moment of death, or if death hurts.

The same objection was raised with regard to the funeral scenes; how horrible for a child to see that box lowered into the ground . . . no, children should not be present at burials. Yet the children, after seeing such a scene, after they know what to expect, are able to talk about how scary it is when one *doesn't know* what to expect. They even recognize that seeing the casket lowered into the ground helps convince you that the dead grandparent isn't just away, soon to return. Most youngsters feel that whether or not to participate in this final, formal good-bye should be their own choice.

In one *joint session*[10] with parents and youngsters, how surprised we adults were to hear an eleven-year-old girl talk about her wish to say good-bye and I love you to her dying grandparent. She responded to *The Day Grandfather Died* with, "It's too bad his grandfather died so suddenly; the boy didn't have a chance to tell him how much he loved him." Pursuing this point I asked how she'd feel about visiting a dying grandparent in the hospital. There was no squeamishness. Yes, the youngsters agreed, they certainly wanted to say good-bye. Yes, they should be allowed into hospitals. "Are heart attacks catching?"

One youngster wanted to know why the picture Linda (*In My Memory*) had made for her grandmother couldn't be placed in the casket. Thinking she didn't understand what death meant and that she believed the grandmother was alive even after burial, I questioned her further. "No. But Linda had made this drawing for her grandmother and why couldn't it be buried with her? Maybe they'd both feel better. *Certainly Linda would*." Why not, indeed?

The affirmation of this joint session was our (adult) discomfiture. The youngsters, with their healthy directness, helped us see afresh. It was something of a role model in reverse. In this case, the youngsters possessed the common sense and assurance and warmth of what humanness is all about.

What materials might be suggested for a junior-high curriculum?

Though there are special concerns and appropriate materials for specific age groups, as already amply illustrated, materials supposedly devised for one age group have just as much value for another. Nursery rhymes and fairy tales are fun even for the most sophisticated (cf. John Ciardi's esoteric analysis of "Humpty Dumpty," and Eric Fromm's or Robert Bly's sexual interpretations of "Little Red Riding Hood").

In the junior-high milieu, the most powerful segment of a unit on death dealt with adolescents facing their own deaths. The protagonists of *Death Be Not Proud, Johnny,* and *Admission to the Feast* all know their diagnoses and we become aware — as they do — of their growing ability to confront their deaths with courage and dignity.[11]

You See . . . I've Already Had a Life[12] (30 minutes, Temple University) is a poignant film in which a thirteen-year-old leukemic boy comes to terms with his fatal illness. In the very real home and hospital settings, Paul interacts with classmates, family, and doctors. He talks out his thoughts about not wanting to be treated differently because he is ill and about feeling depressed, almost suicidal once. As if Paul were a member of their class, the group shared his distresses and their own. They talked openly about uncomfortable feelings with handicapped classmates. They wished the film showed Paul's schoolmates and close friends' reactions. They also wanted to see the emotional breakdown moments of the family and test them against those in *All the Way Home* (the film version of James Agee's *A Death in the Family*) and against their own experiences and gut feelings. In the midst of seriousness they laughed at Paul's substituting cider for a urine specimen. Paul helps us bear the unbearable. He shows us what makes human beings human, and how they can be more so. At the beginning of our death unit the general consensus was for a quick, sudden death in a not-wanting-to-know framework. Something more than admiration for Paul's style accounts for the greater belief in selves and in their own potentialities which finds the class now wanting to know if *they* had fatal diagnoses.

What exists on the senior-high or adult-education levels?

There is no lack of death courses on the secondary or university levels. A *Time* magazine education section featured "Thanatology 1" and photographed Minneapolis high-school students trying out coffins and making detailed plans for their own funerals.[13] The article further reported some seventy colleges and schools throughout the country offering organized courses in death confrontation.

Just as any current newspaper is bound to carry a local story of a class visiting the graveyard, so any church bulletin board is likely to be billing an evening of "Death with Dignity."

High-school youngsters do not lead insular existences. Listen to their music: "Fire & Rain," "Ode to Billy Joe," "Patches," "Vincent," "Teen-Age Blues," "Leader of the Pack," "O.D.," etc. Obviously, Jimi Hendrix, Janis Joplin, drugs, accidents, overdosing, and suicides are not irrelevant in the world of the adolescents. They attend Bergman (*Cries and Whispers*) and Kirosawa (*Ikiru, Redbeard*) films. They will visit funeral homes, hospitals, and cemeteries. They do "life lines,"[14] have their astrological charts read, and interview clergy and Eastern mystics. One such group is planning to spend elective time with patients in a chronic care hospital.

Different segments of the following syllabus, *Perspectives On Death*,[15] designed for a ten-week course at a local adult-education center, have been expanded into mini-courses for the high-school student:

PERSPECTIVES ON DEATH — Sandra Bertman, *The Equinox Institute* — American people have been characterized as death-denying, implying bewilderment when dealing with the death and loss experiences amongst us. In an effort to become more comfortable with the subject of death, grief, and bereavement, we shall explore attitudes and feelings expressed in the written and visual arts; most especially, poetry and film. Materials ranging in tone from Tolstoy to Twain to Brel and the Beatles shall provide the points of departure for reflecting on such concerns as isolation, depersonalization and lack of communication, ritualization; repercussions (creative and non) that accompany loss; growing old; *carpe diem*; a meaningful death; and talking about death with children.

Week 1: "A man sees as he dies death's possibilities" — Roethke

> Film: *How Could I Not Be Among You?*
> Assign: Tolstoy, *The Death of Ivan Ilych*
> Poetry: Some Thoughts on Death and Dying
> (Packet 1)

Week 2: The "sudden" death
> Film: *All the Way Home*
> Assign: *Reacting to the "Accident" of Death* (Packet 2)
> Agee, *A Death in the Family*

Week 3: The hospital:
> "It couldn't be called ungentle
> But how thoroughly departmental"— Frost
> Assign: *"the antiseptic tunnel"* (Packet 3)
> Kubler-Ross, *On Death and Dying*

Week 4: Who owns my life?

> Videotape: *Whose Life Is It Anyway?*
> Assign: *Whose Life Is It Anyway?* (Packet 5)

Week 5: "Will you still need me; will you still feed me" — Beatles

    Film: *Home for Life*
    Assign: *Aging* (Packet 6)

Week 6: "For suicide has cause" — Shapiro

    Film: *The Slender Thread*
    Assign: *Suicide* (Packet 7)

Week 7: The funeral: "Do not bring your dog" — Twain

    Film: *The Loved One*
    Assign: *Funeral Etiquette* (Packet 8)

Week 8: Grief and bereavement: "You cannot prevent the birds of sorrow from flying over your head, but you can prevent them from building nests in your hair" — Chinese proverb
    Tape: *Sing a Song of Dying* WCAS Radio

        (Attitudes toward death reflected in music and song: spirituals, rock & roll, folk)
    Assign: *"the silent language of grief'* (Packet 9)

Week 9: Death rituals in primitive cultures and mythology

    Films: *Dead Birds   Day of the Dead*
    Assign: *love/death* (Packet 10)

Week 10: "About suffering they were never wrong, the old masters" — Auden

    Film: *La Jetée*
        Treatment of death, suffering, bereavement in the visual arts (classicism to surrealism)

Aren't there more oblique ways of handling death education?

Certainly there are. Death education need never be a special or separate unit. The classroom teacher who is aware of the day-to-day happenings in her youngsters' lives is the one to bring in an appropriate experience at a significant moment. Nor is death the only awesome event which calls attention to loss and loneliness. Becoming an adolescent, leaving adolescence, aging, moving to a new neighborhood — all require significant change or adaptation to different life patterns.

For any age group, insert a unit on aging. How old is old? What's aging all about? Ben Shahn describes the excitement of youth approaching the doors in life as new adventure, whereas the aged person opens the doors with the comfortable sense of surprise and recognition at having been through them before. Study the lifestyles of the old. Yeats's "Wild Old Wicked Man" is not the waning gentleman of Ann Sexton's "Old." The loneliness of Brel's "Old Folks" who have lived too long or the nameless man in *Machina* (8 minutes, Vartkes Cholakian) is different from the solitude of the old French woman in *The String Bean* (17 minutes, Contem.) or the gold miner in *Nahanni* (19 minutes, NFB Canada), or the Canadian switchman, *Paul Tomkowitz* (9 minutes, NFB, Canada). The old people's chorus, "I'd Rather Be Dead than Wet My Bed," the Beatles, "will you still need me, will you still feed me,"[16] or Yeats's "Why Should Not Old Men Be Mad?" give audible voice to the fears and concerns of the "golden" generation. *Indian Summer* (28 minutes, McGraw Hill) and *Geronimo Jones* (21 minutes, Learning Corp. of America) are sensitive and insightful treatments of young boys' excitement with change juxtaposed with the old men's roots and lives being cut off by "progress." Close such a unit with *Adventures of an ** (10 minutes, Brandon), a lighthearted animation of the father-son-father cycle illustrating generation gap and rigidities, the sadness of "down they forgot as up they grew."[17]

Social studies, history, and English classes are continually having units on war: "*Dulce et decorum est pro patria mori.*"[18] People don't always die *of* something . . . sometimes they die *for* something. Listen to World War I poetry, to Brooke's "The Soldier," and McCrae's "In Flander's Field," or the World War II airforce theme song, "Wild Blue Yonder," and then try Sassoon's "Base Details," or e. e. cummings's *next to of course god america i love you*, or Country Joe and the Fish's "Viet Nam Rag":[19]

> (chorus) And it's 1 - 2 - 3
> What are we fighting for?
> Don't ask me
> I don't give a damn
> Let's stop this Viet Nam
> And it's 5 - 6 - 7
> Open up the pearly gates
> Ain't no time to wonder why — Whoopee!
> We're all gonna die.

Look at war heroism as portrayed in the visual arts. Contrast Manet's *The Shooting of the Emperor Maximilian* (1867) with Dix's *Dying Soldier* (1924).

Heroes die for reasons other than country. The love/honor paradox uttered in Lovelace's "To Lucasta" ("I could not love thee dear so much/ Loved I not honor more") is the theme of *High Noon*. Big Bad John sacrifices his life in a mine disaster, and it certainly was more than country that inspired *Jesus Christ, Superstar*.

A unit on ecology also raises crisis/death issues. A view of tampering with the balance of nature and its repercussions which affect the natural order of things is charmingly handled in a short French film, *Les Escargots* (15 minutes, Contem.). Follow the showing with the lovely animated *Life Cycle* (8 minutes, NET, *Dream Machine*, 1972) and, perhaps, take a look at those articles and stories which scream out against the medical magics that prolong life and ultimately treat death as a dehumanized, artificial anathema.

Whether in a classroom or at home, watching a television program with your own child, oblique or direct, the approach merely gives the license and willingness to confront painful realities together. It was not a tangential arena that allowed this high-school junior to use poetry's power so creatively as to effectively break through her own emotional isolation. Her uncle's death was not oblique to her:

Their eyes glitter, memories
Sing, as tears wipe the past
Through decades of childhood.

They drift like apparitions

Through timefilled rooms
And only thought conveys the barrenness
Of an empty bedroom,
Absence.
My mother's cheeks are wet.
They sting my throat
And I gulp my uncle's name.

His house melts in the stirring
Of an empty winter.
No Birthday present for me this year,
Only a gap to fear,

To shut me in each cold snowfall.

The light burns up the cigarette, creeping
Like the slash of a razor blade,
Spitting ashes, slicing a lung.

Without lymph glands, first, the face swells.
I smoke, and my hands shake.
One lung, half lung, quarter lung.
The cancer slithered into him

And time was retarded.   That early
Sunday snowfall he let go the others.[20]

NOTES

1. Winsor, Frederick, *The Space Child's Mother Goose*, New York, Simon & Schuster, 1958, p. 41.
2. Jennifer Altschuler, Sixth Grade, John Ward School, Newton, Mass.
3. Film Associates, California, 8 minutes, 1968.
4. M.G.M., Films Incorporated, Boston, Mass.
5. National Instructional Television Center, *Inside Out* Series, Newton, Mass.
6. Seattle, Washington.
7. Clark, Bryan, *Whose Life Is It Anyway?*, London, Grenada Television. Boston, NET, Channel 2, December 2, 1971. "Go on, tear yourself off on the dotted line that separates the woman from the social worker. . . ."
8. Conference: *Helping the Dying Child*, Session: "Talking With Children About Death," University of Pennsylvania, School of Nursing, Philadelphia, April 2, 1973.
9. *The Day Grandfather Died* and *In My Memory*.
10. First Unitarian Society in Newton. West Newton, Mass.
11. Gunther, J., New York, Harper & Bros., 1949. Sanderlin, O., New York, Pyramid, 1970. Beckman, New York, Holt, Rinehart & Winston. 1969.
12. St. Christopher's Hospital for Children, 2600 N. Lawrence St., Philadelphia, Penna. 19133, att. Dr. J. L. Naiman.
13. Chicago, Time, Inc., January 8, 1973, p. 36.
14. Plotting crises experiences in their lives and projecting future crises including, even, age of anticipated death (and writing their own eulogies and obituaries).
15. Cambridge Center for Adult Education, Cambridge, Mass., 1971 - 1972.
16. The Beatles, "When I'm Sixty-Four," London, Northern Songs, 1967
17. cummings, e. e., *op. cit.,* p. 370.
18. Horace, "It is fitting and proper to die for one's country."
19. Country Joe and the Fish, *I Feel Like I'm Fixing to Die*, New York, Vanguard, VSD79266.
20. Shapiro, Amy, Belmont High School, Belmont, Mass., 1971.

For further information on any of the resource materials cited in this chapter, contact Sandra Bertman, Education Director, Equinox Institute, 11 Clinton Road, Brookline, Mass. 02146.

Index

Abandonment, dying person's fear of: 28 - 29

Administrator, estate: 144 - 145

Afterlife: Catholic concept, 110 - 111; Jewish concept, 128 - 137; Protestant concept, 90 - 94

Anger: bereaved's, 276 - 277; child's reaction, 75; dying person's, 19 - 22; grief and, 7; prolonged, 21

Anointing: 103 - 104, 111

Anxiety, child's reaction to death: 76

Atheists, dying persons: 44

Attitudes toward death: dying person, 55 - 56; general public, 50 - 52

Autopsies: 125, 181, 182

Bargaining, reaction of dying person: 22

Ben Sirach: 129

Bereaved: Catholic caring for, 110 - 111; and condolence calls, 268 - 270; Jewish caring for, 135 - 137; loneliness of, 88; Protestant caring for, 94 - 95; by suicide, 328 - 329

Bowlby, John: 73

Business affairs, decedent's: 152 - 153

Casket: 197 - 198; coffin distinguished 197; open/closed, 85, 105, 194 - 195; selection, 198

Catholicism and death: afterlife, 110 - 111; anointing, 103 - 104; cremation, 109, 115; customs, 103 - 108; expressing condolence, 108 - 109; funerals, 104 - 110, 111, 112 - 117; military ritual, 110;

terminology, 111 - 112; theology, 110 - 111; wake, 105 - 106, 112

Cemetery: costs, 216 - 218, 220 - 221; development, 213 - 214; lots, 216 - 218; pre-need selection, 212 - 213, 215 - 216, 218 - 219, 221 - 223; types, 214 - 215

Certificate of death: filing, 191; insurance collection, 166; issuance, 182

Children: ability to accept truth, 69 - 72; dealing with, 77 - 78; and death education, 334 - 351; and funerals, 72 - 73; grief of, 73 - 76, 349 - 351; guardians, 161 - 162; Jewish, 121 - 122; memorials for, 234; and religion, 68 - 69; responses to death, 74 - 76; understanding death, 67 - 68; visiting dying person, 39 - 40; widow(er) and, 294 - 296, 301 - 302, 304 - 305

Civil Service benefits: 163 - 165

Coffin: 197

Columbariums: 241

Committal services: Catholic, 107 - 108; Jewish, 125 - 126; Protestant, 85

Condolence calls: 266 - 279; bereaved and, 268 - 270; caller, 270 - 271; Catholic view, 108 - 109; content, 271 - 276; Jewish view, 122, 126 - 127; Protestant view, 86 - 88

Condolence letters: 89, 282 - 286

Corcoran, Father: 306

Coroner: and certificate of death, 182; and inquests, 183 - 185; medical